MW01077740

Fundamentals of Islamic Thought

MUTAHHARI, Murtaza. **Fundamentals of Islamic thought: God, man, and the universe,** tr. from the Persian by R. Campbell. Mizan, 1985. 235p (Contemporary Islamic thought. Persian series) index 85-15446. 19.95 ISBN 0-933782-14-4; 8.95 pa ISBN 0-933782-15-2. BP 163. CIP

Till his death in 1979, Ayatullah Murtaza Mutahhari had been a close associate of Imam Khomeini. He is among the most prolific and cogent of contemporary Iranian religious scholars; a pragmatic philosopher, addressing issues of immediate social concern. Mutahhari covers the ideological spectrum from Marxism to liberalism; he is not a blind believer. An essay on women's rights in Islam was earlier translated into English (Tehran, 1981), but the essays collected in this volume have never before been made accessible to an English-speaking audience. Mutahhari's approach is fresh and bold. For instance, in assessing modern science as a divine enterprise, he situates it within a triad of worldviews, the most elastic and enduring of which is religious, its linchpin, divine unity (or *tauhíd*, in Arabic/Persian). Some of the technical terms will be tough for the average reader, but the book provides a window of insight for undergraduates and graduate students, for faculty of the sciences and the humanities, and, in short, for all who wish to understand Shi'i Islam as a religious ideology of historical depth as well as of contemporary power.—*B.B. Lawrence, Duke University*

Fundamentals of Islamic Thought
God, Man and the Universe

by **Ayatullah Murtaza Mutahhari**

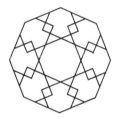

Translated from the Persian by **R. Campbell**
with annotations and an introduction
by **Hamid Algar**

Mizan Press, Berkeley
Contemporary Islamic Thought, Persian Series

Library of Congress Cataloging in Publication Data

Mutahhari, Murtaza.
   Fundamentals of Islamic thought.

   (Contemporary Islamic thought. Persian series)
   Includes index.
   1. Islam—20th century—Addresses, essays, lectures.   2. Shi'ah—
Doctrines—Addresses, essays, lectures.
   I. Algar, Hamid.   II. Title.   III. Series.
   BP163.M945213   1985   297'.2042   85-15446
   ISBN 0-933782-14-4
   ISBN 0-933782-15-2 (pbk.)

                    Designed by Joan Rhine
          Manufactured in the United States of America

Contents

Introduction

Ayatullah Murtaza Mutahhari, one of the principal architects of the new Islamic consciousness in Iran, was born on February 2, 1920, in Fariman, then a village and now a township about sixty kilometers from Mashhad, the great center of Shi'i pilgrimage and learning in Eastern Iran.[1] His father was Muhammad Husayn Mutahhari, a scholar of some renown who studied in Najaf and spent several years in Egypt and the Hijaz before returning to Fariman. The elder Mutahhari was of a different caste of mind from his son, who in any event came to outshine him. The father was devoted to the works of the celebrated traditionalist, Mulla Muhammad Baqir Majlisi; whereas the son's great hero among the Shi'i scholars of the past was the theosophist Mulla Sadra. Nonetheless, Ayatullah Mutahhari always retained great respect and affection for his father, who was also his first teacher, and he dedicated to him one of his most popular books, *Dastan-i Rastan* ("The Epic of the Righteous").[2]

At the exceptionally early age of twelve, Mutahhari began his formal religious studies at the teaching institution in Mashhad, which was then in a state of decline, partly because of internal reasons and partly because of the repressive measures directed by Riza Khan, the first Pahlavi autocrat, against all Islamic institutions. But in Mashhad, Mutahhari discovered his great love for philosophy, theology, and mysticism, a love that remained with him throughout his life and came to shape his entire outlook on religion:

> I can remember that when I began my studies in Mashhad and was still engaged in learning elementary Arabic, the philosophers, mystics, and theologians impressed me far more than other scholars and scientists, such as inventors and explorers. Naturally I was not yet acquainted with their ideas, but I regarded them as heroes on the stage of thought.[3]

Accordingly, the figure in Mashhad who aroused the greatest devotion in Mutahhari was Mirza Mahdi Shahidi Razavi, a teacher of philosophy. But Razavi died in 1936, before Mutahhari was old enough to participate in his classes, and partly for this reason he left Mashhad the following year to join the growing number of students congregating at the teaching institution in Qum.

Thanks to the skillful stewardship of Shaykh 'Abd al-Karim Ha'iri, Qum was on its way to becoming the spiritual and intellectual capital of Islamic Iran, and Mutahhari was able to benefit there from the instruction of a wide range of scholars. He studied *fiqh* and *usul*—the core subjects of the traditional curriculum—with Ayatullah Hujjat Kuhkamari, Ayatullah Sayyid Muhammad Damad, Sayyid Muhammad Riza Gulpayagani, and Hajj Sayyid Sadr al-Din Sadr. But more important than all these was Ayatullah Burujirdi, the successor of Ha'iri as director *(za'im)* of the teaching establishment in Qum. Mutahhari attended his lectures from his arrival in Qum in 1944 until his departure for Tehran in 1952, and he nourished a deep respect for him.[4]

Fervent devotion and close affinity characterized Mutahhari's relationship with his prime mentor in Qum, Imam Ruhullah Khomeini. When Mutahhari arrived in Qum, the *imam* was a young lecturer *(mudarris),* but he was already marked out from his contemporaries by the profundity and comprehensiveness of his Islamic vision and his ability to convey it to others. These qualities were manifested in the celebrated lectures on ethics that he began giving in Qum in the early 1930s. The lectures attracted a wide audience from outside as well as inside the religious teaching institution and had a profound impact on all who attended them. Mutahhari made his first acquaintance with the *imam* at these lectures:

> When I migrated to Qum, I found the object of my desire in a personality who possessed all the attributes of Mirza Mahdi (Shahidi Razavi) in addition to others that were peculiarly his own. I realized that the thirst of my spirit would be quenched at the pure spring of that personality. Although I had still not completed the preliminary stages of my studies and was not yet qualified to embark on the study of the rational sciences *(ma'qulat),* the lectures on ethics given by that beloved personality every Thursday and Friday—lectures that were not restricted to ethics in the dry, academic sense but dealt with gnosis and spiritual wayfaring—intoxicated me. I can say without exaggeration that those lectures aroused in me such ecstasy that their effect remained with me until the following Monday or Tuesday. An important part of my intellectual and spiritual personality took shape under the influence of those lectures and the other classes I took over a period of twelve years with that spiritual master *(ustad-i ilahi).*[5]

In about 1946, Imam Khomeini began lecturing to a small group of students that included both Mutahhari and his roommate at the Fayziya *madrasa*, Ayatullah Muntaziri, on two key philosophical texts, the *Asfar al-Arba'a* of Mulla Sadra and the *Sharh-i Manzuma* of Mulla Hadi Sabzavari. Mutahhari's participation in this group, which continued to meet until about 1951, enabled him to establish more intimate links with the *imam*. Also in 1946, at the urging of Mutahhari and Muntaziri, the *imam* taught his first formal course on *fiqh* and *usul*, taking as his text the chapter on rational proofs from the second volume of Akhund Khurasani's *Kifayat al-Usul*. Mutahhari followed his course assiduously, while still pursuing his studies of *fiqh* with Burujirdi.

In the first two postwar decades, Imam Khomeini trained numerous students in Qum who became leaders of the Islamic Revolution and the Islamic Republic, so that through them (as well as directly), the imprint of his personality is visible on all the key developments of the past decade. But none among his students bore to the *imam* the same relationship of affinity as Mutahhari, an affinity to which the *imam* himself has borne witness. Pupil and master shared a profound attachment to all aspects of traditional scholarship, without in any way being its captive; a comprehensive vision of Islam as a total system of life and belief, with particular importance ascribed to its philosophical and mystical aspects; an absolute loyalty to the religious institution, tempered by an awareness of the necessity of reform; a desire for comprehensive social and political change, accompanied by a great sense of strategy and timing; and an ability to reach out beyond the circle of the traditionally religious and gain the attention and loyalty of the secularly educated.

Finally among the teachers to whose influence Mutahhari was exposed in Qum, mention must be made of the great exegete of the Qur'an and philosopher, Ayatullah Sayyid Muhammad Husayn Tabataba'i. Mutahhari participated in both Tabataba'i's classes on the *Shifa'* of Avicenna from 1950 to 1953 and the Thursday evening meetings that took place under his direction. The subject of these meetings was materialist philosophy, a remarkable choice for a group of traditional scholars. Mutahhari himself had first conceived a critical interest in materialist philosophy, especially Marxism, soon after embarking on the formal study of the rational sciences. According to his own recollections, he began, in about 1946, to study the Persian translations of Marxist literature published by the Tudeh party, the major Marxist organization in Iran and at that time an important force on the political scene. In addition, he read the writings of Taqi Arani, the main theoretician of the Tudeh party, as well as Marxist publications in Arabic emanating from Egypt. At first he had some difficulty understanding these texts because he was not acquainted with modern philosophical terminology, but by dint of continued exertion (which included the drawing up of a synopsis of Georges Pulitzer's *Elementary Principles of Philosophy*), he came to master the whole subject of materialist philosophy. This mastery made him an important contributor to Tabataba'i's circle and later, after his move to Tehran, an effective combatant in the ideological war against Marxism and Marxist-influenced interpretations of Islam.

Numerous refutations of Marxism have been essayed in the Islamic world, both in Iran and elsewhere, but almost all of them fail to go beyond the obvious incompatibilities of Marxism with religious belief and the political failures and inconsistencies of Marxist political parties. Mutahhari, by contrast, went to the philosophical roots of the matter and demonstrated with rigorous logic the contradictory and arbitrarily hypothetic nature of key principles of Marxism. His polemical writings are characterized more by intellectual than rhetorical or emotional force.

However, for Mutahhari, philosophy was far more than a polemical tool or intellectual discipline; it was a particular style of religiosity, a way of understanding and formulating Islam. Mutahhari belongs, in fact, to the tradition of Shi'i philosophical concern that goes back at least as far as Nasir ad-Din Tusi, one of Mutahhari's personal heroes. To say that Mutahhari's view of Islam was philosophical is not to imply that he lacked spirituality or was determined to subordinate revealed dogma to philosophical interpretation and to impose philosophical terminology on all domains of religious concern. It means rather that he viewed the attainment of knowledge and understanding as the prime goal and benefit of religion and for that reason assigned to philosophy a certain primacy among the disciplines cultivated in the religious institution. In this he was at variance with those numerous scholars for whom *fiqh* was the be-all and end-all of the curriculum, with modernists for whom philosophy represented a Hellenistic intrusion into the world of Islam, and with all those whom revolutionary ardor had made impatient with careful philosophical thought.[6] The particular school of philosophy to which Mutahhari adhered was that of Mulla Sadra, the "sublime philosophy" *(hikmat-i muta'aliya)* that seeks to combine the methods of spiritual insight with those of philosophical deduction. Mutahhari was a man of tranquil and serene disposition, both in his general comportment and in his writings. Even when engaged in polemics, he was invariably courteous and usually refrained from emotive and ironical wording. But such was his devotion to Mulla Sadra that he would passionately defend him even against slight or incidental criticism, and he chose for his first grandchild—as well as for the publishing house in Qum that put out his books—the name of Sadra.

Insofar as Sadra's school of philosophy attempts to merge the methods of inward illumination and intellectual reflection, it is not surprising that it has been subject to varying interpretations on the part of those more inclined to one method than the other.[7] To judge from his writings, Mutahhari belonged to those for whom the intellectual dimension of Sadra's school was predominant; there is little of the mystical or markedly spiritual tone found in other exponents of Sadra's thought, perhaps because Mutahhari viewed his own inward experiences as irrelevant to the task of instruction in which he was engaged or even as an intimate secret he should conceal. More likely, however, this predilection for the strictly philosophical dimension of the "sublime philosophy" was an expression of Mutahhari's own temperament and genius. In this respect, he differed profoundly from his great mentor, Imam Khomeini, many of whose political pronouncements continue to be suffused with the language and concerns of mysticism and spirituality.

In 1952, Mutahhari left Qum for Tehran, where he married the daughter of Ayatullah Ruhani and began teaching philosophy at the Madrasa-yi Marvi, one of the principal institutions of religious learning in the capital. This was not the beginning of his teaching career, for already in Qum he had begun to teach certain subjects —logic, philosophy, theology, and *fiqh*—while still a student himself. But Mutahhari seems to have become progressively impatient with the somewhat restricted atmosphere of Qum, with the factionalism prevailing among some of the students and their teachers, and with their remoteness from the concerns of society. His own future prospects in Qum were also uncertain.

In Tehran, Mutahhari found a broader and more satisfying field of religious, educational, and ultimately political activity. In 1954, he was invited to teach philosophy at the Faculty of Theology and Islamic Sciences of Tehran University, where he taught for twenty-two years. First the regularization of his appointment and then his promotion to professor were delayed by the jealousy of mediocre colleagues and by political considerations (for Mutahhari's closeness to the *imam* was well known). But the presence of a figure such as Mutahhari in the secular university was significant and effective. Many men of *madrasa* background had come to teach in the universities, and they were often of great erudition. However, almost without exception they had discarded an Islamic worldview together with their turbans and cloaks. Mutahhari, by contrast, came to the university as an articulate and convinced exponent of Islamic science and wisdom, almost as an envoy of the religious institution to the secularly educated. Numerous people responded to him as the pedagogical powers he had first displayed in Qum now fully unfolded.

In addition to building his reputation as a popular and effective university lecturer, Mutahhari participated in the activities of the numerous professional Islamic associations *(anjumanha)* that had come into being under the supervision of Mahdi Bazargan and Ayatullah Taleghani, lecturing to their members—doctors, engineers, teachers—and helping to coordinate their work. A number of Mutahhari's books consist, in fact, of the revised transcripts of series of lectures delivered to the Islamic associations.

Mutahhari's wishes for a wider diffusion of religious knowledge in society and a more effective engagement of religious scholars in social affairs led him also, in 1960, to assume the leadership of a group of Tehran 'ulama known as the Anjuman-i Mahana-yi Dini ("The Monthly Religious Society"). The members of this group, which included the late Ayatullah Bihishti, a fellow-student of Mutahhari in Qum, organized monthly public lectures designed simultaneously to demonstrate the relevance of Islam to contemporary concerns and to stimulate reformist thinking among the *'ulama.* The lectures were printed under the title of *Guftar-i Mah* ("Discourse of the Month") and proved very popular, but the government banned them in March 1963 when Imam Khomeini began his public denunciation of the Pahlavi regime.

A far more important venture of the same kind was the foundation in 1965 of the Husayniya-yi Irshad, an institution in north Tehran designed to gain the allegiance of the secularly educated young to Islam. Mutahhari was among the members of the directing board; he also lectured at the Husayniya-yi Irshad and edited and contributed to several of its publications. The institution was able to draw huge crowds to its functions, but this success—which doubtless exceeded the hopes of the founders—was overshadowed by a number of internal problems. One such problem was the political context of the institution's activities, which gave rise to differing opinions on the opportuneness of going beyond reformist lecturing to political confrontation. A related but more radical problem was presented by the existence within the Husayniya-yi Irshad of mutually antagonistic concepts and interpretations of Islam and its sociocultural mission. To express it more simply, there was the remarkable personality of 'Ali Shari'ati and the controversies he engendered.

The relationship between Mutahhari and Shari'ati is a delicate subject, fraught with political implications and complicated by the fact that both men are now dead and unable to clarify matters on their own behalves. Elements opposed to the Islamic Republic who claim to be the followers of Shari'ati and the protagonists of a "progressive Islam" suggest that some kind of absolute enmity opposed the two men and cast Mutahhari as the antithesis of their hero. Supporters of the new order in Iran tend, by contrast, to minimize the differences between these two key figures in the recent intellectual history of Iran; while distinctly preferring the work of Mutahhari to that of Shari'ati, they nonetheless wish to preserve for the Islamic Republic the capital that is represented by the lasting appeal of Shari'ati.[8]

Any notion of personal bitterness or discordance between the two men should be dismissed. The only references to Mutahhari in Shari'ati's work are friendly and respectful. It was Mutahhari who solicited from Shari'ati his contribution to *Muhammad, Khatam-i*

Payambaran ("Muhammad, The Seal of the Messengers"), which was later published separately under the title *Az Hijrat ta Vafat* ("From Migration to Death"). Whenever Mutahhari criticizes, in his writings, theories that are unmistakably Shari'ati's, he does so with courtesy and restraint and discreetly refrains from mention of Shari'ati's name. The two men clearly shared important goals: the reorientation of educated youth to Islam and the transformation of Iranian society in accordance with an Islamic vision. Both died while struggling for this goal: Shari'ati exiled in England and Mutahhari assassinated in Tehran.

There were, however, profound differences of outlook between the two men. Mutahhari was deeply rooted in traditional learning and enamored of its exponents; Shari'ati's acquaintance with the legacy of Islamic scholarship was superficial and lacking in reverence. Mutahhari was a systematic thinker who had fully absorbed a rigorous philosophical training; Shari'ati was impatient with philosophical and theological niceties and excelled in novel formulations that were more effective rhetorically and emotionally than intellectually. Mutahhari's thought was of a piece and internally consistent; Shari'ati's was a process of ceaseless exploration and revision. Both Mutahhari and Shari'ati were acquainted with Western thought (the former, it appears, only through Arabic and Persian translations), and both sought to assert Islam's superiority to it. But Mutahhari wielded against it the weapons of the Islamic philosophical tradition; whereas Shari'ati often used terminology and concepts borrowed from the enemy. Most significantly, perhaps, Mutahhari believed firmly in the guiding role of the religious scholars (while conscious of their need for reform); whereas on occasion Shari'ati propounded the fateful thesis of an "Islam minus *akhunds*" and wished to award the leadership of society to the Muslim intellectual.

As a result of these differences, Mutahhari gradually withdrew from the work of the Husayniya-yi Irshad while continuing to lecture elsewhere and avoiding an open conflict with Shari'ati that would have split the developing Islamic movement and served the purposes of the Shah's regime.[9]

The spoken word plays in general a more effective and immediate role in promoting revolutionary change than the written word, and it would be possible to compose an anthology of key sermons, addresses, and lectures that have carried the Islamic Revolution of Iran forward. But the clarification of the ideological content of the revolution and its demarcation from opposing or competing schools of thought have necessarily depended on the written word, on the composition of works that expound Islamic doctrine in systematic form, with particular attention to contemporary problems and concerns. In this area, Mutahhari's contribution was unique in its volume and scope. Mutahhari wrote assiduously and continuously, from his student days in Qum down to 1979, the year of his martyrdom.

Much of his output was marked by the same philosophical tone and emphases already noted, and he probably regarded as his most important work *Usul-i Falsafa va Ravish-i Ri'alism* ("The Principles of Philosophy and the Method of Realism"), the record of Tabataba'i's discourses to the Thursday evening circle in Qum, supplemented with Mutahhari's comments. But he chose the topics of his books in accordance not with personal interest or predilection, but with his perception of need; wherever a book was lacking on some vital topic of contemporary Islamic interest, Mutahhari sought to supply it. Singlehandedly, he set about constructing the main elements of a contemporary Islamic library. Books such as *'Adl-i Ilahi* ("Divine Justice"), *Nizam-i Huquq-i Zan dar Islam* ("The System of Women's Rights in Islam"), *Mas'ala-yi Hijab* ("The Question of the Veil"), *Ashna'i ba 'Ulum-i Islami* ("An Introduction to the Islamic Sciences"), and *Muqaddima bar Jahanbini-yi Islami* ("An Introduction to the Worldview of Islam") were all intended to fill a need, to contribute to an accurate and systematic understanding of Islam and the problems of Islamic society.[10]

These books may well come to be regarded as Mutahhari's most lasting and important contribution to the rebirth of Islamic Iran, but his activity also had a political dimension that, admittedly subordinate, should not be overlooked. While a student and fledgling teacher in Qum, he had sought to instill political consciousness in his contemporaries and was particularly close to those among them who were members of the Fida'iyan-i Islam, the militant organization founded in 1945 by Navvab Safavi. The Qum headquarters of the Fida'iyan was the Madrasa-yi Fayziya, where Mutahhari himself resided, and he sought in vain to prevent them from being removed from the *madrasa* by Burjirdi, who was resolutely set against all political confrontation with the Shah's regime. During the struggle for the nationalization of the Iranian oil industry, Mutahhari sympathized with the efforts of Ayatullah Kashani and Dr. Muhammad Musaddiq, although he criticized the latter for his adherence to secular nationalism. After his move to Tehran, Mutahhari collaborated with the Freedom Movement of Bazargan and Taleghani but never became one of the leading figures in the group.

His first serious confrontation with the Shah's regime came during the uprising of Khurdad 15, 1342/June 6, 1963, when he showed himself to be politically as well as intellectually a follower of Imam Khomeini by distributing the *imam*'s declarations and urging support for him in the sermons he gave.[11] He was accordingly arrested and held for forty-three days. After his release, he participated actively in the various organizations that came into being to maintain the momentum that had been created by the uprising, most importantly the Association of Militant Religious Scholars (*Jami'a-yi Ruhaniyat-i Mubariz*). In November 1964, Imam Khomeini entered on his fourteen years of exile, spent first in Turkey and then in Najaf, and throughout this period Mutahhari remained in touch with the *imam*, both directly—by visits to Najaf—and indirectly. When the Islamic Revolution approached its triumphant climax in the winter of 1978 and the *imam* left Najaf for Paris, Mutahhari was among those who traveled to Paris to meet and consult with him. His closeness to the *imam* was confirmed by his appointment to the Council of the Islamic Revolution, the existence of which the *imam* announced on January 12, 1979.

Mutahhari's services to the Islamic Revolution were brutally curtailed by his assassination on May 1, 1979. The murder was carried out by a group known as Furqan, which claimed to be the protagonists of a "progressive Islam," one freed from the allegedly distorting influence of the religious scholars. Although Mutahhari appears to have been chairman of the Council of the Islamic Revolution at the time of his assassination, it was as a thinker and a writer that he was martyred.[12]

In 1972, Mutahhari had published a book entitled *'Ilal-i Girayish ba Maddigari* ("Reasons for the Turn to Materialism"), an important work analyzing the historical background of materialism in Europe and Iran. During the revolution, he wrote an introduction to the eighth edition of the book, attacking distortions of the thought of Hafiz and Hallaj that had become fashionable in some segments of Iranian society and refuting certain materialistic interpretations of the Qur'an. The source of the interpretations was the Furqan group, which sought to deny fundamental Qur'anic concepts such as the divine transcendence and the reality of the hereafter. As always in such cases, Mutahhari's tone was persuasive and solicitous, not angry or condemnatory, and he even invited a response from Furqan or other interested parties to what he had written. Their only response was the gun.

The threat to assassinate all who opposed them was already contained in the publications of Furqan, and after the publication of the new edition of *'Ilal-i Girayish ba Maddigari,* Mutahhari apparently had some premonition of his martyrdom. According to the testimony of his son, Mujtaba, a kind of detachment from worldly concerns became visible in him; he augmented his nightly prayers and readings of the Qur'an, and he once dreamed that he was in the presence of the Prophet, together with Imam Khomeini.

On Tuesday, May 1, 1979, Mutahhari went to the house of Dr. Yadullah Sahabi, in the company of other members of the Council of the Islamic Revolution. At about 10:30 at night, he and another participant in the meeting, Engineer Katira'i, left Sahabi's house. Walking by himself to an adjacent alley where the car that was to take him home was parked, Mutahhari suddenly heard an unknown voice call out to him. He looked around to see where the voice was coming from, and as he did so, a bullet struck him in the head, entering beneath the right earlobe and exiting above the left eyebrow. He died almost immediately, and although he was rushed to a nearby hospital, there was nothing left to be done but to mourn.[13] The body was left in the hospital the following day, and on Thursday, amid widespread mourning, it was taken for funeral prayers first to Tehran University and then to Qum for burial, next to the grave of Shaykh 'Abd al-Karim Ha'iri.

Imam Khomeini wept openly when Mutahhari was buried in Qum, and he described him as his "dear son," as "the fruit of my life," as "a part of my flesh." But in his eulogy the *imam* also pointed out that with the murder of Mutahhari neither was his personality diminished nor the course of the revolution interrupted:

Let the evil-wishers know that with the departure of Mutahhari, his Islamic personality, his philosophy and learning, have not left us. Assassinations cannot destroy the Islamic personality of the great men of Islam. . . . Islam grows through sacrifice and the martyrdom of its cherished ones. From the time of its revelation down to the present, Islam has always been accompanied by martyrdom and heroism.[14]

The personage and legacy of Ayatullah Mutahhari have certainly remained unforgotten in the Islamic Republic, to such a degree that his posthumous presence has been almost as impressive as the attainments of his life. The anniversary of his martyrdom is regularly commemorated, and his portrait is ubiquitous throughout Iran. Many of his unpublished writings are being printed for the first time, and the whole corpus of his work is now being distributed and studied on a massive scale. In the words of Ayatullah Khamna'i, president of the republic, the works of Mutahhari have come to constitute "the intellectual infrastructure of the Islamic Republic." Efforts are accordingly under way to promote a knowledge of Mutahhari's writings outside the Persian-speaking world, and the Ministry of Islamic Guidance has sponsored translations of his works into languages as diverse as Spanish and Malay.

In a sense, however, it will be the most fitting memorial to Mutahhari if revolutionary Iran proves able to construct a polity, society, economy and culture that are authentically and integrally Islamic. For Mutahhari's life was oriented to a goal that transcended individual motivation, and his martyrdom was the final expression of that effacement of self.

Notes to the Introduction

1. This sketch of the life and work of Ayatullah Mutahhari is based chiefly on Muhammad Va'izzada Khurasani, "Sayri dar Zindagi-yi 'Ilmi va Inqilabi-yi Ustad-i Shahid Murtaza Mutahhari," in *Yadnama-yi Ustad-i Shahid Murtaza Mutahhari*, ed. 'Abd al-Karim Surush, Tehran, 1360 Sh./1981, pp. 319-380, an article rich in information on many aspects of the recent history of Islamic Iran. Reference has also been made to Mujtaba Mutahhari, "Zindagi-yi Pidaram," in *Harakat* (journal of the students at the Tehran Faculty of Theology), no. 1 (n.d.), pp. 5-16; M. Hoda, *In Memory of Martyr Mutahhari*, a pamphlet published by the Ministry of Islamic Guidance, Tehran, April, 1982; and Ayatullah Mutahhari's autobiographical introduction to the eighth edition of *'Ilal-i Girayish ba Maddigari*, Qum, 1357 Sh./1978, pp. 7ff.

2. *Dastan-i Rastan*, first published in 1339 Sh./1960, was chosen as book of the year by the Iranian National Commission for UNESCO in 1965.

3. *'Ilal-i Girayish ba Maddigari*, p. 8.

4. See Mutahhari's article, "Mazaya va Khadamat-i Marhum Ayatullah Burujirdi," in *Bahsi dar bara-yi Marja'iyat va Ruhaniyat*, 2nd. ed., Tehran, n.d., pp. 233-249.

5. *'Ilal-i Girayish ba Maddigari*, p. 9.

6. The authoritative statement of this view was made by Sayyid Qutb in his *Khasa'is al-Tasawwur al-Islami wa Muqawwimatuhu*, Cairo, numerous editions, which was translated into Persian and had some influence on views toward philosophy.

7. See the remarks of William Morris in the introduction to his translation of Sadra's *Wisdom of the Throne*, Princeton, 1982.

8. The approved designation in Iran for Mutahhari is now *ustad-i shahid* ("the martyred master") and that for Shari'ati *mu'allim-i shahid* ("the martyred teacher").

9. It is also said that Mutahhari was critical of Shari'ati's tendencies to give the activities of the Husayniya-yi Irshad a prematurely revolutionary aspect. See Shahrough Akhavi, *Religion and Politics in Contemporary Iran*, Albany, NY, 1980, p. 144, quoting an interview with Mutahhari in October 1975.

10. For a complete bibliography of Mutahhari's writings, published and unpublished, see anon., "Fihrist-i Asar-i Ustad-i Shahid Murtaza Mutahhari," in *Yadnama-yi Ustad-i Shahid Murtaza Mutahhari*, pp. 435-552.

11. Mutahhari's name comes ninth in a list of clerical detainees prepared by the military prosecutor's office in June, 1963. See facsimile of the list in Dihnavi, *Qiyam-i Khunin-i 15 Khurdad 42 ba Rivayat-i Asnad*, Tehran, 1360 Sh./1981, p. 77.

12. See Sayyid Husayn Ta'ib, *Tahlili az Tirur-i Mutafakkir-i Shahid Ustad Mutahhari*, Tehran, n.d., p. 1.

13. Details taken from Mujtaba Mutahhari, "Zindagi-yi Pidaram," pp. 15-16.

14. Text of the Imam's eulogy in *Yadnana-yi Ustad-i Shahid Murtaza Mutahhari*, pp. 3-5.

Man and Faith

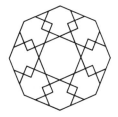

Man and Animal

In the name of God, the Merciful, the Compassionate

Man is a species of animal and thus shares many features with other animals. But many differences distinguish man from animals, and grant him a special virtue, an elevation, that leaves him unrivaled. The basic difference between man and the other animals, the touchstone of his humanity, the source of what have come to be known as human civilization and culture, is the presence of insights and beliefs. Animals in general can perceive themselves and the external world and strive to attain their desires and objects in the light of their awareness and cognition. The same holds true of man, but he differs from the rest of the animals in the scope, extent, and breadth of his awareness and cognitions and in the level to which his desires and objects rise. This grants man a special virtue and elevation and separates him from the rest of the animals.

Awareness and Desire in Animals

First, the animal's awareness of the world comes solely through its external senses and is, accordingly, external and superficial; it does not reach into the interiors and internal relationships of things. Second, it is individual and particular; it enjoys nothing of universality and generality. Third, it is localized, limited to the animal's environment. Fourth, it is immediate, confined to the present, divorced from past and future. The animal is not aware of its own history or that of the world and does not consider or relate its endeavors to the future.

The animal is thus confined in a fourfold prison. If it should perchance emerge, it does so not with awareness, by intelligence and choice, but captive to the compulsions of nature, instinctually, without awareness or intelligence.

The level of the animal's desires and objects is also limited. First, it is material, not rising above eating, drinking, sleeping, playing, nesting, and copulating. For the animal there is no question of abstract desires and objects, moral values, and so on. Second, it is private and individual, related to itself or at the most to its mate and offspring. Third, it is localized and related to its environment. Fourth, it is immediate and related to the present. The animal thus lives within certain confines in this respect as well.

If the animal pursues an object or moves toward an end that is beyond these confines, for instance, if it shows concern for the species rather than the individual or for the future rather than the present, as do such social animals as the honeybee, this behavior arises unconsciously and instinctually, by the direct command of the power that created it and administers the world.

Awareness and Desire in Man

Whether in the area of awareness, insights, and cognitions or desires and objects, the human domain reaches much further and higher than that of the animals. Human awareness and cognition traverse the exterior bounds of objects and phenomena to penetrate into their interiors, their essences and identities, their interrelationships and interdependencies, and the necessities governing them. Human awareness does not remain imprisoned within the limits of locale and place, nor does it remain chained to its moment; it journeys through both time and space. Accordingly, man grows aware both of what is beyond his environment and of his own past and future, discovering his own past history and that of the universe —the histories of the earth, the heavens, the mountains, the seas, the planets, plants and other animals—and contemplating the future to the far horizons. Beyond even this, man sends his thought racing after things limitless and eternal and gains a knowledge of some of them. One who transcends a cognition of the individual and the particular discovers general laws and universal truths that embrace the whole world. Thus, he establishes his dominion over nature.

Man can also attain an elevated level from the standpoint of desires and objects. Man is a being that seeks values and aspires to virtues and ideals that are not material or utilitarian, that are not restricted to self or at most to mate and offspring, that are general and inclusive and embrace the whole of humanity, that are unconfined to a particular environment, locale, or time period. Man is so devoted to ideals and beliefs that he may at times place them above all else and put service to others and their comfort ahead of his own comfort. It is as if the thorn that has pierced another's foot has pierced his own foot, or even his own eye. He commiserates with others; he rejoices in their joy and grieves at their grief. He may grow so attached to his sacred beliefs and ideals that he readily sacrifices to them not only his interests but his whole life and existence. The human dimension of civilization, the spirit of civilization, grows out of just such uniquely human feelings and desires.

The Touchstone of Man's Distinctiveness

Man's breadth of insight into the universe stems from humanity's collective efforts amassed and evolved over the centuries. This insight, expressed through special criteria, rules, and logical procedures, has come to be known as "science." Science in its most general sense means the sum total of human contemplations on the universe (including philosophy), the product of the collective efforts of humanity within a special system of logic.

The elevated and ideal aptitudes of humanity are born of its faith, belief, and attachment to certain realities in the universe that are both extraindividual, or general and inclusive, and extramaterial, or unrelated to advantage or profit. Such beliefs and attachments are in turn born of certain world views and cosmologies given to humanity by prophets of God or by certain philosophers who sought to present a kind of thought that would conduce to belief and idealism. As these elevated, ideal, supra-animal aptitudes in man find an ideational and credal infrastructure, they are designated "faith" (iman).

It is therefore my contention that the central difference between man and the other animals, the touchstone of man's humanity, on which humanity depends, consists in science and faith.

Much has been said about what distinguishes man from the other animals. Although some have denied there is any basic difference between man and other animals, asserting that the difference in awareness and cognition is quantitative or at the most qualitative, but not essential, these thinkers have passed over all the wonders and glories that have drawn the great philosophers of East and West to the question of cognition in man. They regard man as an animal entirely, from the standpoint of desires and objects, not differing from the animals in the least in this respect.[1]

Others think that to have a psyche makes the difference; that is, they believe that only man has a psyche, or anima, that other animals have neither feelings nor appetites, know neither pain nor pleasure, that they are soulless machines only resembling animate beings. They think that the true definition of man is "the animate being."[2]

Other thinkers who do not consider man the only animate being in the universe but maintain basic distinctions between man and the rest of the animals may be grouped according to which one of man's distinguishing features they have dwelt upon. They have defined man as the reasoning animal, the seeker after the Absolute, the unfinished, the idealist, the seeker after values, the metaphysical animal, the insatiable, the indeterminate, the committed and responsible, the provident, the free and empowered, the rebel, the social animal, the seeker after order, the seeker after beauty, the seeker after justice, the one facing two ways, the lover, the answerable, the conscientious, the one with two hearts, the creator, the solitary, the agitated, the devotee of creeds, the toolmaker, the seeker after the beyond, the visionary, the ideal, and the gateway to ideas.

Clearly, each of these distinctions is correct in its turn, but if we wish to advance a definition that comprehends all the basic differences, we can do no better than to speak of science and faith and to say that man is the animal distinguished from the other animals by the two features, "science" and "faith."

Relationship Between Humanity and Animality

Those features man shares with the animal plus those features that distinguish him from the animal result in man having two lives, the animal life and the human life—in other words, the material life and the life of culture. What relationship exists between man's animality and his humanity, between his animal life and his human life, his material life and his cultural and spiritual life? Is one the basis and the other a reflection of it? Is one the infrastructure and the other the superstructure? Since we are considering this question from a sociological, not a psychological point of view, we may express it this way: Among social structures is the economic structure, related to production and production relations, the principle and infrastructure? Do the remaining social structures, especially those in which man's humanity is manifested, all constitute something derivative, a superstructure, a reflection of the economic structure? Have science, philosophy, literature, religion, law, morals, and art at all times been manifestations of economic realities, having no substantive reality?

This sociological discussion automatically leads to a psychological conclusion and likewise to a philosophical argument that concerns humanity, its objective and substantive realities—the question of what today is called humanism. This conclusion is that man's humanity has no substantive reality, that only his animality has any substantive reality. Thus, any basic distinction between man and animal is denied.

According to this theory, not only is the substantive reality of human beliefs denied, including the beliefs in truth, goodness, beauty, and God, but the substantive reality of the desire to know the reality of the universe from a human viewpoint is denied in that no viewpoint can be simply a "viewpoint" and disinterested, but every viewpoint must reflect a particular material tendency. Things cannot be otherwise. Curiously, some schools of thought offer this view and speak of humanity and humanism in the same breath!

The truth is that the course of man's evolution begins with animality and finds its culmination in humanity. This principle holds true for individual and society alike: Man at the outset of his existence is a material body; through an essential evolutionary movement, he is transformed into spirit or a spiritual substance. What is called the human spirit is born in the lap of the body; it is there that it evolves and attains independence. Man's animality amounts to a nest in which man's humanity grows and evolves. It is a property of evolution that the more the organism evolves, the more independent, self-subsistent, and governing of its own environment it becomes. The more man's humanity evolves, in the individual or in society, the more it steps toward independence and governance over the other aspects of his being. An evolved human individual has gained a relative ascendancy over his inner and outer environments. The evolved individual is the one who has been freed of dominance by the inner and outer environments, but depends upon belief and faith.

The evolution of society precisely corresponds to the evolution of the spirit in the lap of the body or the evolution of the individual's humanity in the lap of his animality. The germ of human society is economic structures; the cultural and ideal aspects of society amount to the spirit of society. Just as there is an interaction between body and spirit, so there is one between the spirit and the body of society, that is, between its ideal structures and its material ones.[3] Just as the evolution of the individual leads to greater freedom, autonomy, and sovereignty of the spirit, so does the evolution of society. That is, the more evolved human society becomes, the greater the autonomy of its cultural life and the sovereignty of that life over its material life. Man of the future is the cultural animal; he is the man of belief, faith, and method, not the man of stomach and waistline.

Human society, however, is not moving inexorably and directly to the perfection of human values. At every temporal stage, it is not necessarily one step more advanced than at the preceding stage. It is possible for humanity to pass through an era of social life in which, for all its scientific and technical progress, it declines with respect to human ideal values, as is said today of the humanity of our present century. This idea of human social evolution means rather that humanity is progressing in the sum total of its movements, whether material or ideal, but the movement sometimes twists to the right or left, sometimes stops, or occasionally even reverses itself. However, on the whole, it is a progressive, evolutionary movement. Thus, future man is the cultural animal, not the economic animal; future man is the man of belief and faith, not the man of stomach and waistline.

According to this theory, the evolution of the human aspect of man (because of its substantive reality) keeps step with, or rather anticipates, the evolution of the tools of production. It gradually reduces his dependency on and susceptibility to the natural and social environments and augments his freedom (which is equivalent to his dependence on belief, ideals, principle, and ideology), as well as his influence upon the natural and social environments. In the future, man will attain to ever more perfect spiritual freedom, that is, ever greater independence or ever greater dependence upon faith, belief, and ideology. Past man, while enjoying fewer of the blessings of nature and of his own being, was more captive to nature and to his own animality. But future man, while enjoying more of the blessings of nature and of his own being, will be proportionately freer from the captivities of nature and of his own animal potentials and better able to govern himself and nature.

According to this view, the human reality, despite having appeared along with and in the lap of animal and material evolution, is by no means a shadow, reflection, or function of these. It is itself an independent, evolving reality. Just as it is influenced by the material aspects of being, it influences them. It, not the evolution of the tools of production, determines man's ultimate destiny, his substantive cultural evolution, and his substantive reality. This substantive reality of the humanity of man keeps him in motion and evolves the tools of production along with the other concerns of life. The tools of production do not evolve of themselves, and man's humanity is not changed and transformed like the tools defining a system of production, such that it would be spoken of as evolving because it defined an evolving system of production.

Science and Faith

Relationship of Science and Faith

Now let us see what relationship to each other these two pillars or aspects of humanity bear, or can bear.

In the Christian world, owing to some textual corruptions in the Old Testament (the Torah), the idea of the opposition of science and faith has become widespread, an idea that has cost both of them dearly.[4] This idea has its roots chiefly in the Book of Genesis. In Genesis 2: 16-17, we find, regarding Adam, paradise, and the forbidden tree: "[The LORD God] told the man, 'You may eat from every tree in the garden, but not from the tree of the knowledge of good and evil; for on the day that you eat from it, you will certainly die.'"[5] In Genesis 3: 1-8, it is said:

> The Serpent was more crafty than any wild creature that the LORD God had made. He said to the woman, "Is it true that God has forbidden you to eat from any tree in the garden?" The woman answered the serpent, "We may eat the fruit of any tree in the

garden, except for the tree in the middle of the garden; God has forbidden us either to eat or to touch the fruit of that; if we do, we shall die." The serpent said, "Of course you will not die. God knows that as soon as you eat it, your eyes will be opened and you will be like gods knowing both good and evil." When the woman saw that the fruit of the tree was good to eat, and that it was pleasing to the eye and tempting to contemplate, she took some and ate it. She also gave her husband some and he ate it. Then the eyes of both of them were opened and they discovered that they were naked; so they stitched fig-leaves together and made themselves loincloths.

In Genesis 3:23, it is said:

[The LORD God] said, "The man has become like one of us, knowing good and evil; what if he now reaches out his hand and takes fruit from the tree of life also, eats it and lives forever?"

According to this conception of man and God, of consciousness and rebellion, God's command (din) is that man must not know good and evil, not grow conscious—the forbidden tree is the tree of consciousness. Man, in his rebellion, his mutiny, against God's command (his balking at the teachings of the revealed laws and prophets), attains consciousness and knowledge and so is driven from God's paradise. According to this conception, all satanic suggestions are the suggestions of consciousness; therefore, the suggestor, Satan, is reason itself.

To us Muslims, who have studied the Qur'an, God taught Adam all the names (realities) and then commanded the angels to prostrate themselves before him. Satan was expelled from the court for not prostrating before this viceregent of God, conscious of realities. And the sunna has taught us that the forbidden tree was that of greed, avidity, something of this sort, that is, something connected with the animality of Adam, not with his humanity, that Satan the suggestor always suggests things contrary to reason but conforming to the passions of the animal ego, and that what manifests Satan within man's being is the ego that incites to evil, not the Adamic reason. For us who are thus schooled, what we see in Genesis is quite astonishing.

It is this conception that divides the last fifteen hundred years of European history into the Age of Faith and the Age of Reason and sets faith and science at odds. But the history of Islamic civilization is divisible into the Age of Flowering, or the Age of Science and

Faith, and the Age of Decline, in which science and faith together have declined. We Muslims must eschew this wrong conception that has inflicted irreparable injuries on science and on faith, indeed on humanity; we must not take this opposition of science and faith for granted.

Let us now proceed analytically and ask in a scholarly fashion whether these two aspects or bases of humanity actually each pertain to a certain era. Is man condemned ever to remain half-human, to have only half his humanity in a given era? Is he forever condemned to one of these two species of misfortune: the misfortunes arising from ignorance and the misfortunes arising from want of faith?

Every faith is inevitably based on a special mode of thought and a special conception of the universe and of being. Many conceptions and interpretations of the universe, although they can serve as bases for faith and devotion, are inconsistent with logical and scientific principles and so necessarily deserve rejection. But is there a mode of thought, a kind of conception and interpretation of the universe and of being, that both draws support from the region of science, philosophy, and logic and can be a firm foundation for a felicitous faith? If such a conception, mode of thought, or worldview exists, then it will be clear that man is not condemned to the misfortunes arising from either ignorance or want of faith.

One can address the relationship of science and faith from either of two standpoints. One standpoint is whether an interpretation or conception exists that is both productive of faith and idealism and supported by logic. Are all the ideas that science and philosophy impart to us contrary to faith, devotion, hope, and optimism? (This is a question that I will take up later in discussing the idea of a worldview.)

The other standpoint is that of the influences upon man of science on the one hand and faith on the other. Does science call us to one thing and faith to another, and opposed, thing? Does science seek to shape us one way and faith another, opposed, way? Does our science carry us in one direction and faith in another? Or do science and faith fulfill and complement one another? Does science shape half of us and faith the other half, harmoniously?

Science gives us enlightenment and power; faith gives us love, hope, and ardor. Science makes instruments; faith constructs purposes. Science gives speed; faith gives direction. Science is power; faith is benevolence. Science shows what is; faith inspires insight into what must be done. Science is the outer revolution; faith is the inner revolution. Science makes the universe the human universe; faith makes the psyche the psyche of humanity. Science expands man's being horizontally; faith conveys him upward. Science shapes nature; faith shapes man. Both science and faith empower man, but science gives a power of discrimination, and faith gives a power of integration. Both science and faith are beauty, but science is the beauty of the reason, and faith is the beauty of the spirit. Science is the beauty of thought, and faith is the beauty of feeling. Both science and faith give man security, but science gives outward security, and faith gives inward security. Science gives security against the onslaught of illness, floods, earthquakes, storms; faith, against worry, loneliness, feelings of helplessness, feelings of futility. Science brings the world into greater harmony with man, and faith brings man into greater harmony with himself.

Man's need for science and faith together has greatly excited the interest of both religious and nonreligious thinkers. 'Allama Muhammad Iqbal of Lahore has said:

> Humanity needs three things today—a spiritual interpretation of the universe, spiritual emancipation of the individual, and basic principles of a universal import directing the evolution of human society on a spiritual basis. Modern Europe has, no doubt, built idealistic systems on these lines, but experience shows that truth revealed through pure reason is incapable of bringing that fire of living conviction which personal revelation alone can bring. This is the reason why pure thought has so little influenced men while religion has always elevated individuals, and transformed whole societies. The idealism of Europe never became a living factor in her life and the result is a perverted ego seeking itself through mutually intolerant democracies whose sole function is to exploit the poor in the interest of the rich. Believe me, Europe today is the greatest hindrance in the way of man's ethical achievement. The Muslim, on the other hand, is in possession of these ultimate ideas on the basis of a revelation, which, speaking from the inmost depths of life, internalizes its own apparent externality. With him the spiritual basis of life is a matter of conviction for which even the least enlightened man among us can easily lay down his life.[6]

Will Durant, author of the *History of Civilization,* although nonreligious, says: "[Lucretius would suggest of our progress in mechanization] that this was a difference of means and not of ends. . . . What if all our progress is an improvement in methods, but not in purposes?" He also says: "Our wealth is a weariness, and our wisdom is a little light that chills; but love warms the heart with unspeakable solace, even more when it is given than when it is received."[7]

Today most people realize that scientism and the unalloyed scientific education are incapable of shaping the whole human being. The product of this education is the raw material of humanity, not the fully shaped humanity. It shapes a humanity with capacity, not one with attainment. It shapes a uniform humanity, not a multiform one. Today most people realize that the age of science-and-nothing-but has come to an end. A vacuum in ideals threatens society. Some would fill it with philosophy; others have resorted to literature, the arts, and the humanities. In Iran, too, some propose to fill this vacuum with a humanistic culture, and especially with the literature of *'irfan,* including such writings as those of Rumi, Sa'di, and Hafiz. But they forget that this literature has derived its spirit and attraction from religion. The humanistic spirit of these literatures is that selfsame religious spirit of Islam. Otherwise why are some modern literatures so cold, lifeless, and unattractive, for all their humanist affectations? The humane content of our literature of *'irfan* derives from the kind of thought concerning the universe and man that is specifically Islamic. If we take the spirit of Islam from these literary masterpieces, we are left with nothing more than the dross, or a dead form.

Will Durant feels this vacuum and proposes that literature, philosophy, and art fill it. He says:

> Our schools and colleges have suffered severely from Spencer's conception of education as the adjustment of the individual to his environment; it was a dead, mechanical definition, drawn from a mechanistic philosophy, and distasteful to every creative spirit. The result has been the conquest of our schools by mechanical and theoretical science, to the comparative exclusion of such "useless" subjects as literature, history, philosophy, and art. . . . An education that is purely scientific makes a mere tool of its product; it

leaves him a stranger to beauty, and gives him powers that are divorced from wisdom. It would have been better for the world if Spencer had never written on education.[8]

It is remarkable that although Durant acknowledges that the existing vacuum is, in the first place, a "vacuum of ideals," a vacuum in the area of objects, ends, and aspirations, a vacuum leading to nihilism, although he affirms that it is a vacuum of a kind of thought for and a kind of belief in humane objects and goals, he nonetheless supposes it is remediable through any sort of ideal values, even though they may not go beyond the realm of imagination. He supposes that busying oneself with history, art, aesthetics, poetry, and music can fill this vacuum that arises from the depths of man's aspiring and idealistic nature.

Noninterchangeability of Science and Faith

Science cannot replace faith to give—besides illumination and power—love and hope. It cannot raise the level of our desires. Although it can help us attain objects and goals, to follow the road to them, it cannot take from us those objects, aspirations, and desires that by nature and instinct turn on individuality and self-interest and give us in their place objects and aspirations that turn on love and on ideal and spiritual bonds. Although it is a tool in our hands, it cannot transform our essence and identity. Likewise, faith cannot replace science, to enable us to understand nature, discover its laws, or learn about ourselves.

Historical experiences have shown that the separation of science from faith has brought about irremediable harm. Faith must be known in the light of science; faith must be kept far from superstition in the light of science. When science is removed from faith, faith is deformed into petrification and blind fanaticism; it turns on its own axis and goes nowhere. When there is no science and true knowledge, the faith of an ignorant believer becomes an instrument in the hands of the clever charlatans exemplified in early Islam by the Kharijites and seen in various forms in later times.[9]

Conversely, science without faith is a sword in the hands of a maniac, or else a lamp at midnight in the hands of a thief, so he can pick out the choicest goods. Thus, the scientifically informed person of today without faith does not differ in the least from the ignoramus without faith of yesterday in the nature and essence of his behavior. What difference is there between the Churchills, Johnsons, Nixons, and Stalins of today and the Ghengises and Attilas of yesterday?

But, it might be said, is science not both light and power? Do the light and power of science not only apply to the external world, but also illuminate and reveal to us our inner world and so empower us to change it? If science can shape both the world and man, it can perform both its own function (world shaping) and that of faith (man shaping). The reply is, this is all correct, but the power of science is instrumental—that is, dependent upon man's will and command. In whatever area man wishes to carry out something, he can do it better with the tool of science. Thus, science is man's best aid in attaining the objects he has chosen, in traversing the roads he has decided to follow.

But when man puts the instrument to work, he already has an object in view; instruments are always employed in pursuit of objects. Where has he found these objects? Because man is animal by nature and human by acquisition, that is, because his human potentialities must be gradually nurtured in the light of faith, by nature he moves toward his natural, animal, individual, material, self-interested objects and employs his instruments accordingly. Therefore, man needs a power not among his own instruments and objects but that can rather impel man as an instrument in its own direction. He needs a power that can detonate him from within and activate his hidden potentialities. He needs a power that can produce a revolution in his heart and give him a new direction. This is not accomplished by science, by discovery of the laws governing nature and man. It is born of the sanctification and exaltation of certain values in one's spirit, which values in turn are born of a range of elevated aptitudes in man, which result further, from a particular conception and way of thinking about the universe and man that one can acquire neither in the laboratory nor from syllogism and deduction.

History shows the consequences of disjoining science and faith. Where faith has been, and science not, individuals' humanitarian efforts have produced no great effect—at times, no *good* effect. Sometimes they have given rise to fanaticisms, stagnations, and ruinous conflicts. Human history is filled with such events. Where science has been, with the place of faith left empty, as in some contemporary societies, all the power of science has been expended on selfishness, egoism, acquisitiveness, ambition, exploitation, subjugation, deceit, and guile.

One can regard the past two or three centuries as the age of the worship of science and the flight from faith. Many thinkers came to believe that science could solve all man's problems, but experience has proven the contrary. Today no thinker would deny man's need for some kind of faith—if not religious faith, at least faith in something beyond science. Bertrand Russell, although he had materialistic tendencies, admits "Work of which the motive is solely pecuniary cannot have this value [of bringing a man into fruitful contact with the outer world], but only work which embodies some kind of devotion, whether to persons, to things, or merely to a vision."[10] Today materialists are driven to claim they are materialists in respect to philosophy but idealists in respect to morals, that is, they are materialists in theory, but idealists in practice and aims.[11] The question of how it is possible to be a materialist in theory and an idealist in practice is for the materialists themselves to answer.

George Sarton describes the inadequacy and incapacity of science to humanize personal relationships and man's urgent need for the power of faith: "Science has made gigantic progress in certain fields, but in others, e.g., in politics, national and international, we are still fooling ourselves." He admits that the faith man needs is a religious faith. He says this of man's need for the triad of art, religion, and science: "Art reveals beauty; it is the joy of life. Religion means love; it is the music of life. Science means truth and reason; it is the conscience of mankind. We need all of them—art and religion as well as science. Science is absolutely necessary but it is never sufficient."[12]

Effects and Advantages of Religious Faith

Without ideals, aspirations, and faith, man can neither live a sane life nor accomplish anything useful or fruitful for humanity and human civilization. One lacking ideals and faith becomes either selfish, never emerging from his shell of private interests, or a wavering, bemused being who does not know his own duty in life, in moral and social questions. Man constantly confronts moral and social questions, and must necessarily respond. If one is attached to a teaching, a belief, a faith, one's duty is clear; but if no teaching or method has clarified one's duty, one lives ever in a state of irresolution, drawn sometimes this way, sometimes that, never in balance. So without any doubt, one must attach oneself to a teaching and an ideal.

Only religious faith, however, can make man truly "faithful"— can make faith, belief, and principle dominate selfishness and egoism, can create a kind of devotion and surrender in the individual such that he does not doubt the least point the teaching advances, and can render this belief something precious to him, to the extent that life without it is hollow and meaningless and that he will defend it with zeal and fervor.

Aptitudes to religious faith prompt man to struggle against his natural, individual inclinations and sometimes to sacrifice his reputation and very being for the sake of faith. This grows possible when his ideal takes on an aspect of sanctity and comes to rule his being completely. Only the power of religion can sanctify ideals and effect their rule in its fullest force over man.

Sometimes individuals make sacrifices and relinquish their fortunes, reputations, or lives not for ideals and religious belief but driven by obsessions, vindictiveness, and revengefulness, in short as a violent reaction to feelings of stress and oppression. We see this sort of thing in various parts of the world. The difference between a religious ideal and a nonreligious one is that when religious belief appears and sanctifies an ideal, sacrifices take place naturally and with complete contentment. There is a difference between an act accomplished in contentment and faith—a kind of choice—and an act accomplished under the impact of obsessions and disturbing internal stresses—a kind of explosion.

If man's world view is a purely materialistic one founded on the restriction of reality to sense objects, any sort of social and humane idealism will prove contrary to the sensible realities through which man then feels related to the world.

> What results from a sensual world-view is egoism, not idealism. If idealism is founded upon a world-view of which it is not the logical consequence, it amounts to nothing more than fantasy. That is, man

must figuratively make a separate world of the realities existing within him, from his imagination, and be content with them. But if idealism stems from religion, it rests on a kind of world-view whose logical consequence is to live by social ideals and aspirations. Religious faith is a loving bond between man and the universe, or to put it differently, is a harmony between man and the universal ideals of being. Nonreligious faith and aspirations, on the other hand, constitute a kind of "severance" from the universe and an imaginary construction of a world of one's own that is in no way reinforced by the outer world.[13]

Religious faith does more than specify a set of duties for man contrary to his natural propensities; it changes the mien of the universe in man's eyes. It demonstrates the existence of elements in the structure of the universe other than the sensible ones. It transforms a cold, dessicated, mechanical, and material universe into one living, intelligent, and conscious. Religious faith transforms man's conception of the universe and creation. William James, the American philosopher and psychologist whose life extended into the early part of the present Christian century, says: "The world interpreted religiously is not the materialistic world over again, with an altered expression; it must have, over and above the altered expression, *a natural constitution* different at some point from that which a materialistic world would have."[14]

Beyond all this, there is an aspiration to sacred truths and realities that can be worshipped innate in every human individual. Man is the focus of a range of potential extramaterial aptitudes and capacities waiting to be nurtured. Man's aptitudes are not confined to the material and his ideal aspirations are not solely inculcated and acquired. This is a truth science affirms. William James says: "So far as our ideal impulses originate in this [mystical or supernatural] region (and most of them do originate in it, for we find them possessing us in a way for which we cannot articulately account), we belong to it in a more intimate way than that in which we belong to the visible world, for we belong in the most intimate sense wherever our ideals belong."[15]

Because these impulses exist, they should be nurtured. If they are not rightly nurtured and rightly profited from, they will deviate and cause unimaginable harm leading to idolatry, anthropolatry, nature worship, and a thousand other forms of false worship. Erich Fromm says:

> There is no one without a religious need, a need to have a frame of orientation and an object of devotion . . . He may be aware of his system as being a religious one, different from those of the secular realm, or he may think that he has no religion and interpret his devotion to certain allegedly secular aims like power, money or success as nothing but his concern for the practical and expedient. The question is not *religion or not* but *which kind of religion.*[16]

What this psychologist means is that man cannot live without worship and a sense of the sacred. If he does not know and worship the One God, he will erect something else as the higher reality and make it the object of his faith and worship.

Therefore, because it is imperative for humanity to have an ideal, an aspiration, and a faith and because, on the one hand, religious faith is the only faith that can really penetrate us and, on the other hand, by our nature we seek for something to hold sacred and to worship, the only road open to us is to affirm religious faith.

The Noble Qur'an was the first book:

1. To speak explicitly of religious faith as a kind of harmony with the creation: "Do they seek for other than God's religion, while all in the heavens and on earth bow to Him?" (3:83)

2. To present religious faith as part of the makeup of human beings: "So set your face toward religion as one upright—such is the disposition with which God has created man." (30:30)

Tolstoy, the Russian thinker and writer, says: "Faith is that by which people live." Hakim Nasir-i Khusraw 'Alavi says to his son:

> From the world I turned to religion,
> Without which what's the world but my prison?
> Son, religion imparts to my heart a kingdom,
> That will never fall into ruin.[17]

Religious faith has many beneficial effects, including producing cheer and expansiveness, ameliorating social relationships, and lessening and remedying inevitable troubles that arise from the structure of the world.

Producing Cheer and Expansiveness

Religious faith creates optimism toward the universe, creation, and being. In giving a special form to man's conception of the universe, in representing creation as having an object and the object as goodness, happiness, and evolution, religious faith naturally shapes man's view of the universal system of being and its governing laws into an optimistic one.

The conditions of a person who has faith in the "country" of being resembles the condition of a person who regards as right and just the laws, institutions, and regulations of the country in which he lives and believes in its administrators' good intentions. He will perforce see the way open to progress and elevation for himself and everyone else, and he will believe that only his own laziness and inexperience could hold him back and that the same holds for other responsible beings. Such a person would view himself, not national institutions and regulations, as responsible for his backwardness. He would blame any shortcoming on the failure of himself and his peers to carry out their tasks. This thought would naturally rouse him to zeal and compel him to optimism, hope, and action.

A person without faith in the "country" of being is like a person who regards the laws, institutions, and regulations of the country in which he lives as corrupt and oppressive but must endure them. Such a person is always filled with rancor and vindictiveness. He never thinks of reforming himself; rather he thinks that somewhere earth and sky are askew, that all of being is injustice, oppression, and wrongness. He thinks, "What effect can the rightness of a speck like me have?" Such a person never takes pleasure in the world; the world for him is always like a nightmarish prison. Thus, the Noble Qur'an says: "For whoever turns away from remembrance of Me, life will be narrow" (20:124). Faith gives expanse to the life within us and checks pressures on the spiritual agencies.

Religious faith also illuminates the heart. When through religious faith man sees the world illumined with truth and reality, this clairvoyance illumines the spaces of his spirit. It becomes like a lamp illuminating his inward being. By contrast, an individual without faith, who sees the universe as futile and dark, is devoid of perception, insight, and light. His heart is dark and oppressed in this dark dwelling he has conceived.

Religious faith provides hope, hope of a good outcome for one's efforts. According to the logic of materialism, the universe regards impartially and indifferently those following the road of verity and those following the road of falsity, those following the road of justice and those following the road of injustice, those following the road of right and those following the road of wrong. The outcome of their work depends only on the level of their effort. But according to the logic of the individual with faith, the system of creation supports people who work in the way of truth and reality, in the way of right, justice, and benevolence. "If you aid God, He will aid you" (47:7). The reward to those who do good never goes to waste: "Truly God does not lose the wages of those who do good" (12:90).

Religious faith gives one peace of mind. Man innately seeks his well-being. He becomes immersed in pleasure at the thought of attaining well-being, and he trembles at the thought of a blighted future filled with deprivation. Man's well-being arises from two things:

1. Effort
2. Confidence in environmental conditions

A student's success arises from two things: his own efforts and the appropriateness, or supportiveness, of the school environment, which includes the encouragement and appreciation of the school authorities. If a hardworking student has no confidence in his study environment or in his teachers who will grade him at the end of the year, if he fears he will be the target of unjust conduct, he will be filled with apprehension and anxiety every day of the year.

Plainly one's duty toward oneself does not give rise to anxiety in this area because anxiety arises from doubt and uncertainty. One does not feel doubt or uncertainty in relation to oneself. What does induce such feelings of anxiety, what one feels unsure about one's role in relation to, is the world.

Is there no use in doing good? Are veracity and trustworthiness pointless? Do all our striving and dutifulness lead only to deprivation? Apprehension and anxiety here loom in their most terrible forms.

Religious faith, in relating man, one partner to the transaction, to the universe, the other partner, gives assurance and confidence. It alleviates apprehension and anxiety over how the universe acts upon man and brings peace of mind in their place. Thus, one of the effects of religious faith is peace of mind.

Another effect of religious faith is a greater enjoyment of ideal pleasures. Man knows two kinds of pleasures. Material pleasures are connected with any of the senses and felt when a relationship is set up between an organ and some external object (the pleasures of the eye in seeing, the ear in hearing, the mouth in tasting, the sense of touch in contact). Ideal pleasures are connected with the depths of the human spirit and conscience, not with any particular organ and not dependent upon a relationship with any external object. Such are the pleasures one feels from beneficence and service, from love and respect, or from one's own success or that of one's offspring. These pleasures neither pertain to a particular organ nor arise under the direct influence of an external, material factor.

Ideal pleasures are both stronger and more enduring than material pleasures. For the 'arifs and devotees of Truth, the pleasures of worship of God are of this order. Such worshippers, whose worship is conjoined with presence, humility, and absorption, derive the highest of pleasures from worship, such as are commemorated in the language of religion as "the relish of faith" and "the sweetness of faith." Faith has a sweetness above all sweetnesses. Ideal pleasures are redoubled when such works as scientific study, beneficence, service, and success stem from the religious sense and are carried through for the sake of God, when they fall in the domain of worship.

Ameliorating Social Relationships

Like some other animals, man has been created social. The individual alone is incapable of satisfying his needs; life must assume corporate form in the duties and fruits of which all are to share; a kind of division of labor must exist among individuals. But man differs from the other social animals, such as the honeybee, whose divisions of labor and function nature dictates will take the form of instincts and who are denied any chance to oppose and rebel against these preassigned functions. Man is free and empowered to perform his work freely as a function and duty. Other animals have social needs, but they also have social instincts that govern them.

Man likewise has social needs, but is not governed by social instincts. Man's social instincts consist of a range of demands within him that must be channeled by education.

A sane life for society consists in individuals' respecting the laws, the bounds, and each other's rights; in their regarding justice as sacred; and in their showing kindness to one another. Each should wish for another what he wishes for himself and not deem acceptable for another what he does not accept for himself. All should repose trust and confidence in one another and to guarantee each other's confidence should be their spiritual quality. Each individual should be committed and responsible to his society; each should be as privately pious and honest as he is publicly. All should act with beneficence to one another with the greatest possible degree of disinterestedness. All should rise against injustice and oppression and leave the oppressors and the corrupt no room to practice their oppression and corruption. All should venerate ethical values. All should unite with and support others as the members of a body.

That which above all else honors truth, sanctifies justice, endears hearts to one another, establishes mutual confidence among individuals, causes piety and integrity to penetrate to the depths of the human conscience, invests ethical values with credence, creates courage in the face of oppression, and interlinks and unites all individuals like the members of one body is religious faith. Human beings' humane manifestations, shining like stars in the sky of a tumultuous human history, are those manifestations welling forth from religious faith.

Lessening Troubles

Just as human life has its joys, delights, gains, and successes, it also has suffering, disasters, defeats, losses, hardships, and disappointments. Many of them can be averted or obviated, albeit after great expenditures of effort. Man is clearly obliged to come to grips with nature, to transform the bitter into the sweet. But some of the vicissitudes of the world, such as old age, cannot be averted or obviated. One advances toward old age, and one's life flame dies down. The infirmity and weakness of old age, together with the rest of its adversities, give life a grim face. On top of that, the thought of death and nonbeing, of closing one's eyes to the world, and of entrusting the world to others causes one anguish of another order. Religious faith instills in man the power to resist. It turns bitter to sweet. One with faith knows that everything in the universe has a fixed valuation. If he responds to hardships in the proper manner, even though they are irremediable, God Most High will recompense him in another way. As old age ceases to be seen as the end of man's existence and as the individual with faith regularly fills his leisure time with worship and nearness to God, through remembrance of God, life becomes more pleasant in old age than in youth. The visage of death is different in the eyes of one with faith; death is no longer oblivion and nothingness but is a transfer from an ephemeral world to an enduring one, from a smaller world to a greater one. Death is a transfer from the world of labor and sowing to the world of fruition and harvest. Thus, the individual with faith obviates his anxieties about death through efforts at the good works called in the language of religion "acts of devotion."

According to psychologists, nonreligious individuals experience most of the psychological illnesses arising from spiritual turmoil and life's hardships. The stronger and firmer the religious individual's faith, the greater his immunity to such disorders. One of the features of contemporary life arising from the weakening of the faiths is an increase in mental and nervous disorders.

The Teaching: Ideology

Classifications of Actions

What is a teaching, an ideology? How are these concepts defined? By what necessity does one as an individual or as a member of a society follow a school and cleave to, invest faith in, an ideology? Is the existence of an ideology essential for the human individual or society?

Some prefatory remarks are called for here:

Man's acts are of two kinds: pleasure-oriented and goal-oriented. Man carries out pleasure-oriented acts under the direct influence of instinct, nature, or habit—which is second nature—to attain some pleasure or avoid some form of pain. For instance, he grows thirsty and reaches for water, he sees a snake and flees, or he feels a craving for a cigarette and lights one. Such acts conform to appetite and have to do directly with pleasure and pain. A pleasurable act attracts and a painful act repels.

One is not drawn to or repelled from goal-oriented acts by instinct and nature. One carries them out or leaves them undone according to reason and volition and with a view to the benefit of either course of action. That is, man's final cause and motive force is benefit, not pleasure. Nature discerns pleasure; reason discerns benefit. Pleasure excites appetite; benefit mobilizes will. Man takes pleasure in the midst of performing a pleasure-oriented act, but he does not take pleasure in carrying out goal-oriented acts. Rather he finds satisfaction in conceiving that he has taken a step on an ultimately beneficial course—one leading to a future good, a future attainment, a future pleasure. There is a difference between an act that brings pleasure and happiness and an act that brings neither, that may even bring pain, but that man carries through contentedly, bearing even the pain. Because the result is deferred, goal-oriented acts do not result in pleasure and cheer, but they give satisfaction. Man and animal alike experience pleasure and pain, but satisfaction and dissatisfaction are unique to man, as is hope. Satisfaction, dissatisfaction, and hope belong to the domain of intelligibles and to the thought per se of man, not to his senses and perceptions.

That the goal-oriented acts are performed under the governance of reason means that the evaluative power of the reason sees a good, an attainment, or a pleasure from afar, descries the road to it, which may at times be arduous, and plans for the journey to fulfillment. That these acts are performed through the power of the will means that there exists in man a faculty dependent on the faculty of reason that has the function of executing what reason has sanctioned. At times it puts these things thought has devised and reason has sanctioned into effect in the teeth of all appetites and all natural inclinations. For example, consider a student. His youthful nature calls him to sleep, food, comfort, sensuality, and play; but his evaluative reason, which considers, on the one hand, the disastrous issue of such acts and, on the other, the ultimately happy issue of working hard, foregoing sleep, and abstaining from sensual delights and pleasures, commands him in the name of benefit to adopt the second alternative. In this instance, man elects the governance of reason, which is benefit, over the governance of nature, which is pleasure. As another example, a sick person may loath his bitter and distasteful medicine and recoil from drinking it. But he drinks it, governed by this reason that takes thought for benefit and by this willpower that overrides appetites. The stronger are reason and will, the better they impose their command upon nature, despite nature's inclinations.

In his goal-oriented acts, man is continually implementing some plan, some design, some theory. The more man evolves in the area of reason and will, the greater is the ratio of his goal-oriented acts to his pleasure-oriented acts. The nearer he draws to the animal level, the more the reverse is true because the animal's acts are all pleasure-oriented. Occasionally, animals are observed to act in ways that suggest remote ends and outcomes (nest building, migrations, matings, and reproduction, for example). But none of these are enacted in awareness, with an end in mind, or with thought given to what means to elect to attain that end. Rather, they take place through a kind of irresistible instinctual suggestion from the beyond.

Man has so extended the scope of his goal-oriented acts that it has encompassed his pleasure-oriented acts. That is, the plans benefit dictates may be laid so finely that pleasures are incorporated into the structure of benefits: Each pleasure, just as it is a pleasure, becomes a question of benefit; and every natural act, just as it answers to a natural need, proves obedient to the command of reason as well. If goal-oriented action covers pleasure-oriented acts, and if pleasure-oriented acts assume a role as part of the general plan and program of life under a goal-oriented outlook, then nature will accord with reason and appetite, with will.

Goal-oriented action, in turning on a range of remote ends and objects, as a matter of course calls for planning, programs, methods, and selections of means to reach these ends. Insofar as this action has an individual aspect (that is, insofar as an individual himself plans for himself), the planner, programmer, and theoretician—the one who determines the method and means—is the individual reason, which, of course, is dependent on the level of the individual's qualifications, information, learning, and power of judgment.

Goal-oriented action, even at a hypothetical apogee of perfection, is not sufficient for man's actions to be truly human. Man's goal-oriented action is a necessary condition of humanity in that his reason, science, consciousness, and foresight constitute half of his humanity, but it is not a sufficient condition. Human action is truly human when, in addition to being rational and volitional, it serves the more sublime aptitudes of humanity, or at the very least does not oppose them. Otherwise, the most criminal of human acts may take shape through projections, ingenuity, forethought, planning, and theorizing. The satanic designs of imperialism are the best evidence for this assertion. In Islamic religious terminology, the power of foresight when divorced from human aptitudes and aptitudes for faith and put at the service of material and animal ends is called "abominable" (*nukran*) and "Satanism" (*shaytanat*). Goal-oriented acts are not necessarily human; rather, if they turn on animal objects, they become far more dangerous than the pleasure-oriented animal acts themselves. For instance, an animal may rend another animal or a person to fill its stomach, but man the planner and evaluator will destroy cities and incinerate alive hundreds of thousands of innocent souls to achieve ends of the same order.

The Insufficiency of Reason

To what extent can reason point out an individual's best interests? The power of reason, reflection, and thought is certainly indispensable for one's particular and limited plans in life. One is constantly confronted with such problems as choosing friends, a field of study, a spouse, a job, travel, a social circle, entertainment, charitable activities, struggling against crookedness, and so forth. One needs to think, reflect, and plan in all these instances; and the more and better one considers them, the better one will succeed. At times, one will need to call upon others' reflection and experience (the principle of consultation). In all these particular instances, one first prepares a plan and then puts it into effect.

What of questions of a broad and general scope? Can one draft a plan covering all the problems of his personal life, according with his best interests in every respect? Or is the power of the individual mind to plan confined to limited and particular questions? Is it beyond the allotted power of reason to comprehend one's best interests in life as a totality, embracing happiness in all its aspects? We know that some philosophers believe in such a self-sufficiency. They claim to have discovered the road from adversity to happiness and to be building their own happiness on the strength of reason and will. But we also know that no two philosophers can be found in the world who are of one mind as to where this road lies. Happiness itself, which is the central and ultimate end and which at first appears self-evident, is one of the most ambiguous of concepts. What is happiness? How is it to be realized? What is wretchedness? What factors go into it? These questions point out a great gulf in our knowledge because even now man himself, with his potentialities and possibilities, remains unknown. Is it possible, while man himself remains unknown, to know what constitutes his happiness and the means of attaining it?

Moreover, man is a social being. Social life brings about thousands of problems for him, all of which he must solve, vis-à-vis all of which he must define his responsibility. Because man is a social being, his happiness, aspirations, criteria for good and evil, methods, and choice of means are interwoven with others' happiness, aspirations, criteria for good and evil, methods, and choices of means. One cannot choose one's way independently of others. One must pursue one's happiness on the highway that is leading society to happiness and perfection.

The Need for Ideology Today

If we consider the eternal life of the spirit and the inexperience of reason with respect to the hereafter, the question becomes much more difficult. It is here the need for a teaching, an ideology, becomes apparent—the need for a general theory, a comprehensive, harmonious, and concrete design whose central object is to perfect man and secure universal happiness. Along the lines and through the methods it suggests, musts and must nots, goods and evils, ends and means, needs, ailments and remedies, responsibilities and duties may be discerned, and every individual may derive a sense of his own responsibility from these.

From his first appearance, or at least from the age when the growth and diffusion of his social life culminated in a series of differences and disputes, man has needed an ideology—in the language of the Qur'an, a "revealed law" (*shari'a*).[18] As time has passed and man has evolved, this need has intensified. In the past, tendencies born of consanguinity, race, ethnos, tribe, and nation governed human societies as a collective spirit. This spirit in turn generated a range of collective (if inhuman) aspirations and imparted to society unity and direction. Growth and evolution in reason and science have weakened these ties. An individualistic tendency is an essential property of science. It weakens sympathies and bonds of feeling. *What will give unity, direction, and shared aspirations to the man of today, and* a fortiori *to the man of tomorrow, what will serve as his touchstone of good and evil, of musts and must nots, is an elective, conscious, inspirational philosophy of life armed with logic—in other words, a comprehensive, perfect ideology.* More than the man of yesterday, the man of today needs such a philosophy of life: the philosophy that is able to win him over to realities beyond the individual and his private interests. Today there is no longer any room for doubt that a teaching, an ideology, is among society's most pressing needs.

Designing such a teaching is beyond the power of individual intelligence. But is it within the power of the collective intelligence? Can man design such a thing by using the aggregate of his past and present experiences and learning? If we first assume that man is the greatest of unknowns to himself, knowledge of human society and of what constitutes its happiness would seem to be even more difficult to attain. What is to be done? If we have the correct view of being and creation, if we regard the system of being as a system in equilibrium, if we deny there is emptiness and futility in being, we shall be obliged to admit that this great system of the creation has not ignored this greatest of needs, but has delineated the basic lines of this highway from a plane above human reason, that is, on the plane of revelation (the principle of prophecy). It is the task of reason and science to move along these basic lines. How beautifully and sublimely Avicenna spoke in his *Kitab al-Najat,* where he elucidates people's need for a divinely revealed law expressed by human (prophetic) means. He says: "The need for such a man to preserve the species of man and to bring it to fruition is much greater than the need for a growth of hair on the eyebrows, the arching of the soles of the feet, and other such advantages, which are not essential for man's survival; indeed most of them do not serve that purpose at all."[19] That is to say, how should the great system of creation, which has not neglected these slight and less-than-pressing needs, neglect the most pressing need of all?

But if we are denied the correct view of being and creation, we must acquiesce in man's condemnation to bewilderment and error. Any design, any ideology advanced by this bewildered humanity in this dark edifice of nature, will amount to nothing more than a distraction and an entanglement.

Two Types of Ideologies
Ideologies are of two kinds: human and corporate. Human ideologies are addressed to the human species, not to some special nationality, race, or class, and have for their motive the salvation of the whole human species. They attract supporters from all strata, groupings, nations, and classes. Corporate ideologies are addressed to a certain group, class, or stratum and have for their motive the liberation, or the hegemony, of that group. They thus attract supporters and soldiers from that group only.

These two types of ideology are each based on a vision of man. The catholic and human type of ideology, exemplified by Islam, embodies a kind of realization of man defined by the concept of the primordial nature. According to Islam, in the course of the creation and prior to the influence of historical and social factors, man gained a special existential dimension and lofty capacities that distinguished him from the animals and impart to him his identity. According to this view, man within creation has gained a kind of species-intelligence and species-conscience that exists in all people, and this primordial conscience has given him a species-individuation, an aptitude to be summoned and addressed and to move. These ideologies begin their summons and engender movement in reliance upon the primordial conscience that distinguishes the human species.

Another group of ideologies has a different vision of man. According to these, man as a species has no such aptitude to be summoned and addressed or to move because his intelligence, conscience, and aptitudes coalesce under the influence of historical factors (in the life of nations and peoples) or social factors (in the class situation of man). Man in the absolute, apart from special historical and social factors, has no intelligence, conscience, or aptitude to be summoned or addressed; rather, he is an abstract being, not an objective one. Marxism and the various nationalistic and ethnic philosophies are based on such a vision. These philosophies arise from class interests, national and racial sentiments, or at best from an ethnic culture.

Beyond all doubt, Islamic ideology is human and arises from the primordial nature of man. Thus, Islam is addressed to the *nas,* the people at large, not to a special group or class.[20] Islam in practice has been able to attract supporters from among every group, even from among the very class that it has arisen in struggle against—that is, the class the Qur'an terms the "grandees" and the "affluent" *(mala' wa mutrafin).* To recruit from a class warriors against that class, to engage members of a group against the interests of that group, even to incite an individual against his own corruption are things Islam has done in numerous instances throughout its history. Islam, in being a religion and so penetrating to the deepest strata of man's existence and in resting on the primordial human nature of man, is able to incite the individual against his own corruption and to bring about a revolution of self against self known as repentance *(tawba).* The only power for revolution the corporate and class ideologies have is to incite individual against individual or class against class. They are never able to incite a revolution of individual against self, just as they cannot exert control over an individual in his inwardness, at the locus of his essential selfhood.

Islam, in being a religion—in being, of all the revealed religions, the seal of religions—exists to institute social justice.[21] It follows that its goal is to liberate the deprived and oppressed and to struggle against the oppressors. But Islam is not addressed to the deprived and oppressed alone, just as it has not attracted its supporters from these classes alone. Islam has recruited soldiers even from among the classes that it has risen in struggle against, in reliance on the power of religion on the one hand and on the human primordial nature on the other. Islam is the theory of the victory of humanity over animality, science over ignorance, justice over injustice, equality over discrimination, virtue over iniquity, piety over dissipation, *tauhid* over *shirk*. [22] The victory of the downtrodden over the tyrants and the arrogant is one of the manifestations of these other victories.

Cultural Unity or Diversity

Does the genuine human culture have a single identity? Does culture have an ethnic, national, or class identity, so that what is and always will be are cultures, not culture? These questions, too, relate to whether man has a single and authentic primordial nature, which could bestow a unity on culture, or he has no such single primordial nature, so that cultures must be the products of historical, ethnic, and geographical factors or of profit-oriented class tendencies. Because Islam's world view upholds a single primordial nature, it favors both a single ideology and a single culture.

Only a human ideology, not a corporate ideology, a unitive ideology, not one based on the division and fragmentation of man, a primordial ideology, not a profit-oriented one, can rest on human values and be human in its essence.

Ideological Temporality and Environmental Specificity

Is every ideology tied to a time and a place? Is man condemned to have a particular ideology for each permutation of temporal circumstances and under each set of varying local environmental conditions? Do the principle of variation (according to region and locale) and the principle of abrogation and substitution (according to the time) govern ideology? Or, just as man's ideology is single, not multiple, from the standpoint of grouping, is it likewise single, not multiple, from the standpoints of time and place? In other words, just as it is general, not special, from the standpoint of grouping, is it absolute, not relative, from the standpoints of time and place?

The question of whether an ideology is absolute or relative from the standpoints of time and place relates to the question of whether it arises from the specific primordial nature of man and has for its object the happiness of the human species or whether it arises from corporate interests and ethnic and class sensibilities.

In another respect, it depends on what we regard as the essence of social transformation. When a society undergoes transformation, leaving behind an era and embarking on a new era, does that society undergo a change in identity and so come to be governed by a new set of rules, just as, for instance, water, as its temperature rises, finally vaporizes, thereafter to be governed by the gas laws, not the laws governing liquids? Or are the primary laws of social evolution constant? Is the axis on which social change turns itself fixed? Does society undergo changes in stage, but not in the axis, the law, of evolution, just as animals transform and evolve biologically, while the laws of evolution themselves always remain constant?

In a third respect, the question of whether an ideology is absolute or relative from the standpoints of time and place depends on that ideology's world view. Is it scientific, philosophic, or religious? A scientific ideology, in being founded on an unstable world view, cannot itself be stable. It thus contrasts with the philosophic world view, founded on first principles and first axioms, and with the religious world view, founded on revelation and prophecy.[23]

Ideological Constancy or Change

Does the principle of constancy or the principle of change govern ideology? Whether man's ideology varies as time and place vary is a question of the abrogation and substitution of ideologies, but here I speak of a different question—that of the change and transformation of a single ideology. Whether an ideology is general or special in its content, whether it is absolute or relative, is it as a phenomenon constantly transforming and developing, given that this is the nature of phenomena? Is not the character of an ideology at its inception different from its character as it grows and matures? That is, must it not of necessity constantly undergo modification, augmentation and deletion, and revision at the hands of leaders and ideologues (such as we witness present-day materialistic ideologies undergoing)? Otherwise, will it not soon grow exhausted and dated and lose its authority? Or can an ideology be so ordered and so set along the primary lines of movement of man and society that it needs no revision or deletion and correction, that the role of the leaders and ideologues is only that of *ijtihad* in tenor and content, and that ideological evolution takes place in the realm of these acts of *ijtihad,* not in the substance of the ideology?[24] The answer to this question, too, will grow clear from the answers to the preceding questions.[25]

The Need for Faith

The individual act of cleaving to an ideology takes its true form when it takes the form of faith, and true faith cannot arise through coercion or with a regard to expediency. One may be made to submit to a matter and yield oneself, but ideology is not to yield to. Ideology is to be magnetized by and to embrace. Ideology calls for faith.

An appropriate ideology should, on the one hand, rest on a kind of world view that can convince the reason and nourish the mind and, on the other hand, logically deduce attractive goals from its world view. *At this juncture, love and conviction, the two basic elements of faith, work hand in hand to shape the world.*

Islam: The Comprehensive and All-Encompassing Teaching

Islam, in being founded on such a world view, is a comprehensive and realistic teaching. It considers every aspect of human needs, whether this worldly or otherworldly, physical or spiritual, intellectual or emotional and affectual, individual or social. From one standpoint, the aggregate of Islamic teachings comprises three areas:

1. Principles of belief, that is, things in which it is the duty of every individual to strive to attain belief. The task that man is charged with in this area falls under the heading of investigation and the acquisition of knowledge.

2. Morals, that is, traits that it is the duty of every Muslim to incorporate and adorn himself with and whose opposites it is his duty to shun. The task that man is charged with in this area falls under the heading of self-control and self-molding.

3. Decrees, that is, rules that relate to the overt and objective acts of man, inclusive of acts with this worldly and otherworldly ends, and of individual and social acts.

According to the Shi'i school of thought, the principles of Islamic belief are five: *tauhid,* justice, prophecy, the Imamate, and the

Hereafter (*ma'ad*, the Destination). As regards the principles of belief, according to which each individual is charged with acquiring a right belief, Islam does not regard imitation and blind submission as sufficient; every individual must freely and independently verify the rightness of these beliefs. According to Islam, worship is not confined to physical acts of worship, such as the alms-taxes *zakat* and *khums*. There is another kind of worship, and that is mental worship. Mental worship, or contemplation, if directed at man's admonition and awakening, is superior to years of physical worship.

Where Thought Stumbles

The Glorious Qur'an, in summoning us to reflect and draw conclusions, in regarding reflection as worship, and in not regarding acceptance of the principles of belief as sound without logical reflection, has attended to this basic question: Where do the stumblings in human thought arise? What is the taproot of error and straying? If one wishes to think straight and avoid error and deviation, what must one do?

In the Glorious Qur'an, a series of phenomena are named as the occasions and causes of error and straying: reliance on supposition, psychical tendencies and desires, haste, traditionalism, and obedience to personalities.

Reliance on Supposition Instead of Knowledge and Certainty

The Noble Qur'an, in numerous verses, stringently opposes action based on supposition instead of knowledge and certainty; it says: "Do not pursue that of which you have no knowledge" (17:36) and "The nature of most people is such that if you try to follow them, they will mislead you, because they rely on supposition (not on certainty) and act solely on conjecture and estimation" (paraphrase of 6:116). Modern philosophy has established that this tendency is one of the chief factors in error and confusion. A thousand years after the Qur'an, Descartes made this recognition the first principle of his logic. He says: "The first of these [precepts to which I have adhered] was to accept nothing as true which I did not clearly recognize to be so: that is to say, carefully to avoid precipitation and prejudice in judgments, and to accept in them nothing more than what was presented to my mind so clearly and distinctly that I could have no occasion to doubt it."[26]

Psychical Tendencies and Desires

If one wishes to judge rightly, one must preserve a complete impartiality toward the matter under consideration; that is, one must strive to find only reality and submit to reasons and evidence. One must be just like a judge considering a case, impartial to the two sides of the dispute. If a judge has a personal bias toward one side, he will unconsciously pay more heed to the reasons adduced for that side's case. Such a bias will cause the judge to err.

If in his own reflections one fails to preserve his impartiality relative to the negation or affirmation of a matter, if his psychical tendencies are to one side, automatically, without his being aware, the meter-needle of his thought will swing to the side of his psychical tendencies and desires. Thus, the Qur'an terms the desires of the psyche, along with reliance on supposition, one of the factors in thought's stumbling. It says in the *sura* Najm: "They follow nothing but supposition and what their own psyches desire" (53:23).

Haste

Every judgment or expression of opinion demands a certain amount of evidence. Until sufficient evidence has been gathered on a question, any sort of expression of opinion constitutes haste and occasions stumblings in thought. The Noble Qur'an repeatedly alludes to the paucity of man's stock of knowledge and its insufficiency for some major judgments; it conceives of dogmatic assertions as highly imprudent. For instance, it says: "Only a little knowledge has been given you" (17:85), which is to say that the amount of knowledge and information that has reached us is slight and insufficient for judgment.

Imam Sadiq (peace be upon him) has said:

In two verses of the Qur'an God has singled out His servants and admonished them: first, that they not affirm a thing until they have attained knowledge of it [haste in affirmation], and second, that they not deny a thing until they have attained to knowledge of it—until they have reached the stage of knowledge and certainty [haste in denial]. God says in one verse: "Was not the Covenant of the Book [the book of essential disposition or the revealed books] taken from them that they would not ascribe to God anything but the truth?" (7:169). He said in the other verse: "But they deny what their knowledge does not encompass' (10:39).[27]

Traditionalism and Looking to the Past

In accordance with his first nature, when man sees that a particular thought or belief was accepted by past generations, he automatically accepts it without allowing himself time to consider it. The Qur'an reminds us not to accede to the accepted notions and beliefs of past generations until we have weighed them on the scales of reason, and recommends independence of thought vis-à-vis the beliefs of past generations. It says in the *sura* Baqara, verse 170: "When it is said to them, 'Follow what God has sent down,' they say, 'No, we follow the customs we found our ancestors to believe in.' What! Even though their ancestors were void of reason and unguided?" (2:170).

Obedience to Personalities

Another of the occasions of stumblings in thought is obedience to personalities. Great historical and contemporary personalities, owing to the proportions of grandeur they assume in others' minds, exert an influence on others' thoughts and wills, to the point of overwhelming them. Others think as they think and resolve as they resolve. Others give up their independence of thought and will to them.

The Noble Qur'an summons us to independence of thought and regards blind following of great men and personalities as leading to eternal torment. Accordingly, it has the people who were lost down this road say on the Resurrection: "Our Lord! We obeyed our leaders and great men, and so they misled us as to the path" (33:67).

Wellsprings of Reflection in Islam

The Qur'an, in summoning us to thought and reflection, in addition to pointing out the stumbling points of thought, has also presented the wellsprings of reflection, that is, the subjects that are suitable for man to think upon and avail himself of as the sources of his knowledge and information.

In Islam, there has been a general opposition to the expenditure of mental energy on questions that can have no other issue than mental fatigue (that man has no means to investigate) and on questions that, although they could be investigated, offer no benefit to the human condition.

The Most Noble Messenger characterized as pointless a science that brings no benefit and whose absence brings no detriment, but Islam supports and encourages sciences in which investigation can be pursued and that additionally are beneficial. The Noble Qur'an teaches that three subjects are useful and fruitful to reflect upon:

1. Nature: Throughout the Qur'an, there are many verses mentioning nature (including earth, sky, stars, sun, moon, clouds, rain, winds, movements of ships upon the sea, plants, animals—in sum, all the sensible phenomena that man sees about himself) as something we are to consider closely. As an example, I cite the verse: "Say, 'Observe all that is in the heavens and on the earth' " (10:101).

2. History: There are many verses in the Qur'an that summon us to study peoples of the past and that present such study as a resource for acquiring knowledge. According to the Qur'an, human history, with its transformations, takes shape in accordance with a range of norms and laws. The exaltations and abasements, victories and defeats, successes and failures, joys and miseries of history are subject to exact and ordered calculations. By studying these calculations and laws, one can gain control of present-day history and employ it to further one's own happiness and that of one's contemporaries. Here is one verse as an example: "[Normative] systems have gone away before you. So travel the earth and observe how things came out for those who practiced denial" (3:137). That is,

before your time, norms and laws were actually put into effect. So explore and study the land and the historical remains of those who have gone before and see how things came out for those who took for lies the truth that God revealed to them.

3. The inner being of man: The Qur'an names the human heart as a source of a special kind of knowledge. According to the Qur'an, the whole of creation is a set of signs of God and indications pointing out reality. The Qur'an terms man's external world "the horizons" [afaq] and his internal world "the selves" [anfus]. It thereby points out the special importance of the inner being of man. This is the source for these terms so frequently met in Islamic literature.[28]

The German philosopher Kant has a sentence that has universal renown, and it is inscribed on his tombstone: "Two things fill the mind with ever new and increasing admiration and awe, the oftener and more steadily we reflect on them: the starry heavens above me and the moral law within me."[29]

Notes to "Man and Faith"

1. The English philosopher Hobbes had such a view of man.
2. This is Descartes's theory.
3. The *hukama'* of Islam have a principle for the interrelation of the spirit and the body, worded this way: "The soul and the body reflect each other responsively and preparatorily." [The author makes repeated mention of three classes of traditional Islamic scholars in the course of this work. The *falasifa* (sing. *failasuf*) are concerned with the theory of knowledge, the structure of language, and objective relations. Their field of inquiry is known as *falsafa*. Basically, they are Aristotelians. Avicenna typifies this class. The terms *falasifa* and *falsafa* are translated by their English cognates, philosophers and philosophy.

   [The *hukama'* (sing. *hakim*) are said to be more concerned with ultimate questions of being, the meaning of life, its end, and the human responsibility within it. Their field of inquiry is known as *hikma* (wisdom, *sagesse*). Avicenna would also be included in this group in certain respects. More typical representatives would be Mulla Sadra, Mulla Hadi Sabzavari, and Shihab ad-Din Suhravardi. These terms appear untranslated, except in a few instances where the author has used them in non-Islamic contexts or where *hikma* is translated as "wisdom."

   [The *'urafa*, (sing. *'arif*) are the exponents of the theoretical Sufism codified by Ibn 'Arabi and especially influential in Shi'i thought, known as *'irfan*. These terms, too, appear untranslated.

   [The author seems sometimes to treat *falsafa* and *hikma* as synonyms, particularly in the essay "Philosophy." There he also treats *'irfan* as a synonym for Sufism as such, and many persons familiar in the West as Sufis are introduced throughout as *'urafa'*.

   [My thanks to Muhammad Javad Larijani for his help in clarifying these terms. *Trans.*]
4. Tawrat: This word is cognate with the word Torah, but Muslim commentators hold that the work it refers to is not to be identified with the existing Jewish scripture. See A. Yusuf Ali, translator, *The Holy Qur'an* (n.p., 1946), pp. 282–285. *Trans.*
5. This and the following quotations are from the New English Bible. *Trans.*
6. Muhammad Iqbal, *The Reconstruction of Religious Thought in Islam* (Lahore, 1962), p. 179.

7. Will Durant, *The Pleasures of Philosophy* (New York, 1953), pp. 240, 114.

8. *Ibid.*, pp. 168–169.

9. The Kjarijites: a religiopolitical sect that rejected the claims to rule of both 'Ali and Mu'awiya, founder of the Umayyad dynasty, as well as evolving certain distinctive theological positions.

10. Bertrand Russell, *Marriage and Morals* (London, 1929), p. 102.

11. See, for instance, Georges Politzer, *Cours de philosophie: I. Principes élémentaires* (Paris, 1948).

12. George Sarton, *Six Wings: Men of Science in the Renaissance* (London, 1958), p. 218.

13. This quotation is without attribution and the source is unknown. *Trans.*

14. William James, *The Varieties of Religious Experience* (New York, 1929), p. 508.

15. *Ibid.*, p. 506.

16. Erich Fromm, *Psychoanalysis and Religion* (New York, 1950), pp. 25–26.

17. *Divan-i Ash'ar*, ed., Nasrullah Taqavi (Tehran, 1335 Sh./1956), p. 364. Nasir-i Khusraw was the famous poet, philosopher, and Isma'ili missionary (d. 481/1088). *Trans.*

18. It can be inferred from the noble verses of the Qur'an taken as a whole that these variations and needs appeared in the time of the prophet Noah. No earlier prophet had been given a revealed law. See 'Allama Sayyid Muhammad Husayn Tabataba'i, *Tafsir al-Mizan* (hereafter referred to as *Tafsir al-Mizan*), the commentary to the blessed *sura* Baqara, verse 213: "The people were a single nation, and God sent messengers" (2:213).

19. Exact place of occurrence not found. Trans.

20. Sometimes this word, *nas*, meaning the people at large, is erroneously taken to be synonymous with the masses of the people, as opposed to the privileged classes. Because Islam is addressed to the *nas*, it is claimed that Islam is the religion of the masses, and this is likewise accounted a special feature of Islam. But the real virtue of Islam is that it arose with the support of the masses of the people, not that it is addressed solely to them and so has a corporate or class ideology. What distinguishes Islam even further is that not only does it take hold among the exploited and deprived classes, but, in resting on the human primordial nature, at times it has stirred the conscience of the exploiting classes and capitalists themselves, to the advantage of the exploited.

21. Note Hadid:25: "We had sent our apostles with clear signs, and We sent down with them the Book and the Balance, that the people might

stand up in equity" (57:25). Note also A'raf:29: "Say, 'My Lord has commanded equity' " (7:29).

22. See pp. 84–112 below.

23. I cannot here explore either the question of the primordial nature, which is the "mother of questions" in Islamic theology, or the issue of social transformation.

24. *Ijtihad:* The deduction of particular applications of the law from its principles and ordinances, exercised by a *mujtahid,* here and occasionally elsewhere used in a broad and analogic sense. *Trans.*

25. In "Khatm-i Nubavvat" ("The Seal of Prophecy") appearing in *Muhammad, Khatim-i Payambaran* ("Muhammad, the Seal of the Prophets"), a publication of the Husayniya-yi Irshad, and later published separately as a pamphlet, I have discussed the universality and absoluteness of Islamic ideology along with the role of *ijtihad* in adapting it to the circumstances of different places and changing temporal conditions. I have shown that what is subject to development and change is *ijtihad,* not Islamic ideology. Interested readers should refer to that work.

26. René Descartes, "Discourse on the Method of Rightly Conducting the Reason," in *Philosophical Works* (Cambridge, 1931), vol. 1, p. 92.

27. *Tafsir al-Mizan* (Arabic text), vol. 6, p. 319, commentary to A'raf:169.

28. See Fussilat:53: "Soon We will show them Our signs on the horizons and in their souls, until it grows clear to them that this is the Truth" (41:53).

29. Immanuel Kant, *Critique of Pure Reason* (Indianapolis, 1956), conclusion.

The World View
of Tauhid

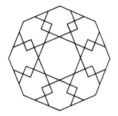

Every path and philosophy of life is based on a belief, outlook, and value system vis-à-vis being or on an explanation and analysis of the world. The kind of conception that a school of thought presents of the world and of being, the manner in which it contemplates it, is considered the intellectual foundation and support of that school. This foundation and support is termed the world view. All religions, customs, schools of thought, and social philosophies rest on a world view. A school's aims, methods, musts and must nots all result necessarily from its world view.

The *hukama'* divide wisdom into theoretical wisdom and practical wisdom. Theoretical wisdom is the realization of being as it is, and practical wisdom is the realization of the practice of life as it should be. What should be derives logically from what is, especially what is as primary philosophy and metaphysics are charged with explaining it.

World Feeling versus World Knowledge

The term "world view" contains the idea of sight, but we must not fall into the error of interpreting world view as world feeling. World view means world knowledge or cosmology; it relates to the well-known question of knowledge, which is an exclusively human property, as opposed to feeling, which man shares with other animals. Therefore, world knowledge is exclusive to man and is a function of his reflection and intellection.

Many animals are more advanced than man from the standpoint of world feeling; they are furnished with certain senses that man lacks (for instance, it is said that some flying creatures have a sort of radar, a sense that man lacks, or that, although some animals have a sense in common with man, it is much better developed in them—such as the eagle's eyesight, the dog's or the ant's sense of smell, and the mouse's hearing). Man's superiority over other animals lies in his knowledge of the world, that is, in a kind of insight into the world. The animals feel the world, but man explains it as well.

What is knowledge? What connection is there between feeling and knowledge? What elements other than sense enter into knowledge? Where do those elements come from and how do they enter the mind? What is the mechanism of the act of knowing? By what standard are valid and invalid knowledge distinguished? These are a series of questions that go to make up an independent essay.[1] What is certain is that sensing a thing is different from knowing it. Everyone sees a stage, a play, and everyone sees it in the same way; yet only a few individuals will explain it, and sometimes they will explain it variously.

Three World Views

World views or schemes of world knowledge (the ways man defines or explains the world) generally fall into three classes: scientific, philosophic, and religious.

Scientific World View

Science is based on two things: hypothesis and experiment. In the scientist's mind, to discover and explain a phenomenon, one first forms a hypothesis, and then one subjects it to concrete experiment, in the laboratory. If the experiment supports the hypothesis, it becomes an accepted scientific principle. As long as no more comprehensive hypothesis, better supported by experimentation, appears, that scientific principle retains its standing. The more comprehensive hypothesis with its advent clears the field for itself. Science thus engages in discovering causes and effects: Through concrete experiments, it discovers a thing's cause or effect; then it pursues the cause of that cause or the effect of that effect. It continues this course of discovery as far as possible.

The work of science, in being based on concrete experiments, has advantages and shortcomings. The greatest advantage of scientific research is that it is exact, precise, and discriminating. Science is able to give man thousands of data about some slight being; it can fill a book with knowledge about a leaf. Because it acquaints man with the special laws of every being, it enables man to control and dominate that being. Thus, it brings about industry and technology. But precisely because of these qualities, the compass of science is also limited to experiment. It advances as far as can be subjected to experiment. But can one bring all of being in all its aspects within the confines of experiment? Science in practice pursues causes and effects to a certain limit and then reaches a point where it must say "I don't know." Science is like a powerful searchlight in the long winter night, illuminating a certain area without disclosing anything beyond its border. Can one determine by experiment whether the universe has a beginning and an end or is limitless in time? Or does the scientist, on reaching this point, consciously or unconsciously mount the pinions of philosophy in order to express an opinion?

From the standpoint of science, the universe is like an old book the first and last pages of which have been lost. Neither the beginning nor the end is known. Thus, the world view of science is a knowledge of the part, not of the whole. Our science acquaints us with the situation of some parts of the universe, not with the shape, mien, and character of the whole universe. The scientist's world view is like the knowledge about the elephant gained by those who touched it in the dark. The one who felt the elephant's ear supposed the animal to be shaped like a fan; the one who felt its leg supposed it to be shaped like a column; and the one who felt its back supposed it to be shaped like a throne.

Another shortcoming of the scientific world view as a basis for an ideology is that science is unstable and unenduring from a theoretical standpoint, that is, from the standpoint of presenting reality as it is or of attracting faith to the nature of the reality of being. From the viewpoint of science, the face of the world changes from day to day because science is based on hypothesis and experiment, not on rational and self-evident first principles. Hypothesis and experiment have a provisional value; so the scientific world view is shaky and inconsistent and cannot serve as a foundation for faith. Faith demands a firmer, an unshakable foundation, a foundation characterized by eternity.

The scientific world view, in accordance with the limitations that the tools of science (hypothesis and experiment) have inevitably brought about for science, falls short of answering a series of basic cosmological questions that an ideology is obliged to answer decisively, such as: Where did the universe come from? Where is it going? How are we situated within the totality of being? Does the universe have a beginning and an end in time or in space? Is being in its totality right or a mistake, true or vain, beautiful or ugly? Do inevitable and immutable norms preside over the universe, or does no immutable norm exist? Is being in its totality a single living, conscious entity, or is it dead and unconscious, man's existence being an aberration, an accident? Can that which exists cease to exist? Can that which does not exist come into existence? Is the return of that which has lapsed from existence possible or impossible? Are the universe and history exactly repeatable, even after billions of years (the cyclical theory)? Does unity truly preside, or does multiplicity? Is the universe divisible into the material and the nonmaterial, and is the material universe a small part of the universe as a whole? Is the universe under guidance and seeing, or is it blind? Is the universe transacting with man? Does the universe respond in kind to man's good and evil? Does an enduring life exist after this transient one?

Science arrives at "I don't know" in trying to answer all these questions because it cannot subject them to experiment. Science answers limited, partial questions but is incapable of representing the totality of the universe. An analogy will clarify this point. It is possible for an individual to be well acquainted with a neighborhood or a quarter of Tehran. For instance, he may know South Tehran or some part of it in detail, such that he can sketch the streets, alleys, and even the houses of that area from memory. Someone else may know another neighborhood, a third person, a third area, and so on. If we bring together everything they know, we shall know enough of Tehran, part by part. But if we learn about Tehran in this way, shall we have learned about Tehran from every standpoint? Can we gain a complete picture of Tehran? Is it circular? Is it square? Is it shaped like the leaf of a tree? Of what tree? What relationships do the neighborhoods have with one another? Which bus lines connect how many neighborhoods? Is Tehran as a whole beautiful or ugly? If we want to inform ourselves on subjects such as these, if, for instance, we want to learn what the shape of Tehran is, or whether it is beautiful or ugly, we must board a plane and take in the whole city from above. In this sense, science is incapable of answering the most basic questions, as a world view must; that is, it can form no general conceptions of the universe as a whole and of its form.

The importance of the scientific world view lies in its practical, technical value, not in its theoretical value. What can serve as the support for an ideology is a theoretical value, not a practical one. The theoretical value of science lies in the reality of the universe being just as it is represented in the mirror of science. The practical and technical value of science lies in science's empowering man in his work and being fruitful, whether or not it represents reality. Today's industry and technology display the practical and technical value of science.

One of the remarkable things about science in today's world is that, to the extent that its practical and technical value increases, its theoretical value diminishes. Those on the sidelines suppose that the progress of science as an illumination of the human conscience and as a source of faith and certitude relative to reality (which is how science represents itself) is in direct proportion to the extent of irrefutable concrete progress, whereas the truth is just the opposite.[2]

An ideology requires a world view that, first, answers the basic cosmological questions of relevance to the universe as a whole, not just to some certain part; second, provides a well-grounded, reliable, and eternally valid comprehension, not a provisional, transient one; and third, provides something of theoretical, not purely practical and technical value, something revealing reality. The scientific world view, for all its advantages from other standpoints, fails to fulfill these three conditions.

Philosophical World View

Although the philosophical world view lacks the exactitude and definition of the scientific world view, it enjoys an assurance and has none of the instability of the scientific world view. The reason for this is that it rests on a series of principles that are in the first place self-evident and undeniable to the mind, carried forward by demonstration and deduction, and in the second place general and comprehensive (in the language of philosophy, they relate to that by virtue of which the being is being). The world view of philosophy answers those same questions on which ideologies rest. Philosophical thought discerns the mien of the universe as a whole.

The scientific world view and the philosophical world view both conduce to action, but in two different ways. The scientific world view conduces to action by giving man the power and capacity to "change" and to "control" nature; it allows him to render nature subservient to his own desires. But the philosophical world view conduces to action and influences action by distinguishing the reasons for action and the criteria for human choice in life. The philosophical world view is influential in the way man encounters and responds to the universe. It fixes the attitude of man to the universe and shapes his outlook toward being and the universe. It gives man ideas or takes them away. It imparts meaning to his life or draws him into futility and emptiness. Thus, science is incapable but philosophy is capable of giving man a world view as the foundation of an ideology.

Religious World View

If we regard every general viewpoint expressed toward being and the universe as philosophical, regardless of the source of that world view (that is, syllogism, demonstration, and deduction or revelation received from the unseen world), we must regard the religious world view as philosophical. The religious world view and the philosophic world view cover the same domain, by contrast with the scientific world view. But if we take into account the source of knowledge, we must certainly admit that the religious and the philosophical cosmologies are different in kind. In some religions, such as Islam, the religious cosmology within the religion has taken on a philosophical quality, that is, a rational quality. It relies on reason and deduction and adduces demonstrations in answering the questions that are raised. From this standpoint, the Islamic world view is likewise a rational and philosophical world view.

Among the advantages of the religious world view (in addition to the two advantages it shares with the philosophical world view

—stability and eternality, and generality and comprehensiveness) is its sanctification of the bases of the world view.

An ideology demands faith. For a school of thought to attract faith calls not only for a belief in that eternity and immutability of its principles, which the scientific world view in particular lacks, but for a respect approaching reverence. Thus, a world view becomes the basis of ideology and the foundation of belief when it takes on a religious character. A world view can become the basis of an ideology when it has attained the firmness and breadth of philosophical thought as well as the holiness and sanctity of religious principles.

Criteria for a World View

The good, sublime world view has the following characteristics:

1. It can be deduced and proven (is supported by reason and logic).

2. It gives meaning to life; it banishes from minds the idea that life is vain and futile, that all roads lead to vanity and nothingness.

3. It gives rise to ideals, enthusiasm, and aspiration.

4. It has the power to sanctify human aims and social goals.

5. It promotes commitment and responsibility.

That a world view is logical paves the way to rational acceptance of it and renders it admissable to thought. It eliminates the ambiguities and obscurities that are great barriers to action.

That the world view of a school of thought gives rise to ideals lends it a magnetism as well as a fervor and force.

That a world view sanctifies the aims of a school of thought leads to individuals' easily making sacrifices and taking risks for the sake of these aims. So long as a school is unable to sanctify its aims, to induce feelings in individuals of worshipfulness, sacrifice, and idealism in relation to the aims of the school, that school of thought has no assurance that its aims will be carried out.

That a world view promotes commitment and responsibility commits the individual, to the depths of his heart and conscience, and makes him responsible for himself and society.

The All-Encompassing World View of Tauhid

All the features and properties that are organic to a good world view are summed up in the world view of *tauhid*, which is the only world view that can have all these features. The world view of *tauhid* means perceiving that the universe has appeared through a sagacious will and that the order of being is founded on goodness, generosity, and mercy, to convey existents to attainments worthy of them. The world view of *tauhid* means the universe is unipolar and uniaxial. The world view of *tauhid* means the universe has for its essence "from Him-ness" (*inna lillah*) and "to Him-ness" (*inna ilayhi raji'un*) [Qur'an, 2:156].

The beings of the universe evolve in a harmonious system in one direction, toward one center. No being is created in vain, aimlessly. The universe is regulated through a series of definitive rules named the divine norms (*sunan ilahiya*). Man enjoys a special nobility and greatness among beings and has a special role and mission. He is responsible for his own evolution and upbringing and for the improvement of his society. The universe is the school for man, and God rewards every human being according to his right intention and right effort.

The world view of *tauhid* is backed by the force of logic, science, and reason. In every particle of the universe, there are indications of the existence of a wise, omniscient God; every tree leaf is a compendium of knowledge of the solicitous Lord.

The world view of *tauhid* gives meaning, spirit, and aim to life because it sets man on the course of perfection that stops at no determinate limit but leads ever onward.

The world view of *tauhid* has a magnetic attraction; it imparts joy and confidence to man; it presents sublime and sacred aims; and it leads individuals to be self-sacrificing.

The world view of *tauhid* is the only world view in which individuals' mutual commitment and responsibility find meaning, just as it is the only world view that saves man from falling into the terrible valley of belief in futility and worship of nothingness.

The Islamic world view is the world view of *tauhid*. *Tauhid* is presented in Islam in the purest form and manner. According to Islam, God has no peer—"There is nothing like Him" (42:11). God resembles nothing and no thing can be compared to God. God is the Absolute without needs; all need Him; He needs none—"You are the ones needing God, and God is the One Free of Need, the Praiseworthy" (35:15). "He is aware of all things" (42:12) and "He is capable of all things" (22:6). He is everywhere, and nowhere is devoid of Him; the highest heaven and the depths of the earth bear the same relationship to Him. Wherever we turn we face Him— "Wherever you turn, there is the presence of God" (2:115). He is aware of all the secrets of the heart, all the thoughts passing through the mind, all the intentions and designs, of everyone—"We created man, and We know what his soul whispers to him, and We are nearer to him than his jugular vein" (50:16). He is the summation of all perfections and is above and devoid of all defect—"The most beautiful names belong to God" (7:180). He is not a body; He is not to be seen with the eye—"No visions can grasp Him, but He comprehends all vision" (6:103).

According to the Islamic world view, the world view of *tauhid*, the universe is a created thing preserved through the divine providence and will. If for an instant this divine providence were withdrawn from the world, it would cease to be.

The universe has not been created in vain, in jest. Wise aims are at work in the creation of the universe and of man. Nothing inappropriate, devoid of wisdom and value, has been created. The existing order is the best and most perfect of possible orders. The universe rests on justice and truth. The order of the universe is based on causes and effects, and one must seek for every result in its unique cause and antecedents. One must expect a unique cause for every result and a unique result for every cause. Divine decree and foreordination bring about the existence of every being only through its own unique cause. A thing's divinely decreed fate is identical with the fate decreed for it by the sequence of causes leading to it.[3]

The intent of the divine will operates in the world in the form of a norm (*sunna*), that is, in the form of a universal law and principle. The divine norms do not change; what changes is based on the divine norms. For man, the world's good and evil depend on the kind of behavior man adopts in the world, how he encounters it and how he acts. The good and evil of actions, apart from the fact that they revert to man in the other world in the form of rewards and punishments, do incur reactions in this world as well. Gradation and evolution are the divine law, the divine norm. The world is the cradle of human evolution.

Divine decree and foreordination preside over the whole universe; in accordance with them, man is free, empowered, and responsible and presides over his own fate. Man has essential nobility and dignity and is worthy to be God's viceregent. This world and the next are related in the way the stage of sowing and the stage of harvest are related, in that each finally reaps what he sows. It is like the relation between childhood and old age in that one's old age is formed in one's childhood and youth.

The Realistic World View

Islam believes in truth, in reality. The word *islam* means surrender; the first condition of being a Muslim is to surrender to realities and truths. Islam rejects and condemns every kind of obduracy, obstinacy, fanaticism, blind imitativeness, partisanship, and selfishness, which are contrary to the spirit that seeks to realize truth and reality. According to Islam, a person who seeks the truth, has no personal considerations, and struggles to attain the truth but fails may be excused, whereas the one who harbors obduracy and obstinacy and accepts the truth through imitation, because of his heritage or for like reasons, has no standing. The real Muslim, man or woman, according to his spirit of search after truth, adopts and integrates wisdom and truth wherever and from whomever he finds it. In searching for truth and knowledge, he does not display the least fanaticism, but instead hastens to find it in the farthest parts of the world. The real Muslim does not confine this search for truth to a certain period of his life, a certain area, or certain persons because the great leader of Islam has ordered that the search for knowledge is incumbent upon all Muslims (men and women alike). He likewise has ordered, "Assimilate wisdom wherever and through whomever you find it, even through a *mushrik.*"[4] He has further ordered, "Seek knowledge, even if you must travel to China." This also has been attributed to him: "Seek knowledge from the cradle to the grave."

Shallow, one-sided conceptions of problems, blind imitation of parents, and submission to inherited traditions are condemned as contrary to the Islamic spirit of surrender and desire that the truth should prevail and as leading to error, deviation, and remoteness from the truth.

God, the Absolute Reality and Source of Being

Man is a realistic being. The human newborn seeks the mother's breast from the first hour of life; it seeks the mother's breast as a reality. Gradually, as the child's body and mind develop, it comes to distinguish between itself and other things, to regard other things as phenomena external to itself. Although a sequence of thought connects it to things, it uses thought as a means, a functional link, and knows that the reality of things is other than the thoughts it has in its mind.

The realities that man perceives through his senses, the sum total of which we call the world, are phenomena from which the following five properties are inseparable:

1. Limitation. The beings we sense and cognize, from the smallest particle to the most immense star, are limited. They are allocated to a particular area of space and interval of time. They do not exist beyond that area of space or interval of time. Some beings occupy a larger space or a longer time and some, a smaller space or a shorter time; but ultimately, all are limited to a region of space and a quantity of time.

2. Change. The beings of the universe are all undergoing change and transformation, are unstable. No being in the world of sense remains in a single state. All are either growing and evolving or eroding and declining. A sensible material being follows a course of continuous exchange with its environment throughout its term of existence. It takes, it gives, or it takes and gives both; that is, it partakes of the realities of other things and makes them part of its

own reality; it transmits something of its own reality to the external environment; or it performs both of these functions.

3. Dependency. Every being's existence is dependent and conditional upon the existence of one or more other beings. If those other beings were not, neither would this being be. Whenever we look into the reality of these beings in their context more closely, we find each of them to be paired with an "if" or with many "ifs." We find no sensible being that can exist unconditionally and absolutely (free of ties to other beings, such that the presence or absence of other beings is of no consequence to it). Each being exists by virtue of the existence of another, which in turn exists by virtue of another, and so on.

4. Need. The beings we sense and cognize, in being dependent and conditional, have needs for all those conditions upon which they depend. And each of those conditions likewise in its turn needs another series of conditions. Among all sensible beings, we cannot find one that is of itself, that does not need things other than itself, that, supposing things other than itself should cease to exist, would remain in existence. Thus, poverty, necessity, and need envelop all these beings.

5. Relativity. The beings we sense and cognize are relative from the standpoints of the origin and the perfections of their existence. If, for instance, we characterize them as great, powerful, beautiful, old, or even existent, we do so by comparing them with other things. If we say the sun is large, we mean it is large by comparison with us, our earth, and the other bodies in our solar system; but the sun is small in relation to some stars. And if we say some ship or animal is powerful, we mean it is powerful by comparison with a man or something weaker. The same holds for objects in which we discern beauty and knowledge. Even the being of a thing is an appearance relative to the being of another. Whatever being, perfection, knowledge, beauty, power, or glory we consider is relative to a lesser, but one can also conceive of a greater, relative to which any of these attributes turns into its opposite. That is, relative to this greater, being becomes appearance; perfection, defect; knowledge, ignorance; beauty, ugliness; and power and glory, paltriness.

The power of man's reason and thought, which, by contrast with the senses, do not remain content with appearances but cause their rays to penetrate behind the curtain of existence, proclaims that being cannot be confined to these limited, mutable, relative, conditional, and necessitous phenomena. This edifice of existence that we see before us as a whole stands by itself and rests on itself. There must necessarily exist some unlimited, enduring, absolute, unconditioned, self-sufficient reality present at all times and places as a support to all beings. Otherwise the edifice of existence could not subsist, or rather there would be no such thing; there would be only sheer nonexistence.

The Noble Qur'an refers to God by such attributes as "the Everlasting," "the Free of Need," and "the Eternal." Thus, it reminds us that the edifice of existence needs that Reality by which it subsists. That Reality is the support and preserver of all limited, relative, and conditional things. He is without need because all other things have needs. He is full and perfect (the Eternal) because all things other than Him are empty within and need the reality that is to fill them with being.

The Noble Qur'an designates sensed and cognized beings as signs (ayat), meaning that each being in turn is a sign of this unlimited Being and of the divine knowledge, power, life, and will. According to the Glorious Qur'an, all of nature is like a book composed by a knowing, wise Author, of Whose boundless knowledge and wisdom its every line, its every word, is a sign. According to the Qur'an, the more man learns through the power of science, the more aware he grows of the effects of divine power, wisdom, providence, and mercy.

Every natural science, just as from one point of view it is a science of nature, from another, more profound, point of view is a science of God. Consider one of the many verses of the Qur'an on this subject:

> Indeed in the creation of the heavens and the earth, the succession of night and day, the ships that sail the seas to the benefit of man, rain that God causes to fall from the skies, and in how by this means He revives a dead earth and scatters all kinds of creatures across the earth, and in the circling of the winds and the clouds that are appointed to work between the sky and the earth—are signs for people who reason and reflect. (2:164)

This noble verse summons us to cosmology in its widest sense, to the art of navigation, to world travel with its economic benefits, to meteorology, to study of the origin and source of wind, rain, and the movements of the clouds, and to biology and zoology. It holds that reflection on the philosophies of these sciences will lead to a knowledge of God.

The Attributes of God

The Noble Qur'an says that God is characterized by all the attributes of perfection: "His are the most beautiful names" (59:24). The most beautiful names and the highest qualities are His: "His is the most sublime similitude in the heavens and the earth" (30:27). The sublime qualities throughout existence are reserved for Him. Thus, God is "the Living," "the Powerful," "the Knowing," "the Intender," "the Merciful," "the Guide," "the Creator," "the Wise," "the Most Forgiving," "the Just"—in sum, there is no attribute of perfection lacking in Him.

From another standpoint, He is not a body, is not compounded, mortal, weak, under compulsion, or oppressive.

The first set of attributes, the attributes of perfection, by which God is characterized are called the affirmative attributes. The second set, which arise from defect and which God is above characterization by, are named the negative attributes.

Our praise of God may take either of the forms termed in Arabic *thana* and *tasbih*. We offer God *thana* when we recall the beautiful names and the attributes of perfection, and we offer Him *tasbih* when we recount how He is beyond and free of what is unworthy of Him. In both cases, we reinforce our knowledge of Him and by this means raise ourselves higher.

The Uniqueness of God

God Most High has no likeness or associate. It is fundamentally impossible that God should have a likeness and in consequence that, instead of one God, we should have two or more gods, because to be multiple, twofold or more, is among the special properties of limited, relative beings. For an unlimited, absolute being, manifoldness and multiplicity have no meaning. We can have one, two, or more children or one, two, or more friends in that the child and the friend are both limited beings, and limited beings can have likenesses on their own level and in consequence will admit manifoldness and multiplicity. But an unlimited being does not admit them. The following analogy, however inadequate it may be from some standpoints, is useful in explaining this point.

As to the dimensions of the sensed material universe (that is, the universe of bodies that we cognize and sense), scientists have presented two kinds of theories. Some advance the theory that the dimensions of the universe are limited (this sensed universe reaches a point and then ends), but some hold that the dimensions of the material universe are limitless, bounded in no direction, that the material universe has no beginning, end, or middle. If we regard the material universe as limited, a question arises: Is there only one material, corporeal universe or more than one? But if the universe is limitless, the supposition of another corporeal universe becomes irrational. Whatever we hypothesize as another universe will turn out to be this same universe or a part of it. This analogy pertains to the universe of bodies and corporeal beings that are limited, conditional, created, and none of which has an absolute, independent, and self-subsistent reality. The material universe, if unlimited in extent, is limited in reality. Because, according to this hypothesis, it is unlimited in extent, no second universe can be conceived of.

God Most High is the Unlimited Being and the Absolute Reality. He encompasses all things and is absent from no time or place. He is nearer to us than our jugular veins. Therefore, it is impossible for Him to have a likeness. Or rather, it is inconceivable that He should. We see the effects of His providence, planning, and wisdom in all beings. We witness a single intent, a single will, a single order throughout the universe, and this fact itself indicates that our universe has only one focus, not more.

If there were two (or more) gods, two (or more) intents and wills would necessarily be involved, both of which would necessarily bear the same relation to events in influencing them. Whatever was to come into existence under that one relation would necessarily constitute two beings if it were to derive from the two foci, and each of those two beings would constitute two further beings in turn, and so on ad infinitum. In consequence, no being would appear and the universe would not exist. Thus, the Noble Qur'an says: "If there were in them gods other than God, [heaven and earth] would be in ruins" (21:22).

Worship

To know the One God as the most perfect Essence, with the most perfect attributes, above all lack and imperfection, and to know His relation to the universe of creation, preservation, and emanation, of kindness and mercy, induce a response in us termed "worship."

Worship is a kind of relation of humility, adoration, and thanksgiving that man establishes with his God and can establish only with his God. It is correct and permissible only in relation to God. To recognize God as the only Source of being, the only Master, and the Lord of all things entails our pairing no created thing with Him in worship. The Noble Qur'an repeatedly affirms and stresses that worship must be reserved for God, that there is no sin like *shirk* toward God.

Two preliminary remarks are required to clarify the meaning of worship:

1. Worship is either verbal or active. Verbal worship consists in reciting a series of phrases and invocations, as in reciting the Opening and another *sura* of the Qur'an as well as invocations during the bows and prostrations of prayer and in pronouncing the *tashahhud* or by calling *Labbayka* during the *hajj*.[5] Active worship is exemplified by the motions of standing, bowing, and prostrating in prayer or, on the *hajj*, by the standing at 'Arafat and the Mash'ar and by the circumambulation of the Ka'ba.[6] Most acts of worship include both verbal and active components, as is the case with the prayer and the *hajj*.

2. Man's actions are of two kinds. Some acts have no special referent; they are not accomplished as signs of something else but only for the sake of their natural and inherent results. For instance, a farmer carries out a series of labors connected with agriculture to reap the natural results of such labors. The farmer does not carry on agriculture as a sign and symbol, as an expression of a series of meanings and sentiments. But we do some things as signs with a series of meanings, as expressions of sentiments of certain kinds. For instance, we nod our heads as a sign of assent; in a gathering, we sit by the door as a sign of humility; and we bow as a sign of veneration and honor to another. Most human actions are of the first kind. But some human actions are of this second kind, done to

represent a meaning, to express sentiments. Such actions have the force of words in conveying a meaning and expressing an intention. Worship, whether verbal or active, is a significant action. Man through his words of worship expresses a truth, or rather truths, and through his acts of worship, such as bowing and prostration, halting and circumambulation, or commencing the fast, expresses the meanings he recites verbally.

Man expresses five things in his verbal and active worship:

1. Praise of God by means of those attributes and qualities that are uniquely God's—that is, those qualities that refer to the Absolute Perfection, such as absolute knowledge, absolute power, absolute will. The meaning of absolute perfection, absolute knowledge, absolute power, and absolute will is that they are not limited or conditional upon anything. They entail God's being free of need.

2. Praise of God by affirming that He is beyond all lacks and defects, such as mortality, limitation, ignorance, miserliness, and injustice.

3. Thanksgiving to God as the original Source of all good things and blessings, affirmation that all the blessings we enjoy come from Him and Him alone, that things other than Him are means He has established.

4. Utter surrender and utter obedience toward Him, acknowledgement that He is to be obeyed unconditionally and deserves obedience and surrender. He, in being God, fittingly gives commands, and we, in being servants, fittingly obey and surrender to Him.

5. Acknowledgment that He has no partner in any of the four matters: There is no absolute perfection but Him; there is no essence beyond defect other than Him; there is no benefactor or original source of blessings to whom all acts of thanksgiving revert but Him; there is no being deserving of absolute obedience and absolute surrender but Him. Every act of obedience, such as obedience to the Prophet, the Imam, the legitimate Islamic ruler, one's mother and father, or one's teacher must in the end equal obedience to Him and satisfaction of Him; otherwise it is impermissible.

This is the response that is appropriate to a servant before the great God. It is neither correct nor permissible in reference to any other being.

Levels and Degrees of Tauhid

Tauhid has levels and degrees, as does its opposite, *shirk*. Until one has traversed all the levels of *tauhid*, one is not a true *muwahhid*.[7]

Essence

Tauhid as regards the Essence means to know the Essence of the God in its unity and uniqueness. The first knowledge anyone has of the Essence of God is of His self-sufficiency. This means that He is the Essence that stands in need of no other being in any respect. In the language of the Qur'an, He is the Self-sufficient. All need Him and receive help from Him, but He is free of need: "O people! You are those in need of God, and God is the Self-sufficient, the Praiseworthy" (35:15). In the language of the *hukama'*, He is the Necessary Being.

They also ascribe to Him priority, which refers to His role as Principle, Source, and Creator. He is the Principle and Creator of other beings, which are all from Him, but He is from nothing. In the language of the *hukama'*, He is the Primal Cause.

This is the first knowledge and first conception anyone has of God. That is, whoever thinks about God, whether in affirmation or denial, belief or disbelief, has such a conception in mind: He asks himself, "Is there a Reality that is dependent upon no other reality, but upon Whom all realities depend, through Whose will all realities have come into being, and Who has not Himself come into being through any other principle?"

Tauhid as regards the Essence implies this Reality does not admit duality or multiplicity, has no likeness: "There is nothing like Him" (42:11). There is no other being at His level of existence: "And there is none comparable to Him" (112:4).

That a being should be considered an individual member of a species, as for instance that Hasan should be considered an individual member of the human species, such that the existence of other members of this species may automatically be inferred, is among the characteristics of creatures and contingent beings. The

Essence of the Necessary Being is above such implications and thus free from them.

Because the Necessary Being is single, the universe is necessarily single in respect to its principle and source and in respect to its point of return and end: The universe neither arises from numerous principles nor reverts to numerous principles. It arises from one Principle, one Reality: "Say, God is the Creator of all things" (13:16). It returns to that same Principle, that same Reality: "Behold, all affairs course to God" (42:53).

The relation of God and the world is a relation of Creator and created, that is, a relation of creative cause and effect, not a relation such as that of light to the lamp or that of man's consciousness to man. God is not separate from the world.[8] He is with all things, but the things are not with Him: "He is with you wherever you may be" (57:4). But that God is not separate from the world does not imply that He is like light to the lamp or consciousness to the body. If this were so, God would be an effect of the world and not the world the effect of God, as light is an effect of the lamp, not the lamp the effect of the light. Likewise, that God is not separate from the world and man does not imply that God, the world, and man all have one mode of being and that they all live and move with one will and one spirit. All these are attributes of the created, the contingent. God is above the attributes of created beings. "Glory to your Lord! The Lord of Power! [He is free] of what they ascribe to Him" (37:180).

Attributes

Tauhid as regards the attributes means to perceive and know the Essence of God in its identity with its attributes and the attributes in their identity with one another. *Tauhid* as regards the Essence means to deny the existence of a second or a likeness, but *tauhid* as regards the attributes means to deny the existence of any sort of multiplicity and compoundedness in the Essence itself. Although the Essence of God is described by the attributes of perfection —beauty and majesty—it does not have various objective aspects. A differentiation between the Essence and the attributes or between attributes would imply a limitation in being. For a boundless being, just as a second for it cannot be conceived, neither can multiplicity, compoundedness, or differentiation between essence and attributes be conceived.

Tauhid as regards the attributes, like *tauhid* as regards the Essence, is among those principles of the Islamic sciences and among those most sublime and elevated of human ideas that have been crystallized most especially in the Shi'i school of thought. 'Ali says in the first sermon of the *Nahj al-Balagha*: "Praise to God, Whom the praise of the speakers does not attain, and Whose blessings the counters do not reckon, and Whose due the strivers do not fulfill, Whom the far-reaching aspirations do not reach, and Whom the plummetings of the sagacious do not attain, of Whom there is no limit to the description, and of Whom there is no qualification." He mentions the limitless attributes of God. A few sentences later, he says: "The perfection of devotion to Him is the rejection of attributes to Him, because any object of attribution bears witness that it is other than the attribute, and any attribute bears witness that it is other than the object of attribution, so whoever ascribes attributes to God (praise Him!) has associated Him, and whoever has associated Him. . . ."[9] In this passage 'Ali has both affirmed attributes of God ("to Whom there is no limit to the description") and negated them ("any attribute bears witness"). The attributes by which God is characterized are clearly the boundless attributes to the boundlessness of the Essence, identical to that Essence, and the attributes God is above and free of are the limited attributes distinct from the Essence and from other attributes. Therefore, *tauhid* as regards the attributes means perceiving and knowing the unity of the Essence and the attributes of God.

Acts

Tauhid as regards acts means perceiving and knowing that the universe, with all its systems, norms, and causes and effects, is God's act and God's work and arises from His will. Just as the beings of the universe are not independent in essence, all subsisting by Him and dependent on Him, He being in the language of the Qur'an the one Self-subsistent by means of Whom the universe subsists, neither are these beings independent in terms of effecting and causality. In consequence, just as God has no partner in essence, neither has He any partner in agency. Every agent and cause gains its reality, its being, its influence and agency from Him; every agent subsists by Him. All powers and all strength are by Him: "Whatever God intend, and there is no strength except by Him—no power and no strength except by God."

Man, like all other beings, has a causal role in and effect on his actions. He is indeed more influential in shaping his own destiny than are the others, but he is by no means a fully empowered being, one left to his own devices.[10] "I stand and sit by God's power and strength."

Belief in complete empowerment of a being, human or otherwise, by way of assignation, entails belief that that being is a partner with God in independence of agency, and independence of agency further entails independence in essence, which is inimical to *tauhid* as regards the Essence, not to speak of *tauhid* as regards acts. "Praise to God, Who does not take a wife and has no son, and with Whom there is no partner in rule, and Who has no supporter from inability, so magnify Him."[11]

Is theoretical *tauhid,* that is, to know God in His unity of essence, unity of essence and attributes, and unity of agency, possible? If it is possible, does such knowledge contribute to human happiness or is it superfluous? I have discussed the possibility or impossibility of such knowledge in *Usul-i Falsafa va Ravish-i Ri'alism* (Principles of Philosophy and the Method of Realism), but how we envision it depends on how we understand man and his happiness. The tide of materialistic thought about man and being has led even believers in God to conceive of questions of theology as useless and vain, as a kind of abstractionism and flight from reality. But a Muslim who views the reality of man as not just the corporeal reality, who views the basic reality of man as the reality of his spirit, whose substance is the substance of knowledge, sanctity, and purity, well understands that so-called theoretical *tauhid* (the three levels I have described), in addition to being the foundation of *tauhid* in practice, is itself in its essence the highest perfection of the soul. It truly elevates man to God and grants him perfection. "To Him ascends the good word, and He exalts the righteous deed" (35:10). Man's humanity is dependent upon his knowledge of God.

Man's knowledge is not separate from man; it is the most basic and dearest part of his existence. To whatever extent man attains knowledge of being, the system of being, and the source and principle of being, he has realized half his substance, which is knowledge, science, gnosis.

According to Islam, and especially according to Shi'i theology, to perceive theological truths, quite apart from the practical and social effects deriving from these truths, is itself the ultimate end of humanity.

Worship

The three levels I have described constitute theoretical *tauhid* and belong to the class of knowledge, but *tauhid* in worship is *tauhid* in practice and belongs to the class of being and becoming. The first three levels of *tauhid* I discussed constitute right thinking; this level means right being and right becoming. Theoretical *tauhid* is an insight into perfection; *tauhid* in practice is a movement aimed at reaching perfection. Theoretical *tauhid* means perceiving the unity of God, but *tauhid* in practice means bringing man into unity. Theoretical *tauhid* is "to see." *Tauhid* in practice is "to go."

Tauhid in practice, or *tauhid* in worship, means worship of the One, to turn to worship of the One God. According to Islam, worship has levels and degrees. The most obvious levels of worship are to carry out the rites of glorification and the affirmation of transcendence in that if they were carried out for something other than God, this act would imply complete departure from the circle of the people of *tauhid* and the pale of Islam. But according to Islam, worship is not confined to this level: every choice of orientation, of an ideal, of a spiritual *qibla*, constitutes worship. "Did you see the one who took his passion for his God?" (25:43). Or the one who obeys the orders of another to whom God has not commanded obedience, who submits to him completely, worships him: "They took their priests and their anchorites as lords, in derogation of God" (9:31). "We do not take some from among us as lords" (3:64).

Accordingly, *tauhid* in practice, or *tauhid* in worship, means to make only God our object of obedience, destination, *qibla*, and ideal, to reject any other object of obedience, destination, *qibla*, or ideal—that is, to bow and rise for God, to stand for God, to serve

God, to live for God, to die for God. It is as Abraham said: "Say: I have set my face to Him Who created the heavens and the earth, in all exclusivity. My prayer, my sacrifice, my life, and my death are for God, the Lord of the worlds. He has no partner; I am commanded of this, and I am of those who surrender" (6:162-163).

This *tauhid* of Abraham's is his *tauhid* in practice. The "good word" *La ilaha illa 'llah* most of all has in view *tauhid* in practice, in meaning that none but God is worthy of worship.

Man and the Attainment of Unity

The questions of how the existential reality of man is to attain unity within a single psychical system and a single humane and evolutionary direction, how human society is to attain unity and integration within a single harmonious, evolving social system, and, conversely, how the personality of the human individual has disintegrated into various poles and his existential reality fragmented into disparate segments and how man's society has disintegrated into conflicting egos and inharmonious groupings and classes, in contradiction and inimical to one another, have stimulated much thought. What must be done to bring the character of man from psychical and social standpoints to the state of unity we know as *tauhid*, within a single humane and evolutionary course? Three theories address this question: the materialistic, the idealistic, and the realistic.

Materialistic Theory

The materialistic theory, which takes only matter into consideration and grants the psyche no sort of substantive reality, holds that private possession (ownership) of objects is what divides and disorders the individual psychically and society socially and makes each of them subject to inharmonious poles. In coming under individual possession, objects fragment man individually (psychically) and socially. Man is a "generic" existent (social by nature).

At the dawn of history, man lived as a social body, as a we. No I existed; that is, man felt no I. He was aware not of his individual existence but of his collective existence. His feelings were the collective's feelings, his pain, the collective's pain. He lived for the collective, not for himself; his conscience was a collective conscience, not an individual one. At the dawn of history, man had a communal life. He lived by hunting. Each was able daily to gain enough from sea and forest to satisfy his individual needs; no surplus production existed. This state of affairs persisted until man discovered agriculture and surplus production grew possible, and with it the growth of one class that worked, and another that consumed without working. This process culminated in the principle of ownership.

Private ownership, also termed the private possession by a special group of property and wealth (the resources for production, such as water and land, and the tools of production, such as the plow), shattered the collective spirit and bisected the society that had lived as a unity: half prosperous and profiting and half deprived, exploited, and toiling. Society, which had lived as a "we," was transformed into a collection of "I"s. Through the appearance of ownership, man grew inwardly alienated from his real self, which was his social self, whereby he had felt his identity with other people. Instead of feeling himself a man, he felt himself an owner; he grew self-alienated and diminished. Only by severing this tie of possession can man return to moral unity and psychical well-being and to social unity and well-being. History flows inexorably toward these unities.

The ownerships that deform human unity into plurality and collectivity into fragmentation are like the battlements that Jalal adDin Rumi speaks of in his beautiful parable as splitting the single and expansive light of the sun and giving rise to shadows. Of course, Rumi is speaking of a truth of 'irfan, the appearance of multiplicity from unity and the return of multiplicity to unity, but with some distortion and forced interpretation, it can be regarded as an allegory for this Marxist theory:

> We were single, of one substance all,
>> We lacked head and foot, that one head all,
> We were one in substance like the sun,
>> We were guileless, pure as water, one.
> First that clear light assumed form, and thence,
>> Number came like shadowed battlements.
> Smash by catapult these battlements,
>> So this party shed all differences.[12]

Idealistic Theory

The idealistic theory considers only the soul and inner being of man, man's relation to his own self; it takes this as its basis and principle. This theory concedes that possession and attachment obstruct realization of unity and lead to multiplicity, work to fragment and disintegrate the collective, and draw the individual into psychical fragmentation and society into dissolution into groups, but it holds that inevitably the thing attached to is the cause of the fragmentation and dissolution of the thing attached, not the thing attached the cause of the fragmentation and dissolution of the thing attached to. The possession of, the attachment to various entities — wealth, wife, position, and so forth — is not the cause of the fragmentation of the psyche and the dissolution of society; rather, the inward attachment of man to such entities causes man's division, decomposition, and alienation. Man's ownership has not separated man from self and society; rather, man's being owned has done this. What fragments me from moral and social standpoints is not my wealth, my wife, or my position, but rather wealth's me, wife's me, and position's me. It is not necessary to sever the possession of things by man to transform me into us; rather, the possession of man by things must be severed. Deliver man from his attachment to objects so that he may revert to his human reality. Do not free things from their attachment to man. Give man spiritual freedom. What has freeing things ever accomplished? Give deliverance, freedom, communality, and unity to man, not to a thing.

Tauhid as an ethical and social factor in man belongs under the heading of educational factors, especially factors in spiritual education, not under that of economic factors. The agent of *tauhid* in man is his inner evolution, not his outer diminution. If man is to attain unity, one must give him spirit, not take from him matter. Man is first an animal and then human. He is an animal innately and human by acquisition. Man regains his humanity, which is his latently and inherently, in the light of faith and through the effects of the factors of correct education and upbringing. So long as man has not regained his spirituality under the effective influence of spiritual factors and become human, he is this same animal by nature, and there is no chance for unity of spirits and animal souls.

The animal soul has no unity
  Seek not from the wind's soul such unity,
If this should eat bread, it sates not then that,
  If this bears a load, it weighs not on that.
But rather this loves to see that one die,
  It dies of sheer spite to see that one thrive.
The souls of the wolves and dogs are at odds,
  But joined are the souls of the lions of God's.
Believers are numbered, but belief one,
  Their bodies are numbered, but the soul one,
Apart from the mind and soul of the cow,
  And ass, we've another mind and a soul.
Ten lamps, if you bring them all to one place,
  Have each their own form distinct from the rest,
One can't make the light out of any one,
  Then turn to its light and with doubt be done.
So seek from the Qur'an the meaning of, "Say,
  We make no distinction among the prophets."
Of apples and peaches each if you count,
  One hundred, when pressed they all become one.
In spirit there are no numbers or parts,
  Are no separate beings, to analyze.[13]

To consider matter the agent of the fragmentation and coalescence of man (such that when it is fragmented, man is fragmented, when it coalesces, man coalesces, and when it is one, man is one) and to regard man's ethical character and social character as dependent and parasitical upon the economic situation and the state of production arise from an ignorance of man and a lack of faith in the substantive reality of man and the powers of his reason and will. It is an antihumanistic theory.

To sever the bond of possession of objects by private persons is impossible. Suppose this were done in the case of property and wealth. What could be done in the case of family, wife and children? Could one propose this area be communalized and advocate a sexual communism? If this were possible, why have those nations that years ago abolished private ownership of wealth stuck with the private family system? Suppose this inherently private system of the family were also communalized. What could one do about posts, positions, reputations, and honors? Could one parcel these out evenly as well? Then what would one do with the individuals' distinct physical, psychical, and mental capacities? These qualities are inseparably attached to each individual's being; they could not be detached and equalized.

Realistic Theory

The realistic theory holds that what divides and disintegrates man individually and socially, the central factor in human fragmentation and multiplicity, is man's attachments to objects, not the objects' attachment to man. Man's captivity arises from his being owned, not from his ownership. Thus, this theory accords the greatest importance to education, to a revolution in thought, to faith, ideology, and spiritual freedom. But it holds that, just as man is not pure matter, neither is he pure spirit. Today's livelihood and the future life are inseparably paired. Body and soul have a reciprocal influence. While in the light of *tauhid* in worship, worship of God, one struggles with the spiritual and psychical agents of fragmentation, one must simultaneously war vehemently against the agents of discrimination, injustice, deprivation, oppression, strangulation, *taghutism*, and subservience to other-than-God.[14] This is the logic of Islam.

When Islam appeared, it simultaneously launched two transformations or revolutions, two movements. Islam did not say "Eliminate discrimination, injustice, or property, and everything will be straightened out." Nor did it say "Reform the heart and leave the outer world alone. Construct a morality, and a society will be constructed automatically." When Islam proclaimed *tauhid* as an inner psychological truth, in the light of faith in God Most High and worship of His single Essence, it simultaneously proclaimed *tauhid* as a social truth, to be realized by means of jihad and struggle against social inequalities.

The following noble verse of the Qur'an shines like a star in the firmament of *tauhid* as we know it. This is the verse that the Most Noble Prophet included in his letters summoning the heads of nations to faith. It presents Islamic realism and the comprehensive outlook of Islam: "Say, 'O people of the book! Come to an agreement between us and you: that we worship none but God, that we associate nothing as a partner with Him . . .'" (3:64). Come to one parlance, one thesis, one truth that is the same for you and for us, that bears the same relation to everyone, under which neither you nor we have any special privilege: We are to worship the One God and nothing else. To this point, the noble verse has covered how unity is granted people through a single faith, a single orientation and *qibla,* and a single ideal, and how spiritual freedom is attained. It continues: " 'and that we not take some from among ourselves as lords other than God. . . .' " Let not some of us people take others as our lords, despite the fact that God is Lord of all. Let us not be disintegrated into lord and serf. Come, let us sever the wrong social ties that lead to such discrimination.

After the disruption of the Islamic caliphate in the time of 'Uthman, the reestablishment of a class structure out of the days of ignorance, the popular uprising, and the killing of 'Uthman, the people flocked to 'Ali (upon whom be peace) to swear allegiance to him. 'Ali had no choice but to accept, although he personally was loath to accept. 'Ali explains his personal loathing and his legal responsibility in this way: "If the people had not gathered, if their support had not made it incumbent upon me, and if God had not extracted a pledge from the *'ulama* to reduce the engorgement of the oppressors and the hunger of the oppressed, I would have laid the bridle [of the caliphate] on its shoulders and left it alone."[15]

After 'Ali undertook the office, he placed two responsibilities at the head of his agenda: One was to advise and counsel the people, to reform their mentalities and morals, and to expound divine knowledge in a way that we see exemplified in the *Nahj al-Balagha.* The other was to struggle against social discrimination. 'Ali did not content himself with inward reform and spiritual liberation, just as he did not consider social reforms enough. He worked for reform in both directions. This is the program of Islam.

Thus, Islam bore in one hand a logic, a summons, and a program for the individual and collective unity of people, directed at worship of God, and in the other hand a sword to sever unjust human relations, to overthrow social classes, and to destroy the *taghuts.*

The Islamic classless society is the society without discriminations, without deprived persons, without *taghuts,* without oppression, the just society. It is not the society without differences; such homogeneity is itself a kind of oppression and injustice. There is a distinction to be made between discrimination and difference. Differences exist in the created system of the universe. And these differences have imparted beauty, diversity, progress, and evolution to the universe, but they do not constitute discrimination. The "virtuous city" of Islam is the city opposed to discrimination, not to differences.[16] *Islamic society is the society of equality and fraternity, not of negative equality, but rather of positive equality. Negative equality means to take no account of natural distinctions among individuals and to deny their acquired distinctions in order to establish equality. Positive equality means creation of equal opportunities for all, possession by each of his acquisitions, and denial of imaginary and unjust distinctions.*

Negative equality is the sort of equality spoken of in the myth [of Procrustes], who lived in the mountains and offered his hospitality to wayfarers. The guest was obliged to sleep on a certain bed. As the host's servants laid him on that bed, if he was neither shorter nor longer than that bed, he was allowed to sleep. But alas for the unfortunate guest if his stature was not equal to the length of the bed! If he was taller, he would be evened with the bed with a saw, at his head or feet. If he was shorter, he would be stretched until he drew even. In either case, it is clear how he wound up.

Positive equality, however, resembles the disinterestedness of a compassionate and sympathetic teacher who regards all students alike. When they give equivalent answers, he gives equal grades; when they give different answers, he gives to each the grade that he deserves.

Islamic society is the natural society. It is neither the discriminatory society nor the society of negative equality. The thesis of Islam is "Work according to ability, merit according to work."

The discriminatory society is the society in which people's relations are based on subjugation and exploitation, that is, on individuals' living by exploiting others' toils, by force. The natural society, however, is the society in which any way one person lives by exploiting another is condemned. The relationship among persons is one of mutual taming. All strive freely and according to their abilities and opportunities, and all are tamed by one another. That is, bilateral employment is the rule. Insofar as natural differences and discrepancies among individuals are the rule, whoever has the greater power and ability will attract the greater number of forces to himself. For instance, an individual who has the greater ability in science will attract the greater number of prospective students of science to himself and tame them to the greater extent. Whoever has the greater ability in technology will necessarily draw the more others, propel them the further in the direction of his own thought and innovation, and tame them the more.

While the Glorious Qur'an negates lordship and servanthood in society, it admits the reality of natural differences and various degrees of abilities from the standpoint of how we are created and affirms the relationship of mutual taming. It is said in the *sura* Zukhruf:

> Do they apportion the mercy of the Lord? [Is it theirs to bestow the mantle of prophecy upon whomever they please?] It is We who portion out among them their livelihood in the life of this world, and we raise them above each other in degree, so they might obtain labor [*yattakhidha . . . sukhriyan*] of each other. But the mercy of your Lord is better than what they amass. (43:32)

The discrepancy in merits is thus not one-sided; that is, people do not fall under one of two classes, one endowed with natural superiority and the other not. In such an event, one class would be the tamers and the other, the tamed. If this were the case, it would have had to be thus expressed: "We raise some of them above others in degree, so that they [the former] might obtain labor of them [the latter]." But the actual wording is "we raise them above each other in degree, so they might obtain labor of each other." That is, all enjoy some superiority and all tame each other. In other words, both merit and the act of taming are bilateral.

The second point relates to the word "taming" (*sukhriyan*). Here the initial letter *sin* bears the short vowel *u*; thus, the word bears the aforementioned sense. In two other verses of the Qur'an, this word occurs with the short vowel *i*. One instance is Mu'minun: 110, addressed to the people of hell, in which their inadmissible behavior toward the people of the faith is attacked: "And there were a party among My servants. . . . But you treated them with derision [*sikhriyan*], to the point that it made you forget to remember Me, while you were laughing at them" (23:109–110). The other is verse 63 of the blessed *sura* Sad, in which the people of hell themselves say, "What has happened to us such that we do not see men whom we used to number among the evil? Did we treat them with derision, or have our eyes failed to perceive them?" (38:62-63). Indications are (and in all the works of exegesis I have consulted—*Majma' al-Bayan, Kashshaf, Tafsir-i Imam,* Bayzawi, *Ruh al-Bayan,* Safi, *Tafsir al-Mizan*—exegetes concur in this interpretation) that *sikhriyan* as it appears in these two verses means as the object of derision. Only the *Majma' al-Bayan* has transmitted (while describing it as unreliable) an assertion by some that it means having been enslaved. Some assert categorically that *sikhriyan* always means as the object of derision and that *sukhriyan* always means tamed (*musakhkhar*).

The verbal noun *taskhir* and its passive participle *musakhkhar* appear repeatedly in the Noble Qur'an with the previously given meanings of to tame and tamed, respectively. The Qur'an speaks of the taming of the moon, sun, night, day, sea, rivers, mountains (for the prophet David), wind (for Solomon), and all that is in the heavens and on earth (for man). The meaning in all these instances is that these phenomena have been so created as to render them tame to man and available for man's use and benefit. These verses speak only of things being tamed for man, not of man being tamed for things. In the verse under consideration, man is spoken of as being tamed for man in a bilateral manner.

The senses of unwillingness and coercion do not enter into the meaning of the word *taskhir*. For instance, the lover is tamed by the beloved, the disciple by the master, the student by the teacher, and the common people, generally, by heroes; but these are under no coercion. Accordingly, the *hukama'* of Islam have perceptively distinguished the expression "agency under 'taming'" (*fa'iliyya bi't-taskhir*) from the expression "agency under coercion" (*fa'iliyya bi'l-jabr*). An act of taming inheres in every act of coercion, but the converse does not hold.

These are the terms in which the Qur'an defines this word. But I do not know whether this terminology is peculiar to the Qur'an —such that the Qur'an has given a new crystallization to the original meaning of the word in order to communicate an extraordinarily novel truth regarding the course of creation, that the activity of natural forces has the character of an activity governed by the action of taming and is neither a predestined activity nor an assigned one—or this terminology was in use prior to the Qur'anic revelations.

Here it grows clear how wide of the mark are the definitions of *taskhir* offered by some dictionaries, such as *Al-Munjid,* which define it as a task performed for another without compensation. First, these lexicographers have applied the word only to the elective social relationships of people. Second, they have had to import the idea of coercion and unwillingness into its meaning, whereas the Qur'an has applied it to a relationship made inherent by creation, without bringing in this idea of coercion and unwillingness.

The verse under consideration expounds this relationship of people in their social life, the relationship of taming of all for all. It is one of the most important verses of the Qur'an from the standpoint of expressing the social philosophy of Islam.

How well, how sublimely have Bayzawi in his well-known *Tafsir* and, after him, 'Allama Fayz expounded this verse, saying that the meaning of the phrase "so that they might obtain labor of each other" is that "they make use of each other in their needs," by this means familiarity and mutual solidarity appear, and thus the order of the world is assured.

It is likewise said in a Tradition that the meaning of the verse is "We have created all in need of one another." The relationship of taming is so composed that, just as it interrelates people's natural needs, it does not lead society out of the arena of free competition, by contrast with determinate relationships. The life of social animals is based on determinate relationships; thus, man's sociality differs from that of honeybees or ants. Determinate laws govern their life. Their life is not an arena for competition. They have no possibility to rise or to fall. Although man is social, he also enjoys a kind of freedom. Human society is the arena for a competition in progress and evolution. Fetters that limit an individual's freedom on the course of evolution block the unfolding of human capacities.

Man as envisioned by materialist theory, in not having attained to freedom within, in finding only his outward fetters broken, is like a wingless bird that has been unfettered but still cannot fly. Man as envisioned by idealist theory is free inwardly but in fetters outwardly, is a bird with wings but with its feet tied to a massive form. Man as presented by the realistic theory, however, is a bird with wings that is fully prepared for flight, from whose feet these heavy fetters have been removed.

Tauhid in practice, individual and social, consists in the individual's growing unified through worship of God alone by means of rejection of all kinds of counterfeit worship (such as worship of carnal desires, money, or prestige) and in society's growing unified through worship of God alone by means of rejection of *taghuts,* of discrimination, and of injustice. So long as individual and society do not attain unity, they will not attain happiness. And except by worship of the Truth, they will not attain unity. In the blessed *sura* Zumar, verse 29, the Noble Qur'an addresses the waywardness and directionlessness of man and the fragmentation and dispersion of his personality in the system of *shirk* and, conversely, his unity, his attainment of a single character and direction, and his evolutionary alignment in the system of *tauhid,* in these words: "God coins a parable: a man in whom partners share ownership, and a man belonging wholly to one man: are these two equal in comparison?" (39:29). Imagine a man with several masters, each of whom angrily and ill-naturedly orders him in a different direction. Man under the system of *shirk* is drawn every moment in a different direction, toward a different pole. He is a piece of straw floating on the sea; the waves wash him in a new direction every instant. But in the system of *tauhid,* he is like a ship equipped with navigational systems, making an orderly, harmonious journey under a benevolent captain.

Levels and Degrees of Shirk

Just as *tauhid* has levels and degrees, so has *shirk.* According to the rule, "Things are known by their contraries," by comparing the levels of *tauhid* with the levels of *shirk,* we can better understand both *tauhid* and *shirk.* Opposite the *tauhid* that the prophets have summoned us to, kinds of *shirk* have always existed.

Essence

Some people have professed belief in two, three, or more independent, eternal, preexistent principles (dualism, trinitarianism, and polytheism, respectively). They have regarded the world as having more than one basis, pole, or focus. What are the roots of such ideas? Is each of them the reflection, the expression, of a people's social situation? Say, for instance, that when a people have professed two eternally preexistent principles, two essential axes for the universe, is it because their society has been divided between two poles and that, likewise, when a people believe in three principles or gods, their society has been a threefold system? That is, has the social system always been reflected in the people's minds as a principle of belief? Does it not follow automatically that when prophets of *tauhid* have professed a belief in *tauhid*, a belief that the universe has a single origin, the social system must already have been gravitating to a single pole?

This theory derives from another philosophical theory I have already considered: that the spiritual and rational aspects of man and the ideal constituents of society, such as science, law, philosophy, religion, and art, are functions of social systems and especially of economics and have no substantive reality of their own. I have already rebutted this theory, and, because I believe in the substantive reality and autonomy of thought, ideology, and humanity, I hold such sociological theories for *shirk* and *tauhid* to be groundless.

It is true, of course, that sometimes a belief system, a religious system, will become a vehicle for abuses in a given social system, just as the particular system of idolatry of the *mushriks* of the Quraysh tribe became a vehicle by which Arab usurers maintained their profits.[17] But these usurers, the Abu Sufyans, Abu Jahls, and Walid ibn Mughiras, had not the least belief in these idols; they defended them only to preserve the existing social system.[18] These defensive actions grew earnest just as Islam, the system of *tauhid* opposed to exploitation and usury, appeared. The idolators, in seeing themselves faced with acute danger of extinction, advanced reverence for popular beliefs as a defense. This point is referred to many times in the verses of the Qur'an, especially in the story of Moses and Pharaoh. But this point is to be distinguished from the idea that, overall, the economic system is the infrastructure of the system of thought and belief or that every system of thought and belief is a determinate reflection of the economic and social systems.

The school of the prophets emphatically denies that every school of thought is necessarily the crystallization of society's demands, which are, in turn, the products of economic conditions. According to this totally materialistic theory, the school of *tauhid* of the prophets is itself the crystallization of society's demands and so the product of the economic needs of their time. That is, the development of the tools of production gave rise to a series of social demands that had to be rationalized as a conception of *tauhid*. The prophets were the vanguard and in fact the envoys of this social and economic need. This is what it means for an idea or belief, such as the idea of *tauhid*, to have an economic infrastructure.

The Qur'an, in maintaining that man has a primordial nature and in accounting this nature a basic existential dimension of man that in turn gives rise to a range of thoughts and desires, regards the prophets' summons to *tauhid* as an answer to these innate needs. It poses no other infrastructure for *tauhid* than the universal primordial nature of man. The Qur'an, in maintaining a primordial nature for man, does not present class conditions as determining factors in thought or belief. If class conditions had the character of an infrastructure, and if there were no such thing as a primordial nature, everyone's thoughts and inclinations would necessarily point where his class background dictated. In this case, no choice or election would exist; there would be neither Pharaohs deserving of blame nor antiPharaohs deserving of praise because man is deserving of praise or blame when he can be other than what he is. If he cannot be other than what he is, as the black in his blackness or the white in his whiteness, he deserves neither. But we know that man is not condemned to thought based on class: He can rise up against his own class interests, just as Moses did after having grown up amid the luxuries of a Pharaoh. This in itself shows that the idea of infrastructure and superstructure, besides negating the humanity of man, is nothing more than a superstition.

I do not, however, mean that one's material situation and one's mental state do not interact or that they are alien to and devoid of influence upon one another. I simply deny that one is the infrastructure and the other, the superstructure. The Qur'an itself says: "man transgresses when he sees himself as self-sufficient" (96:6-7). The Qur'an attests to the special role of the grandees (*mala'*) and the affluent in struggling against the prophets and the special role of the oppressed in supporting them, but in such a way as to uphold the primordial nature in everyone that imparts to man the worth to be summoned and reminded. The difference between the groups lies in the fact that, although, in accordance with the primordial nature, the requisites for acceptance exist in both, one group (the grandees and the affluent) must surmount a great obstacle from a spiritual standpoint, which is their extant material interests and the oppressors' privileges they have acquired, whereas the other faces no such obstacles. In the words of Salman Farsi, "The disencumbered found deliverance."[19]

Not only is there no obstacle to the oppressed responding positively to their primordial nature, but they have an additional inducement—they are leaving behind hard circumstances and attaining a better life. This is why the oppressed compose a majority of the prophets' followers. But the prophets have always gained some adherents from among the other group, who have risen against their class and class background, just as some of the oppressed have joined the ranks of the prophets' enemies, through being ruled by a range of habits, subliminal influences, consanguinary tendencies, and so forth. The Qur'an does not conceive of the pharaohs' and Abu Sufyans' defenses of the *shirk*-ridden systems of their day, which incited the people's religious sentiments against Moses and the Seal of the Prophets, as being the inevitable product of these persons' class situations, such that they could not think in any other way and their social aims were crystallized in these beliefs. The Qur'anic conception is that they acted with duplicity and that, while in accordance with their God-given primordial nature they perceived and recognized the truth, they assumed an attitude of denial: "And they rejected [Our signs], while their souls were convinced of them" (27:14). The Qur'an considers their unbelief to be uncandid (*juhudi*) unbelief, that is, unbelief of the tongue concurrent with belief of the heart. In other words, it conceives of these acts of denial as a kind of rebellion against the rule of conscience.

A great mistake some have made in interpreting the Qur'an is that of supposing it accepts the Marxists' materialistic view of history. This theory neither accords with the objective actualities of history nor proves defensible scientifically.

Belief in multiplicity of origins is *shirk* as regards the Essence, the point diametrically opposite *tauhid* as regards the Essence. Where the Qur'an adduces a demonstration and says, "If there were in them gods other than God, [heaven and earth] would be in ruins" (21:22), it is adducing a demonstration against this group.[20] Such belief occasions departure from the circle of the people of *tauhid* and from the pale of Islam. Islam totally rejects *shirk* as regards the Essence.

Creatorship

Some peoples regard God as the Essence without like or peer and recognize Him as the sole Principle of the universe, but account some created things partners with Him in creatorship. For instance, they say that God is not responsible for the creation of evils, but that evil is the creation of some created things.[21] This kind of *shirk*, *shirk* as regards creatorship and agency, is the point diametrically opposite *tauhid* as regards acts. Islam holds that this form of *shirk* cannot be excused. *Shirk* as regards creatorship also has levels, some of which constitute hidden (*khafi*), not evident (*jali*) *shirk* and thus do not occasion complete exclusion from the circle of the people of *tauhid* and the pale of Islam.

Attributes

Because *shirk* as regards the attributes is too fine a point for the lay public, it is never discussed. *Shirk* as regards the attributes applies only to some thinkers who have considered these questions but lacked the requisite competence and profundity. Among Islamic theologians, the Ash'aris fell into this kind of *shirk*. This kind of *shirk*, too, is hidden and does not occasion departure from the pale of Islam.

Worship

Some peoples have worshipped wood, stone, metal, animals, stars, the sun, trees, or the sea. This kind of *shirk* was once common and is still to be found in parts of the world. This *shirk* is *shirk* in worship and is the point diametrically opposite *tauhid* in worship.

The previously mentioned levels of *shirk* are theoretical and fall under the heading of spurious knowledge, but this kind of *shirk* is *shirk* in practice and falls under the heading of spurious being and becoming.

Shirk in practice has levels. The highest level, which occasions departure from the pale of Islam, is the kind just described and is considered evident *shirk*. But kinds of hidden *shirk* exist, and Islam struggles hard against them in its campaign of *tauhid* in practice. Some of these kinds are so minute and hidden as to require a powerful microscope even to descry with difficulty. The Most Noble Prophet (upon whom and whose family be peace and blessings) says in a Tradition: "[The progress of] *shirk* is more hidden than the passage of an ant over a stone on a dark night. The least of it is that one should love something of oppression or hate something of justice. Is religion anything other than loving and hating for God? God says, '[Say,] if you love God, follow me [my directives that come from God], so that He may love you'" (3:31).[22]

According to Islam, every sort of worship of whim, prestige, position, money, or personality is *shirk*. The Noble Qur'an, in the story of the encounter of Moses and Pharaoh, terms the latter's tyrannical rule over the Israelites "enslavement" (*ta'bid*). It has Moses give this reply to Pharaoh: "And this is the favor you are reminding me of—that you enslaved the Israelites?" (26:22). That is to say, "Having made the Israelites your slaves, are you now trying to make me feel beholden to you because while I was in your house, this and that happened?" It is clear that the Israelites neither worshipped Pharaoh nor were his bondservants; rather, they were completely under the oppressive and *taghut*-styled dominance of Pharaoh, which fact is expressed elsewhere in the Qur'an, in words ascribed to Pharaoh: "we are masters over them" (7:127) (that is, "They are under our power, and we are set over them and subjugate them"). And these words also are ascribed to him: "and their people are in thrall to us" (23:47) (that is, "The people of Moses and Aaron [the Israelites] are slaves for us"). In this noble verse, the expression *lana* (for us) is the best indication that what is meant is not worship, because, supposing that the Israelites were compelled to worship, they would have been worshipping Pharaoh, not all the Pharaoh's henchmen. What had been imposed upon the Israelites by the Pharaoh and his henchmen (in Qur'anic language, Pharaoh's grandees [*mala'*]) was forced obedience.

'Ali (upon whom be peace) in the Qasi'a sermon, as he discussed the imposition of the Pharaoh's oppressive domination upon the Israelites, refers to it as enslavement. He says: "The Pharaohs took them as slaves (*'abidan*)." He goes on to describe this enslavement in this way: "[The Pharaohs] placed them under torture and gave them cups of gall to drink. They lived in deadly abasement and in subjugation from the oppressive dominance of the enemy. They had no means of noncooperation or of defense."

Nothing is more clear and explicit on this matter then the noble verse on the entrusting of the viceregency to the people of faith. "God has promised those of you who have faith and do good that He will make them viceregents on earth [just as He made others viceregents before them], that He will surely establish the religion that He has chosen for them, and that He will transform their state from their prior fear into security: 'They shall worship [only] Me and associate nothing with Me'" (24:55). The final sentence of this verse considers the fact that when the governance of the Truth and the divine viceregency is established, the people of faith will be free from bonds of obedience to any tyrant. It is phrased "They shall worship [only] Me and associate nothing with Me" to make it clear that, according to the Qur'an, every act of obedience to an order constitutes worship. If it is for God, it is obedience to God, and if it is for other than God, it is *shirk* toward God. This sentence is remarkable for holding that the forced obedience that is by no means accounted worship from a moral viewpoint is in fact worship from a social viewpoint. The Most Noble Prophet says: "Whenever the tribe of 'As ibn Umayya [the ancestor of Marwan ibn Hakam and most of the Umayyad caliphs] come to number thirty, they will pass God's wealth from hand to hand, make God's slaves their own servants, and distort God's religion."[23] Reference is made to the oppression and autocracy of the Umayyads. Plainly, they neither called upon the people to worship them nor made them their chattel and bondservants. Rather, they imposed their autocracy and tyranny upon the people. God's Prophet (upon whom and whose family be peace and blessings) with his God-given prescience, called this condition a kind of *shirk*, a tie of master and mastered.

Boundary Between Tauhid and Shirk

What is the precise boundary between *tauhid* and *shirk* (whether in theory or in practice)? What sort of thought is characterized by *tauhid,* and what sort of thought is characterized by *shirk*? What sort of action is characterized by *tauhid,* and what sort of action is characterized by *shirk*? Is belief in a being other than God *shirk* (*shirk* as regards the Essence)? And does *tauhid* as regards the Essence entail our having no belief in the existence of anything other than God (even as His creature)? (This is a form of the doctrine of unity of being [*vahdat-i vujud*].)

It is plain that the creature of God is the act of God; the act of God is itself one of God's modes (*shu'un,* sing. *sha'n*) and not a second entity before Him. God's creatures are manifestations of His effulgence. To believe in the existence of the creature from the standpoint of its creatureliness does not contradict, but fulfills and complements, belief in *tauhid*. Therefore, the boundary between *tauhid* and *shirk* is not belief in the existence or nonexistence of other things, given they are His creatures.

Is belief that creatures have a role in influence and impression, in cause and effect, *shirk* (*shirk* as regards creatorship and agency)? Does *tauhid* as regards acts entail our denying the system of causality of the universe, regarding every effect as stemming directly and without intermediation from God, and professing no role for secondary causes? For instance, are we to believe that fire has no role in burning, water, none in quenching, rain, none in promoting growth, and medicine, none in curing? Thus, God directly burns, directly quenches, directly brings about growth, directly grants healing. The presence or absence of these agents makes no difference. What exists is God's habit of performing His works in the presence of these phenomena. As an analogy, if one is in the habit of writing letters while wearing a hat, the presence or absence of the hat has no effect on the writing of the letter, but the writer does not care to write a letter in the absence of the hat. According to this theory, the presence or absence of the phenomena that are called factors or causes amounts to this. If we profess otherwise, we have professed belief in a partner, or rather partners, with God in agency (the theory of the Ash'ari and predestinarian theologians). This theory, too, is incorrect. Belief in the existence of the creature does not equal *shirk* as regards the Essence and belief in a second god or second pole vis-à-vis God but rather fulfills and complements belief in the existence of the One God. Likewise, belief that things have influence, causality, and a role in the system of the universe does not constitute *shirk* as regards the creation, but rather fulfills and complements belief in the creative agency of God. Just as beings have no independence in essence, they have no independence in influence, but exist by His existence and exert influence by His influence.

It might prove otherwise if we were to profess the doctrine of assignation and the independence of creatures, if we were to conceive of the relation of God to the universe as being the relation of the artificer to his artifact (like that of the maker of the automobile to the automobile). The artifact needs the artificer to come into being, but after it is made, it performs its work in accordance with its mechanism. The artificer plays a role in making the artifact, but not in its subsequent operation. If the maker of the automobile should die, the automobile goes on functioning. If we thus suppose that the constituents of the world—water, rain, electricity, heat, earth, vegetation, animal life, man, and so forth—have such a relation to God (Mu'tazilites occasionally expressed such a view), this is categorically *shirk*. The creature needs the Creator in creation and in continuation.

The universe is pure emanation, pure attachment, pure connection, pure dependency, pure "from Him-ness." From this standpoint, the influence and causality of things is identical with the influence and causality of God. The creativity of the powers and forces of the universe, whether human or extrahuman, is identical with the creativity of God and the unfolding of His agency. In fact, to believe that it is *shirk* to hold that things have a role in the workings of the universe is itself *shirk* because such a belief arises from an unconscious assumption that things have an essential independence vis-à-vis the Essence of the Truth. It would follow that if beings have a role in influence, the influences would be attributable to other poles. Therefore, the boundary between *tauhid* and *shirk* is not that we do or do not profess that things other than God have a role in influence and causality.

Is the boundary between *tauhid* and *shirk* belief in a supernatural power and influence? This view implies that belief that a being, whether angel or man (such as the Prophet or the Imam), has supernatural power is *shirk* but that belief that one has a power and influence within familiar and conventional limits is not *shirk*. Likewise, belief that a deceased person has power and influence is *shirk* in that a dead person is an inanimate being, and, according to natural laws, an inanimate being has no consciousness, power, or will. Thus, to believe that a dead man has perception, to greet him, honor him, venerate him, call upon him, and seek favors of him is *shirk* because it entails imputing a supernatural power to something other than God.

Likewise, belief in objects' harboring an occult and mysterious power, such as belief that a certain kind of earth has an influence that can cure illness or that a certain place can be effective in obtaining an answer to prayer, is *shirk* because it entails belief in a supernatural power in a thing. Such a power cannot be understood, tested, sensed, or felt, as a natural force can. Thus, belief in the absolute that things have influences is not *shirk* (as the Ash'arites supposed). Rather, belief that things have supernatural influences is *shirk*.

Being is thus dichotomized into the natural and the supernatural. The supernatural is the special province of God, and the natural is the special province of His creation or the shared province of God and His creatures. A range of actions has a supernatural aspect, such as giving life, giving death, giving daily provenance, and the like; what remain are usual and normal actions. Paranormal actions are exclusively God's, and those that remain are the domain of His creatures. This part of the argument has to do with theoretical *tauhid*.

From the standpoint of *tauhid* in practice every kind of spiritual contemplation of other-than-God (that is, contemplation that does not take place by way of the face and tongue of the contemplator and the face and outward ear of the contemplated, but rather involves the contemplator's seeking to establish a kind of inner, spiritual bond between himself and his opposite number, calling upon that one to gain his attention, seeking that one's intermediation and granting of pleas) is *shirk* and worship of other-than-God, because worship is nothing if not such actions as these. Worship of other-than-God is

extent have we in this act let go the bond of surrender to other-than-God and become utterly surrendered to His Essence? This aspect of worship depends on the degree of our faith.

Not all individuals have the same degree of veracity and sincerity. Some advance so far that in practice nothing but God's command rules their beings; they have no other commander than God inwardly or outwardly. Psychical impulses and inclinations cannot draw them from this side to that, and no other person can subject them to his command. They permit their psychical inclinations just that scope of activity which conforms to God's pleasure, this being the road that leads man to his real perfection. And they comply with others' orders (father, mother, teacher, and so forth) to please God and within limits of what God has permitted. Some have gone further than this and have no object or beloved other than God. They make God their true Beloved, and they love God's creatures according to the rule "Everyone who loves a thing, loves its traces, signs, and keepsakes as well" because God's creatures are the traces and creations of God, His signs, keepsakes, and remembrances. Some have advanced even beyond this and see nothing but Him and His manifestations (*jilva*); that is, they see Him in everything. They see everything as a mirror and the whole world as a house of mirrors in which wherever they turn they see Him and His manifestations. Their beings declare wordlessly:

> I look on the plain, I see it as You,
> I look on the sea, I see it as You,
> Wherever I look, mount, vale, or plain,
> I see it reveals the beauty of You.[29]

'Ali (upon whom be peace) said, "I saw nothing without seeing God prior to and along with it." What passes between a worshipper in the act of worship and his God that worshipper will enact in his everyday life, and so he will arrive at the stage of veracity.

For a real worshipper, worship is a contract, and the sphere of his life is the fulfillment of that contract. This contract includes two central provisions. One is to free oneself from the rule of other-than-God, from obedience to that rule, whether of psychical impulses and appetites or of beings, objects, persons. The other is utter submission to what God commands, contentment with that, love of that.

Real worship is a major, basic factor in the worshipper's spiritual education. Worship is a lesson to the worshipper: the lesson of liberation, free-spiritedness, sacrifice, love of God, love of God's command, love of, solidarity with, the people of the Truth, beneficence and service to the people.

Islamic *tauhid* accepts no other motive than God. The evolutionary reality of man, the evolutionary reality of the universe, is to Him-ness; whatever is not directed to Him is vain and opposed to the evolutionary course of creation. According to Islam, just as one must do one's own work for God's sake, one must do the people's work for God's sake. It is sometimes said that to work for God means to work for the people, that the way of God and the way of the people are one and the same thing, that "for God's sake" means "for the people's sake," and that to speak of working for God minus the people is *akhundism* or Sufism.[30] But this is wrong. According to Islam, the road is the road to God, period; the goal is God and nothing other. But the road to God passes among the people. To work for oneself is egoism, to work for the people, idolatry, to work for God and the people, *shirk* and worship of two, to do one's own and the people's work for God, *tauhid* and worship of God. In the Islamic method of *tauhid,* tasks must be begun in the name of God. To begin a task in the name of the people is idolatry, in the name of God and the people, *shirk* and idolatry, and in the name of God alone, *tauhid* and worship of the One.

The Glorious Qur'an makes an interesting point concerning the word *ikhlas*: that to be *mukhlis* is something other than to be *mukhlas*.[31] To be *mukhlis* means to exercise *ikhlas* in one's actions, to carry them out purely for God. But to be *mukhlas* means to have been purified for God. To purify one's activity is one thing, and to be pure throughout one's being is another.

Unity of the Universe

Is the universe (nature, the spatiotemporal creation of God) a real unity in its totality? Does *tauhid,* the unity of God in Essence, attributes, and agency, imply that the creation enjoys a kind of unity in its totality? If the whole universe is interrelated as a unity, what form does this interrelatedness take? Is it like the way the parts of a machine are connected, purely contingent and artificial, or is it like the relation of the members of a body to that body? In other words, is the relation of the parts of the universe mechanical or organic?

I have discussed the nature of the unity of the universe in my annotations to *Usul-i Falsafa* (Principles of Philosophy), volume 5. I have also spoken in *'Adl-i Ilahi* (Divine Justice) of how nature is an indivisible unity, how the nonexistence of one part of nature equals the nonexistence of the whole, and how the removal of what are called "evils" from nature would amount to all nature's ceasing to exist. Modern philosophers, especially Hegel, affirm the principle of organicity, that is, the principle that the relation of the parts of nature to the whole is as the relation of the members to the body. Hegel proves this point on the basis of principles whose acceptance is conditional upon acceptance of all the principles of his philosophy. Hegel's materialist followers, the partisans of dialectical materialism, have taken this principle from him and defend it vociferously as the principle of reciprocal influence, the principle of the universal interrelationship of things, or the principle of interdependence of opposites and advocate the position that the relationship of the part to the whole in nature is organic, not mechanical.

But all they can prove is a mechanical relationship. Materialistic philosophical principles cannot prove that the universe in its totality has the character of a body and that the relationship of the part to the whole is the relationship of the member to the body. The theosophers who have held from ancient times that the world is the "great man" and that man is the "little world" have had such a relationship in view. Among Islamic philosophers, the Ikhwan as-Safa particularly stressed this point.[32] The *'urafa'*, too, in their turn looked upon the world and being with the eye of unity, more than did the *hukama'* or the philosophers. According to the *'urafa'*, all of creation and all creatures constitute one flash *(jilva)* bearing witness to the Preeternal:

> Your face mirrored in the cup
> Impelled the *'arif* to raw craving,

In the radiance of the wine.
Your face beautiful, making
This one flash of vision mirrored
All these images appearing
In the mirror of illusion (Hafiz)[33]

The 'urafa' term this other the "holy emanation" (fayz-i muqad-das) and say analogically that the holy emanation is like a cone that at the apex, that is, where it impinges on the Essence of the Truth, is pure simplicity (pure Existence) and at the base, extended and ramified.

I am not going to develop any of the philosophers' or 'urafa's' explanations here. I am pursuing the subject because it relates to my own preceding discussion. I said earlier that the universe has as its reality the properties of from Him-ness and to Him-ness. On the one hand, it is proven that the universe is not a moving, fluid reality; rather, it is motion and flux itself.[34] On the other hand, research on motion has proven that unity of source, unity of end, and unity of course impart to motions a kind of unity and singularity. Therefore, considering that the whole universe runs on one evolutionary course from one source to one end, it necessarily takes on a kind of unity.

The Unseen and the Manifest

The Islamic world view of tauhid regards the universe as a combination of unseen and visible worlds. That is, it divides the universe into two parts: the world of the unseen and the world of the manifest. In the Noble Qur'an repeated mention is made of the unseen and of the manifest, especially of the unseen. Faith in the unseen is the pillar of Islamic faith: "Those who believe in the unseen . . ." (2:2), "With Him are the keys to the unseen—none know them but He" (6:59).

The word ghayb (unseen) can also be translated as hidden. The unseen, the hidden, falls under two categories: the relative unseen and the absolute unseen. The relative unseen embraces things that are concealed from an observer's senses because of his remoteness from them or some similar reason. For instance, for someone who is in Tehran, Tehran is the manifest and Isfahan is the unseen. But for someone in Isfahan, Isfahan is the manifest and Tehran is the unseen.

In the Noble Qur'an, *ghayb* is sometimes used in this relative sense. For instance, where it says, "These are some of the stories of the unseen we have revealed to you" (11:49), it is clear that the stories of the ancients are unseen to present-day people but were manifest to the ancients themselves. But in other instances, the Noble Qur'an applies the term *ghayb* to realities that are inherently invisible. There is a difference between realities that can be sensed and touched but remain hidden because of distance or some other barrier, as Isfahan is hidden to people who are in Tehran, and realities that are unsusceptible to sensation by the outward senses because of their boundlessness and immateriality and so are hidden.

Where the Qur'an characterizes the believers as those who have faith in the unseen, it does not mean the relative unseen. All people, believers and unbelievers alike, admit the existence of the relative unseen. Thus, where it states, "With Him are the keys to the unseen —none know them but He," and so restricts knowledge of the unseen to the Divine Essence, it means the absolute unseen. It does not accord with the definition of the relative unseen. Where it refers to the manifest and the unseen together, as for instance: "the Knower of the manifest and the unseen, He is the Merciful, the Compassionate" (59:22)—that is, He knows the perceptible and the imperceptible—again it means the inherently invisible and not the relative unseen.

What sort of relationship have the world of the unseen and the world of the manifest? Does the perceptible world have a boundary, beyond which lies the world of the unseen? For instance, is from here to the celestial vault the world of the visible and from there onward the world of the unseen? Plainly, such conceptions are vulgar. On the supposition that a physical boundary separates the two worlds, the two worlds would themselves be manifest, physical, material. One cannot explain the relationship of the unseen and the manifest in material, physical terms. The nearest we can come to a definition the mind can grasp is to say that it resembles the relationship between primary and secondary principles or that between figure and shadow. That is, this world amounts to a projection of that. It can be inferred from the Qur'an that whatever is in this world is a being sent down of the beings of the other world. What are termed "keys" in a previously quoted verse are in other verses termed "treasuries": "And there is not a thing but its treasuries are with Us, and We send it down only in assigned quantities" (15:21).

It is by this reckoning that the Qur'an conceives of everything, even things like stone and iron, as sent down: "and We sent down iron" (57:25). Plainly, what is intended is not that "We have transported all things, including iron, from one place to another." So the realities, the principles, and the essential substances of the contents of this world are in another world, which is the world of the unseen. What is in this world are their laminae *(raqiqa)*, their shadows, or these things themselves at the level of descent into this world.[35]

> Lo! The star-studded wheel, so beauteous and splendid!
>> What's above has a form here below correspondent.
> Should this lower form scale the ladder of gnosis,
>> It will ever find union above with its origin.
> The intelligible form that is endless, eternal,
>> Is compendious and single with all or without all.
> No external prehension will grasp this discussion,
>> Be it Bu Nasr Farabi or Bu 'Ali Sina.[36]

Just as the Qur'an presents a species of faith and vision of being under the heading of the unseen and accounts it necessary, it also at times expounds this topic under other headings, such as faith in the angels or in the prophetic mission of the prophets (faith in revelation): "The Messenger believed in what was revealed to him from his Lord, as do the believers: each believes in God, His angels, His books, and His messengers" (2:285). ". . . and whoever denies God, His angels, His books, His messengers, and the Last Day has gone far astray" (4:136). In these two verses, faith in God's books is accorded independent mention. If the celestial books that were sent down to the prophets were meant, this belief in the prophets would suffice. The context shows that realities of a different kind, not that of tomes and pages, are meant. In the Qur'an itself, there is repeated mention of hidden, unseen realities named the Clear Book, the Preserved Tablet, the Mother of the Book, the Inscribed Book, and the Concealed Book.[37] Faith in such supernal books is a part of Islamic faith.

Basically, the prophets have come to impart to man the kind of vision and world view that would allow him to form an image, however sketchy, of the whole system of the creation, to the extent of his allotted powers. Creation is not confined to sensible, palpable phenomena within the scope of the physical and experimental sciences. The prophets sought to raise man's vision from the sensible to the intelligible, from the evident to the hidden, from the limited to the limitless.

Unfortunately, the tide of narrowly materialistic and sensualistic thought has washed so far that some urge that all the sublime, vast, far-reaching concepts of the Islamic world view be brought down to the level of sense objects and material things.

This World and the Hereafter

Another pillar of the Islamic world view is the division of the universe into this world and the hereafter. What I said in the previous section applies to a world prior to this world, a world that makes and governs this world. Although from one point of view the world of the hereafter is the unseen and this world is the manifest, the world of the hereafter merits independent consideration, insofar as it is a world subsequent to this world. It is both the world from which we have come and the world to which we are going. This is the meaning of the discourse by 'Ali (upon whom be peace): "God has mercy upon one who knows: from where? through where? and to where?"[38] 'Ali did not say, "God has mercy on one who knows from what? through what? and to what?" If he had said that, we would have taken him to mean, "Of what were we created? Of the earth. And into what shall we pass? Into the earth. And out of what shall we arise again? Out of the earth." If he had said this, he would have been alluding to this verse of the Qur'an: "From it We created you, into it We will return you, and from it We will extract you another time" (20:55). But 'Ali's assertion here refers to other verses of the Qur'an and bears a higher meaning: What world have we come from? What world are we in? To what world are we going?

Within the Islamic world view, this world and the hereafter, like the unseen and the manifest, are both absolute concepts, not relative ones. In the language of the Qur'an, each is a separate emergence (nash'a). Works are relative: works of this world, works of the hereafter. That is, if a work has for its object egotism, it is a work of this world; if this same work is carried out for God, to satisfy God, it is a work of the hereafter. In a later volume of this series, *Zindagi-yi Javid ya Hayat-i Ukhravi* (Eternal Life, or the Afterlife), I will discuss this world and the hereafter in detail.[39]

Far-Reaching Wisdom and Divine Justice

Within the theosophic world view, some questions concerning the relationship between the world and God are discussed (such as questions of the createdness in time versus the eternality of the world, questions dealing with the order and system of the emergence of beings, and other questions discussed extensively in theology).

What we might appropriately take note of here are the questions of God's far-reaching wisdom and of divine justice, two closely related questions.[40]

The question of God's far-reaching wisdom is set forth in this way: The system of being is a wise system; that is, not only do knowledge, consciousness, intent, and will enter into the workings of this world, but the existing system is the best and most fitting of systems—a better and more fitting system is impossible. The existing world is the most perfect world possible. Questions and objections arise here, given that events and phenomena falling under the categories of defect, evil, ugliness, and inutility are witnessed in the world. Divine wisdom requires that perfection should exist in place of defect, good in place of evil, beauty in place of ugliness, and utility in place of inutility. Congenital defects, plagues and pestilences, ugly features, and superfluous organs and members on the bodies of persons and animals seem to prove the contrary of wisdom. That a system is just implies that injustice and discrimination should not exist in it, that disasters and misfortunes should not exist in it, that mortality and extinction should not exist in it, because it is unjust to bring a being into existence, give it to taste of the pleasure of existence, and then send it to the realm of oblivion. That a system is just implies that such defects as ignorance, impotence, weakness, and poverty should not be found in the beings of that system because it is unjust to withhold from a being the conditions and attainments of existence just as one clothes it in existence.

If the existing system is the just system, then why all this discrimination? Why is one ugly and another beautiful? Why is one healthy and another sickly? Why is one created a man and another a sheep, a scorpion, or an earthworm? Why is one created a devil and another an angel? Why are all not created alike? Why were not the opposite statuses assigned; for instance, why was the beautiful or the healthy not the ugly, or the ailing? The world view of *tauhid,* which regards the world as the act of an absolutely wise and just God, must answer these questions.

My book on this subject, *'Adl-i Ilahi,* presents the detailed means of resolving these difficulties.[41] Here I will simply cite ten principles, acquaintance with which will constitute a groundwork for resolving these difficulties. I leave the task of arriving at conclusions to the reader.

Self-Sufficiency and Perfection of the Divine Essence

God Most High, in being the Necessary Being in the absolute and in lacking no perfection or activity, does nothing in order to attain a goal or a perfection or to compensate for a shortcoming. His work is not movement from defect to perfection. Accordingly, the meaning of wisdom as it applies to Him is not that He in His works elects the best goals and the best means of arriving at His goals. This meaning for wisdom holds for man, not for God. Divine wisdom means that His work is to bring beings to their highest attainments, to the apogee of their being. His work is creation, which itself means bringing things to the attainment of existence (from nonexistence), directing and perfecting them, and impelling them toward their attainments and well-being, which is another kind of effulgence and work of bringing to perfection.

Some of the questions, objections, and difficulties arise from comparing God to man. Usually when it is asked, "What is the use and wisdom of such-and-such a created thing?" the questioner is thinking of God as like a creature that seeks in its actions to employ available creatures and beings to its own ends. If he had borne in mind from the first that the meaning of divine wisdom is that His act, not His selfhood, has an end, that the wisdom of each creature is an end inherent within it, and that God is impelling it toward its essential end, he would find that many of his questions would be answered.

Order

The divine emanation, that is, the emanation of being which envelops the entire universe, has a particular system. An inviolable priority and causality prevail among beings and creatures. That is, no being can exceed or avoid its own particular rank and occupy the rank of another being. Because the ranks of being have degrees and stations, differences and discrepancies from the standpoints of defect or perfection and of vigor or weakness prevail. Differences and discrepancies do not constitute discrimination, which would be considered contrary to wisdom and justice. Discrimination exists when two beings have the capacity for the same specific degree or perfection and it is granted one and withheld from the other. But when discrepancies and differences are traceable to essential deficiencies, they do not constitute discrimination.

Universality

Another human error arising from comparing God to oneself lies here: Man resolves to build a house within a certain time or in a place—of course, under certain prevailing conditions—and he builds it. By a series of artificial bonds, he brings into relation quantities of brick, clay, cement, and iron that have no essential connection with one another. And the product is a certain kind of building called a house. What about God? Is God's work of this nature? Does God's perfectly precise workmanship have this character of an artificial and derivative bond among several unrelated phenomena?

To produce such artificial and derivative bonds is the work of a creature such as man, who is part of this system and avails himself of the existing, created powers, forces, and properties of things, within determinate limits. It is the work of a creature whose agency and creativity are limited to a dynamic agency. That is, they are limited to inducing a motion, a superficial motion at that, not an organic one, in an existing thing. But God is the Creative Agent; He is the Creator of things, with all their faculties, powers, properties, and traits.

For instance, man uses fire and electrical energy when it is advantageous to him and prevents their appearance when they would harm him. But God is the Creator and Originator of fire and electricity with all their properties. The existence of fire or electricity entails that it give heat, create motion, or cause combustion. God has not created fire or electricity for a particular person or occasion (for instance, to heat a poor man's shack, but not to burn his clothing should it fall into the fire). He has created it with the property of combustion. Therefore, if one is to see that the existence of fire is necessary, useful, and consistent with wisdom, one must consider its total role in the system of the universe, not some particular role it has in some narrow circumstance in regard to some individual and personal motive.

In the case of divine wisdom, the end must be taken to be the end of the act, not the end of the agent. God's wisdom means not God's effecting the best means to deliver Himself from defect to perfection, from potentiality to act, and to arrive at His own objects of perfection, but His creating the best possible system to bring beings to their ends. Further, the ends of divine acts are universal, not particular. The end of the creation of fire is combustion in general, not some particular instance of combustion that might prove useful to some individual or some other particular instance that might prove harmful to another.

Subject's Capacity

For a truth, a reality, to come into being, the effulgence and completeness of agency of the agent are not sufficient; the subject's capacity is also necessary. The absence of this capacity becomes in many instances the source of deprivation for some beings of some boons and attainments. This is why some deficiencies, such as ignorance and weakness, crop up from the standpoint of the total system and the aspect of relationship with the Necessary Being.

Necessary Being

Just as God Most High is the Necessary in Essence, He is the Necessary Being in every respect. Accordingly, it is impossible that a being should find the capacity for existence but fail to be filled with His effulgence and so grow impoverished.

Categories of Evils

Evils belong either to the category of nonbeing (ignorance, weakness, and poverty) or to the category of being, but derive their evilness from the fact that they become sources of nonbeing (earthquakes, microbes, floods, hailstorms, and the like). The evil of beings that become sources of non-being arises from their existence incidental and relative to other beings, not from their intrinsic existence. That is, whatever is evil is not evil in and of itself but for something else. The real existence of any thing is its intrinsic existence; its incidental and relative existence is a nominal and abstract circumstance that is an inseparable concomitant of its real existence.

Goods and Evils

Goods and evils do not form two separate and independent ranks; rather, evils are inseparable concomitants and attributes of goods. The root of evils that belong to the category of nonbeing is the lack of capacity of the subject; given the subject's capacity, the effulgence of being from the Necessary Being is certain and inevitable. On the other hand, the root of evils that do not belong to the category of nonbeing is their inseparability from goods.

Good in Evil

No evil is absolute. Deprivation and nonbeing are in their turn the antecedents of beings, goods, and attainments. Evils in their turn are the thresholds and steps of evolution. Thus a good lies hidden in every evil, and a being is hidden in every nonbeing.

Laws and Norms

The universe of being, in functioning according to a universal cause-and-effect system, operates according to laws and norms. The Noble Qur'an affirms this point explicitly.

Essential Unity

Just as the universe has a universal and inviolable system, it is an indivisible unity in its essence. That is, the whole creation forms a unity like that of the body with its members. Therefore, not only are evils and nonbeing inseparable from goods and being, but all the parts of the universe, in composing a unity and a single manifestation (*jilwa*), are inseparable from one another.

In accordance with these ten principles, what has the possibility to exist is a determinate, universal, and immutable system. Therefore, the phenomenon of the universe has the possibilities of existing with this determinate system and of not existing at all. That it should exist and have no system or have a system with a different configuration as, for instance, one in which causes replace effects and effects, causes, is absurd. Therefore, either the universe exists with a determinate system or nothing exists. Wisdom requires the optimum, that is, being, not nonbeing.

Furthermore, things have the possibility to exist only with all their inseparable concomitants and attributes. That goods and beings, however, should prove separable from evils and nonbeing is no more than sheer fantasy and absurd illusion. Therefore, from this standpoint as well, the paired existence or nonexistence of goods and evils, not the existence of goods and the nonexistence of evils, is the choice confronting wisdom.

Lastly, the whole universe as an interdependent unity, not one part in the absence of another, has the possibility to exist. Therefore, what can be contemplated by wisdom is the existence or nonexistence of the whole, not the existence of one part and the non-existence of another part.

These principles, if rightly assimilated, reduce all the uncertainties and problems of far-reaching wisdom and perfect divine justice to the level of a phantasm. I again refer those requiring more detail to my work '*Adl-i Ilahi* (Divine justice).

The Principle of Justice
in Islamic Culture

In Shi'ism, the principle of justice is one of the principles of religion. Justice in Islamic culture is divided into divine justice and human justice. Divine justice is subdivided into creative justice and legislative justice. Human justice is subdivided into individual justice and social justice. The concept of justice considered unique to Shi'ism that has taken its place among the principles of religion in Shi'ism is divine justice. This type of justice specifically arises in the context of the Islamic world view.

To believe in divine justice means to believe that God acts in accordance with truth and justice, both in the system of the creation and in the system of legislation, and never shows injustice. Justice has become one of the principles of Shi'ism because some who denied human choice and freedom appeared among the Muslims. They arrived at a belief regarding divine decree and foreordination that was wholly inconsistent with human freedom. They denied the principle of cause and effect in the overall system of the universe and in the system of human conduct. They came to believe that divine decree acts directly and without intermediation. According to this belief, fire does not cause to burn, but God causes to burn; a magnetic field in no way attracts iron, but God directly draws the iron to the lines of the magnetic field; man does not the good or evil deed, but God directly carries out the good or evil deed through the human form.

Here a major question arose. If the system of cause and effect has no reality, and if man himself has no real role in choosing his actions, then what function is served by rewarding or punishing the individual for his acts? Why does God mete out rewards to some people and take them to paradise and punish others and take them to hell when He Himself has carried out both the good deed and the evil one? To punish human individuals when they have not possessed the least choice and freedom of their own is injustice and contrary to the categorical principle of divine justice.

The Shi'a at large and a party among the Sunnis called the Mu'tazilites, relying on decisive rational and transmitted proofs, denied that man is determined and that divine decree and foreordination act directly on the universe; they regarded these ideas as inimical to the principle of justice and so became known as the People of Justice ('adliyya). Although justice is a divine principle (that is, linked with one of the attributes of God), it is likewise a human principle because it is linked with human freedom and choice. Therefore, among the Shi'a and the Mu'tazilites, belief in the principle of justice means belief in the principle of human freedom, human responsibility, and human creativity.

The question concerning divine justice that generally—especially in our own time—draws the most attention has to do with certain social inequalities: How is it that some individuals are beautiful and others ugly, some healthy and others sickly, some comfortable and affluent and others empty-handed and indigent? Would divine justice not require all individuals to be equal with respect to wealth, lifespan, offspring, social position, reputation, and receipt of love? Can anything but divine decree and foreordination be responsible for these inequalities?

The roots of this question and the confusion underlying it are two. One is inattention to the nature of the operation of divine decree and foreordination. The questioner has imagined that they work directly.[42] For instance, wealth would be directly and without the intervention of any cause or agency transported from the divine treasuries of the unseen and parceled out at people's doors, and the same would hold for health, beauty, power, position, love, offspring, and other blessings. The questioner has failed to note that no sort of sustenance, whether material or spiritual, is apportioned directly from the treasury of the unseen. Rather, divine decree has produced a system and originated a series of norms and laws. Whatever anyone seeks, he must seek through that system and those norms. The second root of this error is inattention to the station and situation of man as a being who seeks to better his own life, to struggle with the factors in nature on the one hand and to struggle with the evil factors in society and the misdeeds and oppression of human individuals on the other—who has these as his responsibilities. If there are certain inequalities in society, if some are rich and have wealth by the shiploads at their disposal, while others are destitute and in despair on oceans of affliction, the divine decree is not responsible. Man, free, empowered, and responsible, bears the blame for these inequalities.

Notes to "The World View of Tauhid"

1. The first essay in the series, "Darsha'i az Ma'arif-i Qur'an" ("Lessons from the Teachings of the Qur'an), to be titled *Shinakht dar Qur'an* ("Knowledge in the Qu'ran"), in which the problems of knowledge will be considered, will be published soon through the Hawza-yi 'Ilmiya-yi Qum, God willing. [This essay was later published in an undated pamphlet of sixty-eight pages. *Trans.*]

2. See *The Scientific Outlook* (New York, 1931), "Limitations of Scientific Method," the chapter title being a polite way of denying the theoretical value of science.

3. See my *Insan va Sar Nivisht* ("Man and Fate"), Tehran, 1345 Sh./ 1966.

4. Shaykh Abu Muhammad al-Halabi, *Tuhaf al-'Uqul*, p. 198.

5. *Tashahhud:* the pronouncement of the Islamic declaration of faith, *"Ashhadu an la ilaha illa 'llah, wa ashhadu anna Muhammadan Rasulu 'llah"* ("I bear witness that there is no god but God, and I bear witness that Muhammad is God's Messenger"), in prayer. *Trans.*

6. 'Arafat: The plain just outside of Mecca dominated by a low mountain where all the pilgrims on the *hajj* must be present on the ninth day of Dhu 'l-Hijja, the pilgrimage month.

   Mash'ar: More fully, the Mash'ar al-Haram, literally "the Sacred Waymark" and also known as Muzdalifa, a site eight kilometers from 'Arafat where the pilgrims must perform the sunset and night prayers on the ninth day of the pilgrimage month. *Trans.*

7. *Muwahhid:* Practitioner of *tauhid. Trans.*

8. "He is not external to things, and He is not internal to them" (*Nahj al-Balagha*).

9. Exact place of occurrence not found. *Trans.*

10. 'Ali Shari'ati has compared the concept of assignation (*tafviz*, passive participle *mufavvaz*) in Muslim philosophy with that of *délaissement* in the existentialism of Sartre. See his *Marxism and Other Western Fallacies* (Berkeley, 1980), p. 46. *Trans.*

11. This is virtually the Qur'anic verse 17:111. *Trans.*

12. "This party" is interpreted to mean the Sufis. *Trans.*

13. Phrases such as "Say,/We make no distinction among the prophets" are found in 2:136, 2:285, and 3:84. *Trans.*

14. *Taghutism:* The *taghut* is a typification of evil mentioned in the Qur'an

(for example, 4:76) and characterized by an overrunning of all bounds, as in tyranny. (For a discussion of the term, see Mahmud Taleghani, *Society and Economics in Islam* [Berkeley, 1982], pp. 80–82). Revolutionary figures often characterized the Shah's régime as the régime of *taghutism. Trans.*

15. Nahj al-Balagha, Shaqshaqiya sermon.

16. Virtuous City: *Madina-yi Fazila*, a conception of an idealized political order having its roots in Plato's *Republic* and in Muslim philosophy associated most closely with Abu Nasr Muhammad Farabi (259/ 872–339/950). *Trans.*

17. Quraysh: The Meccan mercantile family into which the Prophet Muhammad was born and which was, as an influential ruling family, the source of many of Islam's early enemies. *Trans.*

18. Abu Sufyan, Abu Jahl, Walid ibn Mughira: Early Qurayshi opponents of the Prophet and of Islam. *Trans.*

19. Salman Farsi: An early companion of the Prophet of Iranian origin, also closely associated with 'Ali ibn Abi Talib. *Trans.*

20. I have discussed the import of this verse earlier in this chapter (see "The Uniqueness of God"). For an account and explanation of this demonstration, called demonstration of interobstruction (*burhan-i tamanu'*), refer to my annotations to 'Allama Sayyid Muhammad Husayn Tabataba'i, *Usul-i Falsafa va Ravish-i Ri'alism* ("The Principles of Philosophy and the Method of Realism" Qum, 1350 Sh./1971 [Hereafter referred to as *Usul-i Falsafa*]), vol. 5.

21. They term misfortunes, deformities, defects, deficiencies, and all unsought-for occurrences "evils." I have discussed in detail the manner evils are to be predicated of God in the book *'Adl-i Ilahi* ("Divine Justice," Tehran 1349 Sh./1970).

22. See *Tafsir al-Mizan,* under the above verse [3:31].

23. From Ibn Abi'l-Hadid's *Sharh* to the *Nahj al-Balagha*, the section treating Discourse 128.

24. People living under the influence of Wahhabism without acknowledging it. *Trans.*

25. I discuss the question further in *Muqaddima'i bar Jahan Bini-yi Islami*, volume 7: *"Hayat-i Javid, ya Hayat-i Ukhravi* ("Eternal Life, or the Afterlife"), Qum, 1358 Sh./1979.

26. See Additional Notes.

27. All three quotes are from *Ziyarat-i Jami'a-yi Kabira* [a litany recited when visiting the tombs of the Imams; for the text, see 'Abbas Qummi, *Mafatih al-Jinan,* Tehran, n.d., pp. 750–759. *Trans.*]

28. See my treatise, *Vala'ha va Vilayatha* ("Allegiances and Sovereignties"), Tehran, 1349 Sh./1960.

29. Unknown. *Trans.*
30. See Additional Notes.
31. *Ikhlas* is the verbal noun; *mukhlis* is the active participle; and *mukhlas* is the passive participle. *Trans.*
32. Ikhwan as-Safa: A philosophical association of fourth-century Basra and Baghdad, noted for their collective authorship of the *Rasa'il,* an encyclopedia of the philosophy and high culture of the time, written in a notably simple and clear Arabic. *Trans.*
33. See Hafiz Shirazi, *Divan,* Na'ini and Ahmad, eds. (Tehran, 1352 Sh./1973), p. 268. *Trans.*
34. Only Islamic philosophy has demonstrated that the natural universe is motion and flow. Some Western systems have advanced this idea, but they are incapable of demonstrating it. For further consideration of this point, refer to the essay "Tazadd va Harakat dar Falsafa-yi Islami" ("Contradiction and Motion in Islamic Philosophy") in my collection *Maqalat-i Falsafi* ("Philosophic Essays"). [See also "The Mutable and the Constant" in the third essay, "Philosophy," in this book. *Trans.*]
35. See *Tafsir al-Mizan* (Arabic text), vol. 7, under the *sura* An'am, verse 59.
36. Bu Nasr Farabi: Abu Nasr Muhammad Farabi, the tenth-century philosopher. Bu 'Ali Sina: the famous philosopher and physician better known in the West as Avicenna (d. 1037 C.E.). The poem is by the Safavid-era philosopher, Mir Abu'l-Qasim Findiriski (d. 1640 C.E.). See "Illuminationism and Peripateticism" in the third essay, "Philosophy," in this book.
37. See *Tafsir al-Mizan,* under the verses in which these terms occur.
38. Unknown.
39. Published in Qum in 1358 Sh./1979. *Trans.*
40. "Far-reaching wisdom" (*hikma balagha*): a term found in the Qur'an, 54:5. *Trans.*
41. Published in Qum in 1349 Sh./1970. *Trans.*
42. Refer to my *Insan va Sar Nivisht* ("Man and Fate"), where questions related to divine decree and foreordination are discussed at length.

Philosophy

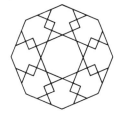

What Is Philosophy?

Literal and Semantic Definitions

The logicians say that when one asks about the whatness of a thing, one is actually asking various things. Sometimes one is asking the conceptual meaning of a word. That is, when we ask what a thing is, we are asking about the very word. In asking about its whatness, we seek to know the lexical or idiomatic meaning of that word. Suppose in reading a book we run across the word *pupak* (hoopoe) and do not know its meaning. We ask someone, "What is a *pupak*?" He replies, "*Pupak* is the name of a bird." Or suppose we run across the word *kalima* (word) in the terminology of the logicians and we ask someone, "What does *kalima* mean in the terminology of the logicians?" He says, "*Kalima* in the terminology of the logicians is equivalent to *fi'l* (verb) in the language of the grammarians." Plainly, the relation between word and meaning is conventional and terminological, whether the terminology is restricted or general.

In answering such a question, one must search out instances of usage or consult a dictionary. Such a question may have numerous answers, all of them correct, because it is possible for a single word to have various meaning in various contexts. For instance, a word may have a special meaning in the usage of the logicians and the philosophers, and another in that of the grammarians. The word *kalima* has one meaning in common usage and in the usage of grammarians and another meaning in the usage of the logicians. Or, the word *qiyas* (analogy, syllogism) has one meaning in the usage of the logicians and another in the usage of the jurists and the legists. When a word has two or more meanings within a single body of usages, one must say that it has this meaning in this expression, and that in that. Answers given to such questions are called verbal definitions.

Sometimes when one inquires into the whatness of a thing, what one seeks is not the meaning of the word, but the reality of its referent. We do not ask, "What is the meaning of this word?" We know the meaning of the word, but not the reality and suchness of its referent. For instance, if we ask, "What is man?", we do not seek

135

to know what the word "man" has been coined to mean. We all know that this word is applied to this bipedal, upright-postured, speaking being. We seek instead to know the identity and the reality of man. Plainly, in this case there can be only one correct answer, called the real definition.

The verbal definition is prior to the real definition. That is, one must ascertain first the conceptual meaning of the word, and then the real definition of the referent so delineated. Otherwise fallacies and pointless disputes will arise because a word has numerous lexical and idiomatic meanings, and this multiplicity of meanings is easily overlooked. Any party may define a word by a special meaning and idiomatic usage, heedless of the fact that it is envisioning something different from what another party has envisioned. So they dispute pointlessly.

The failure to distinguish the meaning of the word from the reality of its referent sometimes results in the transformation and evolution that take place in the meaning of the word being ascribed to the reality of its referent. For instance, a certain word may at first be applied to a whole and then, through changes in usage, to a part of that whole. If one fails to distinguish the meaning of the word from the reality of its referent, he will suppose that that whole actually has been fragmented, whereas in fact no change has occurred in the whole, but rather the word applying to it has been displaced in meaning to apply to a part of that whole.

Just such an error in regard to the word "philosophy" has overtaken all of Western philosophy and its imitators in the East. Philosophy is an idiomatic word and has found numerous and various idiomatic meanings. Various parties of philosophers have defined philosophy each in a special way, but this discrepancy in definition does not bear on any reality. Each party has used this word in a special sense, which it has defined as its object. What one party calls philosophy, another does not call philosophy; the latter will completely deny its value, call it something else, or regard it as part of another science. So neither party will regard the other as philosophers. I shall take these various usages into account.

The Word "Philosophy"

Falsafa has a Greek origin. This word is an Arabic verbal noun derived from the Greek word *philosophia,* which is a compound of *philos* and *sophia*, the former meaning love, the latter, wisdom. Therefore, *philosophia* means love of wisdom. Plato called Socrates a *philosophos* in the sense of his being a lover of wisdom.[1] Therefore, the word *falsafa* is an Arabicization, a verbal noun, meaning the work or pursuit of philosophers.

Before Socrates, a party appeared calling themselves the Sophists, meaning the scholars. They made human perception the measure of reality and used fallacious arguments in their deductions. Gradually, "sophist" *(sophistes)* lost its original meaning and came to mean one who makes use of fallacious arguments. Thus we have the word "sophistry," which has the cognate in Arabic *safsafa*, with the same meaning.

Socrates, out of humility and also perhaps a desire to avoid being identified with the Sophists, forbade people to call him a *sophistes*, a scholar.[2] He therefore called himself a *philosophos*, a lover of wisdom. Gradually, *philosophos*, with its original sense of lover of wisdom, displaced *sophistes* as meaning scholar, and the latter was downgraded to its modern sense of one who uses fallacious reasoning. *Philosophia* became synonymous with wisdom. Therefore, *philosophos* as a technical term had been applied to no one before Socrates, and it was not applied to anyone immediately after him. The term *philosophia*, too, had no definite meaning in those days; it is said that not even Aristotle used it. Later, use of the terms *philosophia* and *philosophos* became widespread.

Muslim Usage

The Muslims took the word "philosophy" from the Greeks. They gave it an Arabic form and an Eastern nuance, using it to mean pure rational knowledge. Philosophy in the common Muslim usage did not refer to a special discipline or science; it embraced all rational sciences, as opposed to transmitted sciences, such as etymology, syntax, declension, rhetoric, stylistics, prosody, exegesis, tradition, and jurisprudence. Because this word had a generic meaning, only one who comprehended all the rational sciences of his time, including theology, mathematics, the natural sciences, politics, ethics, and domestic economy, would be called a philosopher. Thus it was said, "Whoever is a philosopher becomes a world of knowledge, analogous to the objective world."

When Muslims sought to reproduce Aristotle's classification of the sciences, they used the words *falsafa* or *hikma*. They said, "Philosophy, that is, the rational science, has two divisions: the theoretical and the practical."

Theoretical philosophy addresses things as they are; practical philosophy addresses man's actions as they ought to be. Theoretical philosophy is threefold: theology or high philosophy, mathematics or middle philosophy, and natural science or low philosophy. High philosophy, or theology, in turn comprehends two disciplines, general phenomenology and theology per se. Mathematics is fourfold, each of its areas being a science in itself: arithmetic, geometry, astronomy, and music. Natural science has numerous divisions. Practical philosophy is divisible into ethics, domestic economy, and civics. The complete philosopher comprehends all these sciences.

True Philosophy

In the philosophers' view, one area enjoys a special prominence among the numerous areas of philosophy. It is called first philosophy, high philosophy, the supreme science, the universal science, theology, or metaphysics. The ancients believed that one of the features distinguishing this science from all others is its firmer foundation on demonstration and certainty. Another is that it presides over all other sciences; it is in truth the queen of the sciences because the others depend on it totally, but it has no such dependence on them. A third distinguishing feature is that it is more general and universal than any other science.[3] According to these philosophers, this science is the true philosophy. Accordingly, sometimes the word "philosophy" is restricted in application to this science, but this usage is rare.

Therefore, in the view of the ancient philosophers, the word "philosophy" had two meanings: one, the prevalent meaning of rational knowledge as such, including all but the transmitted sciences, and the other the rare meaning of theology, or first philosophy, one of the three divisions of theoretical philosophy.

Accordingly, there are two possibilities if we choose to define philosophy according to the usage of the ancients. First, if we adopt the common usage, because here philosophy is a generic term applying to no special science or discipline, it will have no special definition. It will mean all nontransmitted science. To be a philosopher will mean to comprehend all such sciences. It was in accordance with such a generalized conception of philosophy that it was said, "Philosophy is the perfection of the soul of man from both a theoretical standpoint and a practical one."

Second, if we adopt the rarer usage, defining philosophy as that activity the ancients called true philosophy, first philosophy, or the supreme science, this will constitute a special definition for philosophy. The answer to the question "What is philosophy?" will be that philosophy consists of a science of the states of being from the standpoint that is being, not from the standpoint of its having a special individuation, for instance, of its being body, quantity, quality, man, vegetable, or what have you.

Our knowledge of things is of two kinds: It may be restricted to a certain species or genus; it may apply to the special states, determinations *(ahkam),* and accidents *('avariz)* of a certain species or a certain genus, as does, for instance, our knowledge constituting the science of the determinations of numbers (arithmetic), of quantities (geometry), of the states and properties of plants (botany), or of the states, properties, and determinations of the human body (medicine or physiology).[4] This sort of knowledge embraces the rest of the sciences, such as meteorology, geology, minerology, zoology, psychology, sociology, and atomics.

Or our knowledge may not be restricted to a certain species; that is, we may say that being has these determinations, states, and properties not from the standpoint that it is of a certain species but from the standpoint that it is being. Sometimes we study the universe from the standpoint of its plurality and discrete subjects, whereas sometimes we study it from the standpoint of unity; that is, we regard being from the standpoint that it is being as a unity, and we pursue our studies with a regard to this unity that embraces all things.

If we liken the universe to a body, we see that our studies of that body will be of two kinds. Some of our studies will pertain to the members of that body (for instance, its head, hands, feet, or eyes); others will pertain to the whole of that body, as we ask, for instance, "When did this body come into being, and how long will it persist?"

Or is it at all meaningful to ask when in relation to the body as an aggregate? Does this body have a real unity, the multiplicity of the members being an apparent, not a real, multiplicity? Or is its unity nominal, on the level of a mechanical interrelationship; that is, does it not exceed the unity of a manufactured device? Has this body a source member from which the other members have sprung? For instance, has this body a head, which is the source for the other members? Or is it a body without a head? If it has a head, does this head have a sensible and perceiving mind, or is it hollow and empty? Does the whole of the body down to the nails and bones enjoy a kind of life, or is the intelligence and perception of this body confined to some entities that have appeared by chance, like worms on a corpse—these worms being what we call the animals, including man? Does this body as a whole pursue an end, course toward a perfection and a reality, or is it an aimless being? Are the appearance and decline of the members an accident, or does the law of causation govern them, no phenomenon being without cause and every particular effect arising from a particular cause? Is the system governing this body certain and inescapable? Or does no necessity or certainty govern this body? Is the order and priority of the members of this body real or not? How many are the basic organs of this body?

The portion of our studies that pertains to an organology of the universe of being is science, and the portion that pertains to a physiology of the universe as a whole is philosophy.

There is thus a special class of questions that resemble those of none of the world's sciences, which investigate particular beings, but that compose a class of their own. When we take up the study of this class of questions as an exploration of the parts of the sciences, and when we wish to understand of what subject questions of this class are, technically speaking, accidents, we see that they are accidents of being *qua* being.

Whenever we inquire into the identities (*mahiyat*, essences) of things—as, for instance, to ask what is the identity, the whatness, the true definition of a body or of man—or whenever we inquire into the being of things—as, for instance, to ask whether a real circle or line exists—this same discipline is involved because to inquire into [these] phenomena is to inquire into the accidents of being *qua* being. That is, these identities, so to speak, are among the accidents and determinations of being *qua* being.

If one of us should ask, "What is philosophy?" before answering we must state that this word has a special sense in the usage of any given party. Among Muslims, it is most commonly a generic noun representing all the rational sciences, not the name of a particular science and less commonly a name for first philosophy, a science of the most universal aspects of being, pertaining to no particular subject but to all subjects. This is a science that investigates all of being as a unified subject.

Metaphysics

Aristotle was the first to discern a series of questions that belong to none of the natural, mathematical, ethical, social, or logical sciences and must be seen as belonging to a separate science. He may have been the first to discern the pivot on which all these questions turn as accidents and states, which is being *qua* being. He may also have been the first one to discover the factor that interconnects the questions of any one science and the standard by which they are to be distinguished from the questions of another science—in other words, what is called the subject of a science.

The questions of this science, like those of any other, were later to be greatly expanded and augmented. This fact grows clear through a comparison of the metaphysics of Aristotle with the metaphysics of Avicenna, not to mention the metaphysics of Mulla Sadra. But Aristotle was the first to elaborate this science as an independent field, to give it a special place among the sciences.

Aristotle gave this science no name. His works were posthumously compiled into an encyclopedia. The section in question followed that on natural philosophy in sequence and, having no special name, came to be known as *metaphysika*, meaning after physics. It was translated into Arabic as *ma ba'd at-tabi'a.*

It was eventually forgotten that this name was given this science because it occurred after natural philosophy in Aristotle's work. It was supposed that this had occurred because at least some of the questions this science addresses, such as God and the pure intelligences, are external to nature. Accordingly, it occurred to some persons, such as Avicenna, that this science should be called not metaphysics but prophysics because it includes the subject of God, Who is prior to nature, not posterior to it.[5]

This verbal error in translation later led to an error in meaning among some modern students of philosophy. Many Europeans supposed that metaphysics is equivalent to hyperphysics and that the subject of this science consists of phenomena external to nature. In fact, this science includes the natural and the supernatural, in sum, all that exists. This group has erroneously defined this science as follows: Metaphysics is that science which deals solely with God and phenomena separate from nature.

Philosophy in Modern Times

The watershed between the modern era (beginning in the sixteenth Christian century) and the ancient was marked by the displacement of the syllogistic and rational method of science by the experimental and empirical method, a change instituted by a group foremost among whom were the Frenchman, Descartes, and the Englishman, Bacon. The natural sciences *en bloc* departed the domain of syllogistic reasoning and entered that of the experimental method. Mathematics took on a semisyllogistic, semiexperimental character.

After this course of events, some decided that the syllogistic method is unreliable. So, if a science is beyond the reach of concrete experiment, if it calls exclusively for syllogistic reasoning, it is groundless. Because this is the case with metaphysics, that is, because concrete experiment has no place in it, this science is groundless. Its questions are beyond confirmation or refutation through research. These persons draw a red line through the science that once had stood above all others and had been called the most noble of sciences and the queen of the sciences. According to them, the science of metaphysics or first philosophy did not and could not exist. They took from man the questions his reason most keenly feels the need to address.

Others maintained that the syllogistic method is not in all cases unreliable and must be employed in metaphysics and ethics. They created a new terminology: What could take the form of research through the experimental method they called science, and what had to be approached through the syllogistic method, including metaphysics, ethics, and logic, they called philosophy. Philosophy consists of those sciences that consist in research through the syllogistic method only and in which concrete experiment plays no part.

In this view, as in the view of the ancient scholars, philosophy is generic, not specific, in meaning: It is not the name of one science, but comprehends several sciences. But philosophy in this sense encompasses less than it did according to ancient usage. It includes metaphysics, ethics, logic, law, and perhaps a few others, but mathematics and the natural sciences are outside its compass.

Members of the first group totally denied metaphysics and the syllogistic method, trusting in the empirical and experimental sciences. In time, they realized that if all that is falls into the domain of the experimental sciences, and if the questions they address are restricted to particular subjects, then we are going to be wholly deprived of an overall understanding of the universe, which philosophy or metaphysics had undertaken to provide. Thus, they founded a scientific philosophy, that is, a philosophy resting completely on the sciences. Through comparative study of the sciences, inquiry into how their questions connect to other questions, and discovery of the kind of relationships among the laws and questions of the sciences, the totality they compose, a range of more general questions would devolve. They called these more general questions philosophy. The Frenchman Auguste Comte and the Englishman Herbert Spencer took up this method.

Philosophy was no longer an autonomous science either in its subject matter or in its sources, since such an autonomous science had for its subject being *qua* being and had its sources—at least its chief source—in first axioms. Philosophy had become a science whose function was to study the products of the other sciences, to interrelate them, and to derive general questions from their more limited questions. Auguste Comte's philosophy of positivism and Herbert Spencer's synthetic philosophy are of this sort. According to this view, philosophy is not a science apart from the other sciences, but constitutes a broader and fuller view of things seen and learned through the sciences.

Some others, such as Kant, thought it necessary first to study knowledge itself, along with the faculty that is its source, that is, reason. They made a critique of human reason and designated their researches philosophy as such or critical philosophy. However, this, too, has nothing but the word in common with what the ancients called philosophy or with Comte's positivism or Spencer's synthetic philosophy. Kant's philosophy has more to do with logic, which is a special form of ideology in the strict sense *(fikr shinasi)*, than with philosophy in its original meaning, which is cosmology.

In the European cultural sphere, whatever was not science, that is, whatever did not fit into any of the natural or mathematical sciences but was a theory of the universe, man, or society, gradually came to be known as philosophy. If someone were to collect all the "isms" that have been called philosophy in Europe and America and list all their definitions, one would see that they have nothing in common except being not science.

The difference between ancient and modern philosophies is dissimilar in kind to the difference between ancient and modern sciences. Compare ancient and modern medicine, geometry, psychology, or botany. Ancient science is not different in identity from modern science (for example, the word "medicine" did not refer to one science in ancient times and another in modern times). Ancient and modern medicine share a single definition; medicine has always consisted in knowledge of the states and symptomatic conditions of the human body. But ancient and modern medicine differ in how they approach questions. Modern medicine is the more empirical; ancient medicine is the more deductive and syllogistic. Modern medicine is also the more developed. This sort of difference holds for all other sciences.

The term "philosophy," however, has had various referents, and a separate definition for each referent, in the course of the ancient and modern periods. In ancient times, philosophy sometimes designated rational science as such and sometimes had a specialized meaning applying to one of the branches of this science (such as metaphysics or first philosophy). In modern times, the word has been applied to numerous referents, having a different definition in accordance with each.

Divorce of the Sciences from Philosophy

An egregious but prevalent error of our time that arose in the West and has grown widespread among Eastern imitators of Western thinkers is the myth of the divorce of the sciences from philosophy.

A linguistic change pertaining to a convention of usage has been mistaken for a change of meaning pertaining to a real referent. In the language of the ancients, the words "philosophy" and *"hikma"* generally were used to mean rational, as opposed to transmitted, knowlege. Thus, these words comprehended all of man's rational and intellectual ideas in their meanings. In this usage, philosophy was a generic, not a proper, noun.

In modern times, this word became restricted to metaphysics, logic, aesthetics, and the like. This change in the name has led some to suppose that in ancient times philosophy was a single science embracing theology and the natural, mathematical, and other sciences and that later the natural and mathematical sciences were divorced from philosophy and grew independent of it. It is as if the word "body" once meant the human frame, as opposed to the spirit, and included the whole human form from head to feet and later acquired the secondary sense of the trunk and limbs, minus the head. Suppose some came to imagine that the head of man thus had become separated from his body. A linguistic change would have been mistaken for a change in meaning. Consider also the word "Fars," which once referred to the whole of Iran but today refers only to one of its southern provinces. Someone might think the province of Fars had seceded from Iran. This is the status of the divorce of the sciences from philosophy. The sciences were once lumped under the name "philosophy," but today this name is applied to only one of the sciences.

This change in name has nothing to do with a divorce of the sciences from philosophy. The sciences have never been part of philosophy proper; so they could not be divorced from it.

Illuminationism and Peripateticism

Islamic philosophers are divisible into two groups: illuminationists and peripateticists. Foremost among the illuminationist philosophers of Islam is the sixth-century scholar Shaykh Shihab ad-Din Suhravardi (otherwise known as Shaykh-i Ishraq, but whom I shall refer to as Suhravardi), and foremost among the peripatetic philosophers of Islam is Shaykh ar-Ra'is Abu Ali ibn Sina (Avicenna).

The illuminationists are considered to be followers of Plato and the peripatetics, of Aristotle. The principal and essential difference between the two methods is that the illuminationists consider deduction and rational thought insufficient for study of philosophical questions, especially of divine wisdom *(hikmat-i ilahi)*, and the path of the heart, asceticism, and purification of the soul as incumbent if one is to realize inner realities. Peripatetics rely solely on deduction.

The word *ishraq*, meaning illumination, aptly conveys a sense of the illuminationist method, but the word *mashsha'* or peripatetic, which means ambulant or much ambulant, is purely arbitrary and conveys nothing of the peripatetic method. Aristotle and his followers were called the *mashsha'in*, the peripatetics, because Aristotle held forth while taking walks. "Deductionist" actually describes the peripatetics' method. Thus, it is more accurate to label the two kinds of philosophers illuminationists and deductionists, although I shall continue to use the more common term, peripatetic.

The major questions over which illuminationists and peripatetics differ in Islam today generally pertain to Islam and not to Plato or Aristotle. They include the questions of essentialism *(isalat-i mahiya)* versus existentialism *(isalat-i vujud)*, the unity versus the multiplicity of being, the question of fabrication *(ja'l)*, the question of whether a body is compounded of matter and form, the question of ideas *(muthul)* and archetypes *(arbab-i anva')*, and the question of the principle of the more noble possibility *(imkan-i ashraf)*.[6]

Did Plato and Aristotle actually have two different methods? Did such a difference in outlook exist between the master, Plato, and the pupil, Aristotle? Was Suhravardi's method, propounded in the Islamic era, actually Plato's method? Did Plato follow the way of the Heart, asceticism and the discipline of the soul, or the illumination and witness of the heart? Was he an exponent of what Suhravardi later called experiential wisdom *(hikmat-i dhawqi)*? Do the questions that illuminationists and peripatetics have been known to differ over since the time of Suhravardi (questions of essence and existence, of fabrication, of the compoundedness or simplicity of the body, of the formula of the more noble possibility, and of the unity or multiplicity of being) actually date back to differences of opinion between Plato and Aristotle? Or are the questions, at least some of them, later developments unknown to Plato or Aristotle? There were certainly differences of opinion between the two; Aristotle refuted many of Plato's theories and countered them with different ones.

In the Alexandrian period, which was the watershed between the Hellenic and Islamic eras, the followers of Plato and Aristotle formed two opposed ranks. Farabi, in *Al-Jam' Bayn Ra'yay al-Hakimayn* (The reconciliation of the views of the two sages), discusses the questions over which the two philosophers disagree and strives to resolve these disagreements. There are three basic questions on which Plato and Aristotle differed, questions different from those discussed during the Islamic era.

It is highly doubtful that Plato advocated a spiritual way, with asceticism and discipline of the soul, and witness of the heart. Thus, the notion that Plato and Aristotle had two distinct methods, the illuminationist and the peripatetic, becomes highly debatable. It is by no means clear that Plato was recognized as an illuminationist, an exponent of inner illumination, in his own time or any time soon thereafter. It is not even clear that the term peripatetic was applied exclusively to Aristotle and his followers in his own time. As Shahristani says: "Now the strict peripatetics then are the members of the Lyceum. Plato, honored for his wisdom, always taught them while taking walks. Aristotle followed his example, and accordingly he [apparently Aristotle] and his followers were called peripatetics."[7] Aristotle and his followers surely were called peripatetics, and this usage was simply continued in Islamic times. However, it is doubtful and even deniable that Plato was called an illuminationist.

Prior to Suhravardi, we never find any of the philosophers, such as Farabi and Avicenna, or any of the historians of philosophy, such as Shahristani, speaking of Plato as a sage advocating experiential or illuminationist wisdom.[8] It was Suhravardi who gave this term currency, and it was he who, in his *Hikmat al-Ishraq* (Wisdom of Illumination), called a party among the ancient sages, including Pythagoras and Plato, exponents of experiential and illuminationist wisdom and who called Plato chief of the illuminationists.

I believe Suhravardi adopted the illuminationist method under the influence of the *'urafa'* and the Sufis; the admixture of illumination and deduction is his own invention. But he—perhaps in order to improve acceptance of his theory—spoke of a party among the ancient philosophers as having this same method. Suhravardi offers no sort of documentation on this subject, just as he offers none on the matter of the ancient Iranian sages. Certainly, if he possessed such documentation, he would have presented it and so avoided leaving an idea to which he was so devoted in ambiguity and doubt.

Some writers on the history of philosophy, in writing on Plato's beliefs and ideas, have not mentioned his supposed illuminationist method. Shahristani's *Al-Milal wa'n-Nihal*, Dr. Human's *Tarikh-i Falsafa*, Will Durant's *History of Philosophy*, and Muhammad 'Ali Furughi's *Sayr-i Hikmat dar Urupa* do not mention such a method in the sense Suhravardi intends. Furughi mentions Platonic love, which is a love of the beautiful that in Plato's belief—at least as expressed in the Symposium—is rooted in divinity. It bears no relation to what Suhravardi has said about the purification of the psyche and the gnostic way to God. Plato is said to hold: "Before coming to the world, the spirit beheld absolute beauty; when in this world it sees outward beauty, it remembers absolute beauty and feels pain at its exile. Physical love, like formal beauty, is metaphysical. But true love is something else; it is the basis for illuminative perception and realization of eternal life."[9]

In his *History of Western Philosophy*, Bertrand Russell repeatedly mentions the admixture of ratiocination and illumination in the philosophy of Plato. However, he offers no documentation or quotations that would shed light on the question of whether Plato's illumination arises from discipline and purification of the soul or is just that experience born of love for the beautiful.[10] Further investigation of this question must include direct study of Plato's entire corpus.

Pythagoras may have employed the illuminationist method, apparently under the inspiration of Oriental teachings. Russell, who regards Plato's method as illuminationistic, maintains that Plato came under the influence of Pythagoras in this regard.[11]

Whether or not we see Plato as an illuminationist in method, there are pivotal ideas among his beliefs that define his philosophy, all of which Aristotle opposed. One such concept is the theory of ideas, according to which all we witness in this world, substances and accidents alike, have their origin and reality in the other world. The individual beings of this world amount to shadows or reflections of other-worldly realities. For instance, all the human individuals who dwell in this world have a principle and reality in the other world; the real and substantive man is that man of the other world.

Plato called these realities ideas. In Islamic times, the Greek word for idea was translated as *mithal* (likeness, idea), and these realities were called collectively the *muthul-i aflatuni* (Platonic ideas). Avicenna strenuously opposed the theory of Platonic ideas, and Suhravardi just as strenuously advocated it. Among later philosophers holding to the theory of ideas are Mir Damad and Mulla Sadra. However, these two sages' definitions of idea, especially Mir Damad's, differ from Plato's and even from Suhravardi's.

Mir Findiriski is another advocate of the theory of ideas from the Safavid era. He has a well-known *qasida* in Persian in which he propounds his own views on this theory. Here is how it begins:

> Lo! The star-studded wheel, so beauteous and splendid!
> What's above has a form here below correspondent.
> Should this lower form scale the ladder of gnosis,
> It will ever find union above with its origin.
> The intelligible form that is endless, eternal,
> Is compendious and single with all or without all.
> No external prehension will grasp this discussion,
> Be it Bu Nasr Farabi or Bu 'Ali Sina.[12]

Another of Plato's pivotal theories concerns the human spirit. He believes that, prior to being attached to bodies, spirits were created and dwelt in a world above and beyond this, which is the world of ideas (or of similitudes, *'alam-i muthul*), and that they are attached to and settled in bodies subsequent to the latter's creation.

The third of Plato's theories is based on the first two and amounts to a corollary of them. It holds that knowledge comes through recollection, not through actual learning. Everything we learn in this world, although we suppose it to be something we were previously ignorant of and have learned for the first time, is in reality a recollection of those things we knew before in that, prior to being attached to the body in this world, the spirit dwelt in a higher world in which it witnessed ideas. Because the realities of all things are the ideas of those things, which the spirits perceived earlier, these spirits knew realities prior to coming to this world and finding attachment to bodies. After finding this attachment, we forgot these things.

For the spirit, the body is like a curtain hung across a mirror that prevents the transmission of light and the reflection of forms from the mirror. Through dialectics (discussion, argument, and rational method), through love, or, as Suhravardi and like-minded people infer, through asceticism, discipline of the soul, and the spiritual way, the curtain is lifted, the light shines through, and the forms are revealed.

Aristotle differs with Plato on all three of these ideas. First, he denies the existence of ideal, abstract, and celestial universals; he regards the universal, or, more properly speaking, the universality of the universal, as a purely subjective phenomenon. Second, he believes that the spirit is created after the body, that is, as the creation of the body is completed and perfected. Third, Aristotle considers the body in no way a hindrance or curtain to the spirit; on the contrary, it is the means and instrument by which the spirit acquires new learning. The spirit acquires its learning by means of these senses and bodily instruments; it had no prior existence in another world in which to have learned anything.

Plato's and Aristotle's differences of opinion over these basic questions, as well as over some less important ones, were kept alive after them. They each had their followers in the Alexandrian school. Plato's followers there became known as neo-Platonists. This school was founded by the Egyptian Ammonius Saccas. Its most celebrated and outstanding exponent was the Egyptian of Greek descent, Plotinus, whom the Islamic historians called the Greek master (Ash-Shaykh al-Yunani). The neo-Platonists introduced new topics, perhaps borrowing from ancient Oriental sources. Aristotle's Alexandrian followers and expositors were numerous. The most famous were Themistius and Alexander of Aphrodisias.

Islamic Methods of Thought

There have been other methods of thought in the Islamic world, at variance with the illuminationist and peripatetic methods, that have played genuine and basic roles in the development of Islamic culture. Two such methods are *'irfan* (gnosis) and *kalam* (scholastic theology).

Neither the *'urafa'* nor the *mutakallimin* have regarded themselves as followers of the philosophers, whether illuminationists or peripatetics. They have taken stands against the philosophers and clashed with them. These clashes have had an appreciable effect on the fate of Islamic philosophy. *'Irfan* and *kalam* have both motivated Islamic philosophy through conflict and clashes and opened up new horizons for philosophy.

Four Islamic Approaches

Many of the questions Islamic philosophy addresses were first addressed by the *mutakallimin* or the *'urafa'*, although they express themselves in a way different from that of the philosophers. Islam comprehends four methods of thought, and Islamic thinkers are of any of four sorts. I am discussing methods of thought having a philosophical character in the most general sense, that is, constituting an ontology and a cosmology. I am treating the universals of philosophy, and not the methods of thought of jurisprudence, exegesis, tradition, letters, politics, or ethics, which are another matter entirely. Each of these methods has taken on a special character under the influence of Islamic teachings and differs from its counterparts outside the Islamic sphere. Each is governed by the particular spirit of Islamic culture.

One method is the deductive method of peripatetic philosophy. It has numerous adherents in history. Most Islamic philosophers, including Al-Kindi, Farabi, Avicenna, Khwaja Nasir ad-Din Tusi, Mir Damad, Ibn Rushd of Andalusia, Ibn Baja of Andalusia, and Ibn as-Sa'igh of Andalusia, have followed this method. The perfect exemplar of this school is Avicenna. Such philosophical works of his as the *Kitab ash-Shifa'* (The book of healing [the so-called *Sufficientia*]), *Isharat va Tanbihat* (Allusions and admonitions), *Najat* (Deliverance), *Danishnama-yi 'Ala'i* (The book of knowledge, dedicated to 'Ala ad-Dawla), *Mabda' va Ma'ad* (The source and the destination), *Ta'liqat-i Mubahathat* (Annotations to the discussions), and *'Uyun al-Hikma* (Wellsprings of wisdom) are all works of peripateticism. This method relies exclusively on rational deduction and demonstration.

A second method is the illuminationist method. This has fewer adherents than the first method. It was revived by Shihab ad-Din Suhravardi and followed by Qutb ad-Din Shirazi, Shahrazuri, and a number of others. Suhravardi is considered the perfect exemplar of this school. He wrote numerous books, including the *Hikmat al-Ishraq* (Wisdom of illumination), *Talvihat* (Intimations), *Muta-rahat* (Conversations), *Muqavamat* (Oppositions), and *Hayakil an-Nur* (Temples of light). The best known of them is the *Hikmat al-Ishraq*; only this work is wholly devoted to the illuminationist method. Suhravardi has written some treatises in Persian, among them *Avaz-i Par-i Jabra'il* (The song of Gabriel's wing) and *'Aql-i Surkh* (The red intelligence).

The illuminationist method rests on rational deduction and demonstration and on endeavor and purification of the soul. According to this method, one cannot discover the underlying realities of the universe through rational deduction and demonstration alone.

The wayfaring method of *'irfan,* or Sufism, is the third method. It relies exclusively on a purification of the soul based on a concept of making one's way to God and drawing near to the Truth. This way is said to culminate in the attainment of Reality. The method of *'irfan* places no confidence at all in rational deduction. The *'urafa'* say that the deductionists stand on wooden legs. According to the method of *'irfan,* the goal is not just to uncover reality, but to reach it.

The method of *'irfan* has numerous adherents, some of whom have grown famous in the Islamic world, including Bayazid Bistami, Hallaj, Shibli, Junayd of Baghdad, Dhu'n-Nun Misri, Abu Sa'id-i Abi'l-Khayr, Khwaja 'Abdullah Ansari, Abu Talib Makki, Abu Nasr Sarraj, Abu'l-Qasim Qushayri, Muhyi 'd-Din Ibn 'Arabi of Andalusia, Ibn Faridh of Egypt, and Mawlana Rumi. The perfect exemplar of Islamic *'irfan,* who codified it as a science and had a compelling influence on all who followed him, is Muhyi 'd-Din Ibn 'Arabi.

The wayfaring method of *'irfan* has one feature in common with the illuminationist method and two features at variance with it. Their shared feature is reliance on reform, refinement, and purification of the soul. The distinguishing features of each are as follows: The *'arif* wholly rejects deduction; the illuminationist upholds it and uses thought and purification to aid each other. The illuminationist, like any other philosopher, seeks to discover reality; the *'arif* seeks to attain it.

Fourth is the deductive method of *kalam*. Like the peripatetics, the *mutakallimin* rely on rational deduction, but with two differences. First, the principles on which the *mutakallimin* base their reasoning are different from those on which the philosophers base theirs. The most important convention used by the *mutakallimin*, especially by the Mu'tazilites, is that of beauty and ugliness. However, they differ among themselves as to the meaning of this convention: The Mu'tazilites regard the concept of beauty and ugliness as rational, but the Ash'arites regard it as canonical. The Mu'tazilites have derived a series of principles and formulae from this principle, such as the formula of grace *(qa'ida-yi lutf)* and the incumbency of the optimal *(wujub-i aslah)* upon God Most High.

The philosophers, however, regard the principle of beauty and ugliness as a nominal and human principle, like the pragmatic premises and intelligibles propounded in logic, which are useful only in polemics, not in demonstration. Accordingly, the philosophers call *kalam* "polemical wisdom," as opposed to "demonstrational wisdom."

Second, the *mutakallimin*, as opposed to the philosophers, regard themselves as committed, committed to the defense of the bounds of Islam. Philosophical discussion is free; that is, the philosopher has not the predetermined object of defending a particular belief. The *mutakallim* does have such an object.

The method of *kalam* is subdivided into three methods: the Mu'tazilite, the Ash'arite, and the Shi'ite.

Mu'tazilites are numerous in history. There are Abu'l Hudhayl 'Allaf, Nazzam, Jahiz, Abu 'Ubayda, and Mu'ammar ibn Muthanna, all of whom lived in the second or third centuries of the Hijra. Qazi 'Abd al-Jabbar in the fourth century and Zamakhshari around the turn of the fifth-sixth centuries also exemplify this school.

Shaykh Abu'l-Hasan Ash'ari (d. 330) perfectly exemplifies the Ash'arite school. Qazi Abu Bakr Baqillani, Imam al-Haramayn

Juvayni, Ghazali, and Fakhr ad-Din Razi all followed the Ash'ari method. Shi'i *mutakallimin* are also numerous. Hisham ibn al-Hikam, a companion of Imam Ja'far Sadiq (upon whom be peace) was a Shi'i *mutakallim*. The Nawbakhti family, an Iranian Shi'i family, produced some outstanding *mutakallims*. Shaykh Mufid and Sayyid Murtaza 'Alam al-Huda are also ranked among Shi'i *mutakallimin*. The perfect exemplar of Shi'i *kalam* is Khwaja Nasir ad-Din Tusi. His *Tajrid al-'Aqa'id* (Refinement of beliefs) is one of the most famous works of *kalam*. He was also a philosopher and mathematician. After him, *kalam* took a wholly different course and assumed a more philosophical character.

Among the Sunnis' works of *kalam*, the most famous is the *Sharh-i Mavaqif* (Elucidation of the stations), with text by Qazi 'Azud ad-Din Iji (a contemporary of Hafiz, who praised him in his poetry) and annotations by Sharif Jurjani. This work was deeply influenced by the *Tajrid al-'Aqa'id*.

Sublime Wisdom

The four streams of thought continued in the Islamic world until they reached a point of confluence called "sublime wisdom" *(hikmat-i muta'aliya)*. The science of sublime wisdom was founded by Sadr al-Muta'allihin Shirazi (or Mulla Sadra) (d. 1050/1640).[13] The term "sublime wisdom" occurs in Avicenna's *Isharat*, but Avicenna's philosophy never became known by this name.

Mulla Sadra formally designated his philosophy sublime wisdom, and it became so known. His school resembles Suhravardi's in method in seeking to combine demonstration with mystic vision and direct witness, but it differs in its principles and conclusions.

In Mulla Sadra's school, many of the points of disagreement between peripateticism and illuminationism, between philosophy and 'irfan, or between philosophy and *kalam* have been definitively resolved. Mulla Sadra's philosophy is not a syncretism, however, but a unique philosophical system, that, although the various Islamic methods of thought had an impact on its formation, one must regard as autonomous.

Mulla Sadra has written numerous works, among them the *As-*

far-i Arba'a (The four journeys, or books), *Ash-Shavahid ar-Rubu-biya* (Witnesses to lordship), *Mabda' va Ma'ad* (The source and the destination), *'Arshiya* (On the Empyrean), *Masha'ir* (The perceptual faculties), and *Sharh-i Hidaya-yi Athir ad-Din Abhari* (An elucidation of Athir ad-Din Abhari's guidance).

Among Mulla Sadra's followers is Hajj Mulla Hadi Sabzavari (1212/1798–1289/1878), author of the *Kitab-i Manzuma* (The rhymed book) and the *Sharh-i Manzuma* (The elucidation of the rhymed book). A typical basic library for study of the ancient sciences might consist of Sabzavari's *Sharh-i Manzuma,* Mulla Sadra's *Asfar,* Avicenna's *Isharat* and *Shifa',* and Suhravardi's *Hikmat al-Ishraq.*

Mulla Sadra organized the philosophical topics concerning the intellectual and rational way in a manner paralleling the manner in which the *'urafa'* had propounded the way of the heart and spirit. The *'urafa'* hold that the wayfarer accomplishes four journeys in carrying through the method of the *'arif*:

1. The journey from creation to God. At this stage, the wayfarer attempts to transcend nature as well as certain supernatural worlds in order to reach the Divine Essence, leaving no veil between himself and God.

2. The journey by God in God. After the wayfarer attains proximate knowledge of God, with His help the wayfarer journeys through His phases, perfections, names, and attributes.

3. The journey from God to creation by God. In this journey, the wayfarer returns to creation and rejoins people, but this return does not mean separation and remoteness from the Divine Essence. Rather, the wayfarer sees the Divine Essence with all things and in all things.

4. The journey in Creation by God. In this journey, the wayfarer undertakes to guide the people and lead them to the Truth.

Mulla Sadra, considering that philosophical questions constitute a "way," if a mental one, sorted them into four sets:

1. Topics that constitute a foundation or preliminary to the study of *tauhid.* These (the ordinary matter of philosophy) constitute our mental journey from creation to God.

2. Topics of *tauhid,* theology, and divine attributes—The journey by God in God.

3. Topics of the divine acts, the universal worlds of being—the journey from God to creation by God.

4. Topics of the soul and the Destination *(ma'ad)*—the journey in creation by God.

The *Asfar-i Arba'a,* which means the Four Journeys, is organized on this basis.

Mulla Sadra, who called his special philosophical system sublime wisdom, referred to conventional philosophy, whether illuminationist or peripatetic, as common or conventional philosophy.

Overview of Philosophies and Wisdoms

Philosophy and wisdom, in the widest sense, are variously classified from different perspectives; but if we consider them from the standpoint of method, they fall under four headings: deductive wisdom, experiential wisdom, experimental wisdom, and polemical wisdom.

Deductive wisdom rests on syllogism and demonstration. It has to do only with greater and lesser, result and concomitant, contradictory and contrary, and the like.

Experiential wisdom pertains not only to deduction but to experience, inspiration, and illumination. It takes its inspiration more from the heart than from the reason.

Experimental wisdom pertains neither to a priori reasoning and deduction nor to the heart and its inspirations. It pertains to sense, trial, and experiment. It takes the products of the sciences, the fruits of trial and experiment, and, by interrelating them, welds them into wisdom and philosophy.

Polemical wisdom is deductive, but the premises for its deductions are what logicians call common knowledge *(mashhurat)* and accepted facts *(maqbulat).* There are several kinds of premises to deduction, including first axioms *(badihiyat)* and common knowledge. For instance, the idea that two things each equal to a third are equal to each other, which is expressed in the phrase "the equal to the equal are equal," and the idea that it is absurd for a proposition and its contradictory to hold true at once are considered axiomatic.

The idea that it is ugly to yawn in the presence of others is considered common knowledge.

Deduction on the basis of axioms is called demonstration, and deduction on the basis of common knowledge is considered an element of polemics. Therefore, polemical wisdom means a wisdom that deduces global and universal ideas from common knowledge. The *mutakallimin* generally base their deductions on the beauty or the ugliness of a thing, on rational beauty and ugliness, so to speak. The *hukama'* hold that all beauty and ugliness relate to the sphere of human life; one cannot evaluate God, the universe, and being by these criteria. Thus, the *hukama'* call *kalam* polemical wisdom.

The *hukama'* believe that the central principles of religion may be better deduced from the premises of demonstration and in reliance on first axioms than from the premises of common knowledge and polemics. In Islamic times, especially among the Shi'a, philosophy, without departing from its mission of free inquiry and committing itself in advance, gradually proved the best source of support for Islamic principles. Accordingly, polemical wisdom, in the hands of such persons as Khwaja Nasir ad-Din Tusi, gradually took on a demonstrational and illuminationistic character. Thus, *kalam* came to be overshadowed by philosophy.

Although experimental wisdom is extraordinarily valuable, it has two shortcomings. One is that its compass is confined to the experimental sciences, and the experimental sciences are confined to what is sensible and palpable. Man's philosophical needs extend beyond what is in the domain of sense experience. For instance, when we discuss the possibility of a beginning of time, an end to space, or an origin for causes, how are we to find what we seek in the laboratory or under the microscope? Thus, experimental wisdom cannot satiate man's philosophical instinct and must elect silence on basic philosophical questions.

The other shortcoming lies in the fact that the value of experimental questions is rendered precarious by their confinement to and dependence upon nature. Questions of experimental science have a time-bound value and may grow obsolescent at any moment. A wisdom based on experiment is naturally precarious and so does not meet a basic human need, the need for certainty. Certainty arises in questions having mathematical abstraction or philosophical abstraction, and the meanings of mathematical and philosophical abstractions can be clarified only by philosophy.

There remain deductive wisdom and experiential wisdom. The questions discussed in the following sections should elucidate these two wisdoms and spell out their value.

Problems in Philosophy

Being

Philosophical questions pivot on being. That which is to philosophy what the body is to medicine, number is to mathematics, or quantity is to geometry is being *qua* being. It is the subject of philosophy and all philosophical topics turn on it. In other words, philosophy has for its subject existence.

Several kinds of questions turn on being. One is questions pertaining to being, or existence, and its opposites in the two respective senses: nonbeing and essence *(mahiya)*.[14] There is nothing but being in the objective world. Being has no opposite outside the mind. But the conceptualizing mind of man has formed two concepts vis-à-vis being or existence: nonbeing and essence (of course, essence*s*). A range of philosophical questions, especially in sublime wisdom, pertains to existence and essence, and another range pertains to being and nonbeing.

A second group of questions pertains to divisions of being. Being in its turn has divisions that are regarded as amounting to species of being; in other words, being is divisible (for instance, into the objective and the subjective, the necessary and the possible, the eternal and the created in time, the stable and the changing, the singular and the plural, the potential and the act, and the substance and the accident). Of course, these are the primary divisions of being, that is, the divisions that enter into being by virtue of the fact that it is being.

To illustrate, divisions into black and white, large and small, equal and unequal, odd and even, or long and short are divisions not in being *qua* being but in being *qua* body or in being *qua* quantifiable. Corporeality in being corporeality, or quantity in being quantity, admits of such division. However, division into singular and plural, or division into necessary and possible, is division of being *qua* being.

Close research has been done in philosophy as to the criteria for these divisions, what distinguishes the divisions of being *qua* being from other divisions. Some philosophers have regarded certain divisions as applying to body *qua* body and thus falling outside the scope of first philosophy, but other philosophers for various reasons have regarded these divisions as applying to being *qua* being and thus falling under this same domain.

A third group of questions pertains to the universal laws governing being, such as causality, the correspondence of cause and effect, the necessity governing the system of cause and effect, and priority versus synchronism among the levels of being.

A fourth group of questions pertains to demonstration of the planes of being or worlds of being. Being has particular planes or worlds. The *hukama'* of Islam believe that there are four general worlds or four emergences *(nash'a)*:

1. The world of nature, or the *nasut*
2. The world of ideas, or the *malakut*
3. The world of [separate] intelligences, or the *jabarut*
4. The world of divinity, or the *lahut*

The world of *nasut* is the world of matter, motion, and space-time. It is the world of nature and sense objects, this world.

The world of [Platonic] ideas [similitudes], or the *malakut*, is a world superior to nature, having forms and dimensions, but lacking motion, time, and change.

The world of *jabarut* is the world of the [separate] intelligences or the world of the [abstract] idea *(ma'na)*, free of forms and images and thus superior to the world of *malakut*.

The world of *lahut* is the world of divinity and unity.

A fifth group of questions pertains to the relations between the world of nature and the worlds above it, the descent of being from *lahut* to nature, and to the ascent from nature to the higher worlds. With special reference to man, these are called questions of the destination *(ma'ad)* and figure very prominently in sublime wisdom.

Existence and Essence
Is existence substantive, or is essence? We always distinguish two valid senses in which things may be spoken of: the isness of a thing

and the whatness of a thing. For instance, we know that man is, the tree is, number is, and quantity is, but number has one whatness, one essence, and man has another.[15] If we ask, "What is number?", we receive one answer. If we ask, "What is man?", we receive another.

Many things have a patent isness; that is, we know that they are. But we may not know what they are. For instance, we know that life is or that electricity is, but we may not know what life is or what electricity is. We know what many things are—for instance, we have a clear definition of a circle and so know what a circle is—but we do not know whether the circle exists in objective nature. Thus, isness is something other than whatness.

This plurality, this dichotomy of essence and existence, is purely subjective. In extensional reality, no thing is twofold. Therefore, one of these two is objectively so and substantive, and the other is nominal and not substantive.

The whole question of existentialism versus essentialism has no ancient historical antecedents. This topic originated in the Islamic world. None of the early philosophers, Farabi, Avicenna, Khwaja Nasir ad-Din Tusi, or even Suhravardi, discussed anything under this heading. The topic made its debut in philosophy in the time of Mir Damad (the beginning of the eleventh century of the Hijra). Mir Damad was an essentialist. However, his famous pupil, Mulla Sadra, made a compelling case for existentialism, and from then onward, every philosopher of note has been an existentialist.[16] In the third volume of *Usul-i Falsafa va Ravish-i Ri'alism,* I have discussed the respective ideas of the *'urafa',* the *mutakallimin,* and the philosophers as precursors to this philosophical conception of Mulla Sadra's.

Another philosophy sometimes known as existentialism has flourished in our own time. This form of existentialism pertains to man and has reference to the idea that man, by contrast with all other beings, has no definite, preassigned essence and no form determined by nature. Man designs and builds his own whatness. This idea is largely correct and supported by Islamic philosophy, except that, what in Islamic philosophy is called existentialism does not apply to man alone, but to the whole universe, and, second, when we speak of existentialism or *isalat-i vujud* in an Islamic context, we are using the term *isalat* (-ism) in its sense of substantive reality or objective being, as opposed to nominal or mental existence. When we use it in the Western context of modern existentialism, we are using it in its sense of primacy or priority. One should by no means conflate the two senses.

The Objective and the Subjective

A thing is either objective or subjective. Objective being means being external to and independent of man's mind. We know, for instance, that mountain, sea, and plain have being external to our minds and independent of them. Whether our minds conceive of them or not, indeed, whether ourselves and our minds exist or not, mountain, sea, and plain exist.

But that mountain, sea, and plain have an existence in our minds as well. When we imagine them, we give them being in our minds. The being things find in our minds is called subjective being or mental being.

Two questions arise here. One is why the images of things appearing in our minds should be conceived of as a kind of being for those things in our minds. If they are, one might say that the image of a thing painted on a wall or printed on a sheet of paper deserves to be called another kind of being, a parietal being or a papyraceous being. If we term mental images a form of being for the thing imagined, to be just, we have employed a metaphor and not spoken the literal truth, but philosophy ought to deal with the literal truth.

The relation of a mental form to an external object (for instance, the relation of a mental mountain or sea to an external mountain or sea) is far more profound than the relation of the picture of a mountain or a sea on a sheet of paper or a wall to that external mountain or sea. If what appears in the mind were only a simple image, it would never give rise to consciousness, just as the image on the wall does not give rise to consciousness in the wall. Rather, the mental image is consciousness itself.

The other question is whether mental being, as a concept actually relating to man and the human psyche, belongs to the realm of psychology. Philosophy deals with general questions, and such particular questions pertain to the sciences.

Philosophers have demonstrated that we are conscious of external objects because our mental images, far from being simple, are a kind of realization of existence in our minds for the essences *(mahiya)* of the objects. Although, from one standpoint, the question of mental images is a question of the human psyche and so belongs to the field of psychology, from another standpoint, that man's mind is in fact another emergence *(nash'a)* of being, resulting in being in its essence taking two forms, subjective and objective, it is a question for philosophy.

Avicenna and Mulla Sadra have said (the former allusively, near the beginning of the "Ilahiyat" of his *Shifa'*, and the latter explicitly and at length in his commentary to the same work) that at times a question may pertain to two different disciplines from two standpoints; for instance, a question may pertain to philosophy from one standpoint and to the natural sciences from another.

Truth and Error
The question of mental being has another angle that has been studied: It has to do with the validity of perceptions, the extent to which our perceptions, sensations, and conceptions of the external world are valid. From ancient times, philosophers have asked whether what we perceive of an object by means of our senses or our reason corresponds to actuality, the thing in itself.

Some postulate that some of our sense perceptions or rational perceptions do correspond to actuality, the thing in itself, and some do not. Those that correspond to actuality are termed "truth," and those that do not are termed "error." Sight, hearing, taste, touch, and smell are all subject to error. But most of our sense perceptions correspond fully to reality. Through these same senses, we accurately distinguish night from day, far from near, large from small in volume, tough from smooth, and cold from hot.

Our reason is likewise subject to error. Logic was compiled to avert errors of the reason in its deductions. But most of our rational deductions are valid. When we add up all the debits and all the credits in a ledger and subtract the former from the latter, we are performing a mental and rational procedure that we are perfectly assured will hold true if we are sufficiently careful and exact.

However, the Sophists of Greece denied the distinction between truth and error. They said that whatever some person feels and thinks is for that person the truth. They said that man is the measure of all things. They radically denied reality and, having denied it, left nothing in corresponding to which man's perceptions and sensations could be true and in failing to correspond to which they could be erroneous.

The Sophists were contemporaries of Socrates (Socrates came along near the close of the Sophist period). Protagoras and Gorgias are two famous Sophists. Socrates, Plato, and Aristotle rebelled against them.

After Aristotle's time, another group appeared in Alexandria, called the Skeptics, the most famous of whom is Pyrrho. The Skeptics did not deny actuality in principle but denied that human perceptions correspond to it. They said that one perceives an object in a certain way under the influence of internal states and certain external conditions. Sometimes two people experiencing different states or viewing from different angles will see the same event in two different ways. A thing may appear ugly in one's eyes and beautiful in another's, or single in one's eyes and double in another's. The air may feel warm to one and cold to another. A flavor may taste sweet to one and bitter to another. The Skeptics, like the Sophists, denied the validity of knowledge.

Bishop Berkeley wholly rejects external reality. No one has been able to refute his reasons for his position, although everyone knows they are fallacious.

Those who have sought a reply to the ancient Sophists exemplified by Berkeley have not taken the approach that could resolve the sophism. The philosophers of Islam have held that the basic approach to resolving this sophism consists in our perceiving the reality of mental being. Only thus is the puzzle solved.

In approaching mental being, the *hukama'* of Islam first define knowledge, or perception, as consisting in a kind of being for the object perceived within the being of the perceiver. They go on to cite certain demonstrations in support of this position, and then they recount and reply to certain objections to mental being or allegations of problems in it.

This topic did not exist in this form early in the Islamic period and *a fortiori* did not exist in Hellenic times. Nasir ad-Din Tusi was the first to speak of the objective and the subjective in his works of philosophy and *kalam*. Thereafter, it came to occupy a major place in the works of such comparatively recent philosophers as Mulla Sadra and Mulla Hadi Sabzavari. Farabi, Avicenna, and even Suhravardi, as well as their followers, never broached the subject of mental being or even used the term in their works. The term first appeared after Avicenna's time.

However, what Farabi and Avicenna said on other subjects shows that they believed perception to consist of a simulacrum of the reality of the object perceived within the being of the perceiver. But they neither sought to demonstrate this point nor conceived of it as an independent question of being, an independent division of being.

The Created in Time and the Eternal

The Arabic word *hadith* has the lexical and customary meaning of new, and *qadim* means old. However, these words have other meanings in the terminologies of philosophy and *kalam*. Like other people, when philosophers speak of the *hadith* and the *qadim,* they seek to know what is new and what is old, but in speaking of a thing as new, they mean that before it was, it was not—that is, that first it was not, then it was. In speaking of a thing as old, they mean that it always has been and never was not. Suppose there is a tree that has lived for billions of years. In common usage, it would be spoken of as old, quite old indeed, but according to the terminologies of philosophy and *kalam,* it is *hadith* (new) because there was a time billions of years ago when it was not.

Philosophers define createdness in time *(huduth)* as the precedence of a thing's nonbeing to its being, and they define eternality *(qidam)* as the nonprecedence of a thing's nonbeing to its being. Therefore, an entity is created in time whose nonbeing precedes its being, and an entity is eternal for which no nonbeing prior to its being can be conceived.

Discussion of the question of the created in time and the eternal turns on this point: Is everything in the universe created in time and nothing eternal, such that whatever we consider first was not and then was? Or is everything eternal and nothing created in time, such that everything has always been? Or are some things created in time, and some eternal, such that, for instance, shapes, forms, and externals are created in time, but matter, subjects, and invisible things are eternal? Or are individuals and parts created in time, whereas species and wholes are eternal? Or are natural and material phenomena created in time, whereas abstract and suprameterial phenomena are eternal? Or is only God, the Creator of the whole and Cause of causes, eternal, whereas all else is created in time? Overall, is the universe created in time, or is it eternal?

The *mutakallimin* of Islam believe that only God is eternal. All else—matter and form, individuals and species, parts and wholes, abstract and material—constitutes what is called the world or 'other' *(masiva)* and is created in time. The philosophers of Islam, however, believe that createdness in time is a property of the material world, whereas the supernatural worlds are abstract and eternal. In the world of nature, too, principles and universals are eternal, whereas the phenomena and particulars are created in time. Therefore, the universe is created in time with respect to its phenomena and particulars but eternal with respect to its principles and universals.

Debate over createdness in time and eternality has excited acrimonious disputes between the philosophers and the *mutakallimin*. Abu Hamid Ghazali, who, although leaning to *'irfan* and Sufism in most of his works, leans to *kalam* in some, declares Avicenna an unbeliever for his stand on several questions, among them his belief in the eternality of the world. In his famous *Tahafut al-Falsafa* (The incoherence of the philosophers), Ghazali has criticized philosophers on twenty points and exposed what he believed to be the incoherencies in their thought. Ibn Rushd of Andalusia has rebutted Ghazali in *Tahafut at-Tahafut* (The incoherence of the "incoherence").

The *mutakallimin* say that if a thing is not created in time but eternal—if it has always been and never not been—then that thing has no need of a creator and cause. Therfore, if we suppose other eternal things exist than the Essence of the Truth, it follows that they will have no need of a creator and so in reality be necessary beings in their essence, like God, and the demonstrations that show the Necessary Being in Essence to be singular do not permit us to profess more than one such Necessary Being. Accordingly, no more than one Eternal Being exists, and all else is created in time. Therefore, the universe is created in time, including the abstract and the material, principles and phenomena, species and individuals, wholes and parts, matter and form, visible and invisible.

The philosophers have rebutted the arguments of the *mutakallimin* decisively, saying that all the confusion turns on one point, which consists in supposing that, if a thing has a continuous existence into the indefinite past, it has no need of a cause, whereas this is not so. A thing's need or lack of need for a cause pertains to its essence, which makes it a necessary being or a possible being; it has nothing to do with its createdness in time or eternality.[17] By analogy, the sun's radiance stems from the sun and cannot exist apart from it. Its existence depends on the sun's existence. It is the sun's luminence and issues from the sun whether we suppose there was a time this radiance did not exist or we suppose it has always existed, along with the sun. If we suppose that the sun's radiance has coexisted with the sun itself from preeternity to posteternity, this does not entail its having no need of the sun.

The philosophers maintain that the relation of the universe to God is as the relation of the radiance to the sun, with this difference: The sun is not conscious of itself or of its action and does not perform its function as an act of will; the contrary is true of God.

At times we encounter expressions in the primary texts of Islam that compare the relation of the universe and God to the relation of radiance and the sun. The noble verse of the Qur'an states, "God is the Light of the heavens and the earth" (24:35). Exegetes have interpreted this verse to mean that God is the light-giver of the heavens and the earth (that the being of heaven and earth is a ray of God).

The philosophers do not adduce any evidence for the eternality of the universe from the universe itself; rather, they approach this argument from the position that God is the Absolutely Effulgent and the Eternally Beneficent—we cannot possibly conceive of His effulgence (emanation) and beneficence as limited, as terminating somewhere. In other words, the theistic philosophers have arrived at the eternality of the universe through an a priori demonstration, that is, by making the being and attributes of God the premise to the eternality of the universe. Generally, those disbelieving in God advance the position of the eternality of the universe, but the theistic philosophers say that the same thing nonbelievers adduce as a reason for God's nonexistence in their view implies God's existence. The eternality of the universe is a hypothesis to nonbelievers, but it is an established fact to theistic philosophers.

The Mutable and the Constant

Change means transformation and constancy means uniformity. We continually witness changes in the universe. We ourselves continually make transitions from state to state, from period to period, beginning when we are born and ending when we die. The same holds for earth and sea, for mountains, trees, animals, stars, solar systems, and galaxies. Are these changes outward, pertaining to the configuration, form, and accidents of the universe, or are they profound and fundamental, such that no constant phenomenon exists in the universe? Are the changes that occur in the universe transient and instantaneous, or are they gradual and protracted?

These questions, too, date from remote times; they were discussed in ancient Greece. Democritus, known as the father of the atomic theory and also as the laughing philosopher, maintained that all change or transformation is superficial because natural being is based on atomic particles, which are forever in one state and unchangeable. The changes we witness are like those in a heap of gravel, massed sometimes in one shape, sometimes in another, but never changing in identity or real nature. This is the mechanistic outlook and constitutes a kind of mechanistic philosophy.

Another Greek philosopher, Heraclitus, maintains that nothing remains in the same state for two successive instants. As he says, you cannot set foot twice in the same river because at the second instant you are not who you were before and that river is not the same river. This philosophy stands opposite to Democritus's in seeing everything in a state of flux and inconstancy, but it says nothing contrary to mechanism; that is, it advances no idea of dynamics.

Aristotle's philosophy has no quarrel with the idea that all the parts of nature change, but undertakes to determine which changes are gradual and protracted and which are transient and instantaneous. It terms the gradual changes "motion" and the transient changes "generation and corruption" (that is, a transient coming into being is called generation, and a transient extinction is called corruption). Because Aristotle and his followers consider the basic changes occurring in this world, especially those that appear in substances, as transient, they term this "the world of generation and corruption."

At other moments, constancy obtains. If we regard changes as transient, because they occur in an instant, although at other instants or through time things are constant, such mutable things have a relative mutability and a relative constancy. Therefore, if change is in the mode of motion, it is absolute change. If it is in the mode of generation and corruption, if it is in an instantaneous mode—it is relative.

According to the Aristotelians, although nothing absolutely constant and uniform exists in nature, but everything is mutable (contrary to the view of the Democriteans), because substances are basic to nature and changes in substances are transient, the world has a relative constancy along with relative change. But constancy governs the world to a greater extent than does change.

Aristotle and the Aristotelians regard all things as falling under ten basic generic classes, which they call the ten categories: substance, quantity, quality, determination in space, position, determination in time, relation, condition, action, and passion.

Motion occurs only in the categories of quantity, quality, and determination in space. In all other categories change is transient; in other words, all other categories enjoy a relative constancy. Even those three categories in which motion occurs—because the motion is intermittent—are governed by a relative constancy. Therefore, in Aristotle's philosophy, one encounters more constancy than change, more uniformity than transformation.

Avicenna believed that motion occurs in the category of position as well. He demonstrated that certain motions, such as the rotation of the earth about its axis, constitute a positional motion, not a motion in spatial determination. Thus, after Avicenna, motion in spatial determination was restricted to transferential motion. Avicenna did not demonstrate the existence of a new sort of motion, but reclassified as positional what had previously been categorized as a motion in spatial determination. His reclassification is generally accepted.

Mulla Sadra effected a major transformation in Islamic philosophy by demonstrating substantial motion. He demonstrated that, even on the basis of the Aristotelian principles of matter and form, we must accept that the substances of the world are in continuous motion; there is never so much as an instant of constancy and uniformity in the substances of the world. The accidents (that is, the nine other categories), as functions of the substances, are also in motion. According to Mulla Sadra, nature equals motion, and motion equals continuous, uninterrupted creation and extinction.

Through the principle of substantial motion, the visage of the Aristotelian universe is wholly transformed. According to this principle, nature, or matter, equals motion. Time consists in the measure or tensile force of this substantial motion, and constancy equals supernatural being. What exists consists of, on the one hand, absolute change (nature) and, on the other, absolute constancy (the supernatural). The constancy of nature is the constancy of order, not the constancy of being; that is, a definite, immutable system governs the universe, and the contents of the system are all mutable (they are change itself). Both the being and the system of this universe stem from the supernal. Were it not for the governance of the other world, this world, which is wholly flux and mutation, would be cut off from its past and future. "Many times has the water exchanged in this stream,/Still the moon's and the stars' reflections remain."[18]

Prior to Mulla Sadra, the topic of the mutable and the constant was felt to belong to the natural sciences, in that any determination or any division that applies to a body *qua* body belongs to the natural sciences. It was said that it is such-and-such a body that is either constant or mutable, or that is either still or in motion. In other words, motion and stasis are among the accidents of a body. Therefore, the topic of the constant and the mutable ought to fall wholly within the domain of the natural sciences.

This all changed with Mulla Sadra's realization of existentialism (the substantive reality of being), his realization of substantial motion, and his demonstration that the natures of the universe constitute the mobile *qua* mobile and the mutable *qua* mutable (that is, that a body is not something to which motion is merely added as an accident, whereby at times this motion can be annulled, leaving the motionless state we call stasis). Rather, the natures of the universe are motion itself, and the contrary of this substantial motion is constancy, not stasis. Stasis holds for the accidental motions the state of whose absence we call stasis but is inconceivable in the case of essential, substantial motion. The contrary of this substantial motion that is the substance itself consists of substances for which constancy is the very essence. These are entities beyond space and time, devoid of spatiotemporal forces, potentialities, or dimensions. Therefore, it is not the body that is either constant or mutable. Rather, it is being *qua* being that appears either as constancy itself (as supramaterial beings) or as continuous flux/becoming/creation itself (the world of nature). Therefore, just as being is in its essence divisible into necessary and possible, so is it in its essence divisible into the constant and the fluid.

Thus, according to Mulla Sadra, only certain kinds of motions —the accidental motions of a body having stasis for their opposite— ought to be studied under the heading of the natural sciences. Other motions, or indeed these very motions when not regarded from the standpoint of their being accidents of natural bodies, ought to be discussed and studied in first philosophy. Mulla Sadra himself brought in his discussions of motion under "general phenomena" in the *Asfar* in the course of discussing potentials and acts, although it warranted a chapter to itself.

Among the key conclusions arising from this great realization —basically, that being in its essence is divisible into the constant and the fluid and that constant being is one modality of being, while fluid being is another—is that becoming is precisely a plane of being. Although, nominally speaking, we may regard becoming as a synthesis of being and nonbeing, this synthesis is actually a kind of notion or metaphor.[19]

In truth it is the realization of the substantive reality of being and of the nominal status of essences *(mahiyat)* that permits us to perceive this key reality. Without a grasp of the substantive reality of being, neither a conception of substantial motion nor a conception that flux and becoming are precisely a plane of being would be possible.

Motion has recovered its proper place in the modern philosophy of Europe by other avenues. Some philosophers came to believe that motion is the cornerstone of nature, that nature equals becoming. However, because this idea was not based on existentialism (the substantive reality of being) and the primary division of being into the constant and the fluid, these philosophers supposed that becoming was the same union of opposites that the ancients had deemed absurd. They likewise supposed that becoming falsified the principle of identity *(huhuya)*, which the ancients had taken for granted.

These philosophers said that the presiding principle in the thought of the ancients was the principle of constancy and that, in deeming beings constant, the ancients had supposed that either being or nonbeing must hold sway over things. Therefore, one alone of these holds true (the principle of the impossibility of union and cancellation of opposites). That is, either there is always being or there is always nonbeing; no third alternative obtains. Similarly, because the ancients thought things constant, they supposed of everything that is itself (the principle of identity). But with the realization of the principle of motion and change in nature, the realization that nature is continually in a state of becoming, the two principles are groundless because becoming is a union of being and nonbeing; where a thing is both being and non-being, becoming has been demonstrated. A thing in a state of becoming both is and is not; at every instant, its self is its not-self; its self is at once its self and not its self; the self of its self is progressively negated. Therefore, if the principle governing things were that of being and nonbeing, both the principle of the impossibility of the union of opposites and the principle of identity would hold true. Because the principle governing things is the principle of becoming, neither of these other principles holds true.

The principle of the impossibility of the union of opposites and the principle of identity, which held unrivaled sway over the minds of the ancients, arose from a further principle that they also accepted implicitly: the principle of constancy. As the natural sciences showed the invalidity of the principle of constancy, these two principles, too, lost their credibility. This development represents the conception of many modern philosophers, from Hegel onward.

Mulla Sadra invalidated the principle of constancy by other means. Motion, according to his realization, implies that nature equals inconstancy and constancy equals abstraction. Unlike the modern philosophers, however, he never concludes that because nature equals flux and becoming, the principle of the impossibility of the union and cancellation of opposites is falsified. Although Mulla Sadra regards becoming as a kind of union of being and nonbeing, he does not treat this as a union of opposites because he has realized a more important principle: that being is divisible in its essence into the constant and the fluid. Constant being is a plane of being, not a synthesis of being and nonbeing. The synthesis of becoming from being and nonbeing is not a union of two opposites just as it is not the negation of the self of a thing.

The modern philosophers' confusion has two roots: their failure to perceive the division of being into the constant and the fluid and their inadequate conception of the principles of contradiction and contrariety.

Cause and Effect

The most ancient of philosophical questions is that of cause and effect. The concept of cause and effect appears in every philosophical system, unlike such concepts as existentialism and subjective being, which have a prominent place in some philosophies and pass unnoted in others, the concept of potential and act, which plays an important role in Aristotelianism, or the concept of the constant and the mutable, which has a deservedly prominent position in the philosophy of Mulla Sadra.

Causation is a kind of relation between two things, one of which we call the cause and the other, the effect. This is the most profound of relations. The relation of cause and effect consists in the cause's giving being to the effect. What the effect realizes from the cause is its whole being, its whole reality; therefore, if the cause were not, the effect would not be. We find such a relation nowhere else. Therefore, the effect's need of the cause is the keenest of needs, a need at the root of being. Accordingly, if we would define cause, we must say, "A cause is that thing an effect needs in its essence and being."

Every phenomenon is an effect, and every effect needs a cause; therefore, every phenomenon needs a cause. That is, if a thing is not being itself in its essence—if it has appeared as an accident, a phenomenon—it must have arisen through the intervention of a factor we call a cause. Therefore, no phenomenon is without a cause. The hypothesis contrary to this theory is that a phenomenon may appear without a cause. This hypothesis is called coincidence (sudfa) or chance (ittifaq). The philosophy of causality radically rejects this hypothesis.

Philosophers and *mutakallimin* concur that every phenomenon is an effect and needs a cause, but the *mutakallimin* define such a phenomenon as created in time *(hadith),* and the philosophers define it as possible *(mumkin).* That is, the *mutakallimin* say that whatever is created in time is an effect and needs a cause, and the philosophers say that whatever is possible is an effect and needs a cause. These two definitions lead to the different conclusions previously discussed in "The Created in Time and the Eternal."

A certain cause produces only a certain effect, and a certain effect proceeds only from a certain cause. There are special relations of dependence among the beings of the universe such that any one thing cannot necessarily give rise to any other thing and any one thing cannot necessarily arise from any other thing. We rely on this truth in our everyday experience. For instance, eating is the cause of satiety, drinking water is the cause of quenching of thirst, and study is the cause of literacy. Therefore, if we wish to realize any of these qualities, we have resort to the appropriate cause. For instance, we never drink water or study for the sake of satiety, nor do we consider eating sufficient for the attainment of literacy.

Philosophy demonstrates that such a clear relation obtains among all the processes in the universe. It makes this point through this definition: A unique correspondence and symmetry govern every single cause-and-effect relation and appear in no other such relation. This is the single most important principle in giving order to our thought and in presenting the universe to our thought not as a chaotic aggregate in which nothing is conditional upon anything else but as an ordered, systematic cosmos in which every part has a special place, in which no one thing can displace another.

There are four kinds of cause in the philosophy of Aristotle: the efficient cause, the final cause, the material cause, and the formal cause. These four causes are well illustrated in human industry: If we build a house, the builder or workman is the efficient cause; to dwell in that house is the final cause; the building materials are the material cause; and the configuration of the house, in being appropriate to a dwelling and not, say, to a granary, a bathhouse, or a mosque, is the formal cause. In Aristotle's view, every natural phenomenon, whether a stone, a plant, or a human being, has these same four causes.

Cause as defined by natural scientists differs somewhat from cause as defined by theologians. In theology, or what we now call philosophy, cause means giver of existence. Philosophers call what brings something into existence its cause. Otherwise they do not call it cause, although they may at times call it contributory (mu'idd). The natural scientists, however, use the word "cause" even where the relation between two things is simply one of transfer of momentum. Therefore, in the natural scientists' terminology, the builder is the cause of the house in being the point of issue for its construction, through a series of transfers of materials. The theologians, however, never call the builder the cause of the house, in that he does not bring the house into being. Rather, the materials for the house existed beforehand, and the builder's work has been confined to organizing them. Likewise, according to the natural scientists, the relation of mother and father to child is causal; but according to philosophy, it is that of an antecedent, a contributory factor, or a channel, not that of a cause.

The sequence of causes (causes in the terminology of the philosophers, not that of the natural scientists, that is, causes of being, not causes of motion) terminates. It is absurd that it should be interminable. If the being of a thing proceeds from a cause, arises from a cause, and if the being of that cause arises from a further cause, and if the being of that cause arises from a yet further cause, this process could go on through thousands, millions, billions of causes and more. However, it must finally terminate in a cause that arises through its own essence and not through another cause. Philosophers have often demonstrated that an endless regress of causes is absurd, which phrase they shorten to a regress of causes is absurd or usually even further to regress is absurd.

The word tasalsul (regress) is derived from the word silsila (sequence, series, range), with the root meaning of chain. Therefore, tasalsul means an endless chain of causes. Philosophers thus liken the ordered system of causes and effects to a chain whose links interlock in sequence.

The Necessary, the Possible, and the Impossible

Logicians say that if we attribute a predicate to a subject, if, for instance, we say a is b, the relation of b to a will have one of three qualities. First, it may be necessary, that is, certain, inevitable, and inviolable; in other words, reason may refuse to accept anything contrary to it. Second, the opposite may be true. That is, the relation may be impossible, meaning it is absurd that the predicate should be an accident of the subject. In other words, reason refuses to accept that it should be one. Third, the relation may be such that it may be affirmed or negated; that is, it is susceptible both to affirmation and to negation. In other words, reason refuses to accept neither this relation nor its contrary.

For instance, if we consider the relation of the number four to evenness, we see that it is necessary and certain. Reason refuses to accept its contrary. Reason says that the number four is certainly and necessarily even. Therefore, necessity governs this relation.

But if we say that the number five is even, this relation is impossible. The number five has no possibility of being even, and our reason in perceiving this relation rejects it. Therefore, impossibility and inconceivability govern this relation.

But if we say that today the weather is sunny, this is a possible relation. That is, the nature of the day does not require that the weather be sunny or that it be cloudy. Either may accord with the nature of the day. Possibility governs this relation.

It follows that, whatever subject and whatever predicate we consider, their relation will not be devoid of these three qualities, which at times from a certain standpoint we term the three modalities. I have described the logicians' approach.

The philosophers, who study being, say that any idea or concept we consider, take as a subject, and predicate being of will fall under one of these three categories. The relation of being to that idea or concept may be necessary; that is, that thing must necessarily exist. We then call that thing a necessary being.

God is discussed in philosophy under the heading of proofs for necessary being. Philosophical demonstrations show that there is a Being for which nonexistence is absurd and existence is necessary.

If the relation of being to that idea is impossible, that is, if it is absurd that it should exist, we call it an impossible being. An example is a body that is at once spherical and cubical.

If the relation of being to that idea is possible, that is, if that idea is an essence for which reason rejects neither the existence nor the nonexistence, we call it a possible being. All the beings in the universe, in appearing and then disappearing according to a sequence of causes, are possible beings.

Every possible being in itself becomes a necessary being through its cause, but a being necessary through other, not a being necessary in itself. That is, whenever all the causes and preconditions for a possible being exist, it must exist and so becomes a being necessary through other. If it does not come into existence—if so much as one of its preconditions or one of the elements of its causal nexus is lacking—it becomes a being impossible through other.

The philosophers accordingly say that as long as a thing is not necessary, it does not exist. That is, until the existence of a thing reaches the stage of necessity, it will not come into being. Therefore, whatever comes into being does so according to necessity, within a definite and inviolable system. Thus, the system governing the universe and all that is in it is a necessary, certain, and inviolable system. In the language of modern philosophers, it is a determinate system.[20]

In discussing cause and effect, I said that the principle of correspondence between cause and effect imparts a special order to our thought and marks out a special connection between principles and ramifications, between causes and effects, in our minds. This principle—that every possible being gains necessity from its cause—which, from one standpoint, pertains to cause and effect and, from another, to necessity and possibility, imparts a special character to the system of our cosmology in making it a necessary, certain, and inviolable system. Philosophy succinctly terms this point the principle of cause-and-effect necessity. If we accept the principle of the final cause in reference to nature (if we accept that nature pursues ends in its evolutionary journey and that all these ends revert to one primary end that is the end of ends), the system of our cosmology takes on a further special character.

Notes to "Philosophy"

1. See Muhammad Shahristani, *Kitab-i Milal va Nihal*, ("Nations and Sects") vol. 2, p. 231, and Dr. Human, *Tarikh-i Falsafa* ("History of Philosophy"), vol. 1, p. 20.
2. Human, *Tarikh-i Falsafa*, vol. 1, p. 69.
3. To explicate or demonstrate these three features is beyond the scope of these brief discussions. See Avicenna, *Danishnama-yi A'la'i: Ilahiyat*, the first three chapters, and Mulla Sadra, *Al-Asfar al-Arba'a*, the first few sections.
4. *Ahkam:* the plural of *hukm*, a term in logic, meaning conformity to the affirmative or negative relation between subject and predicate. *Trans.*
5. See the *Ilahiyat* of *ash-Shifa'* (old edition), p. 15.
6. Existentialists are said to hold that what is "fabricated in itself" (*maj'ul bi'dh-dhat*) is being, but essences are nominal. Essentialists are said to hold the contrary.

   That "more base" (i.e., natural) possible beings should arise directly from the Essence of the Truth is said to violate the law of correspondence between cause and effect. Thus, "more noble" possible beings, such as intelligences and souls, must exist as intermediate causes. Suhravardi is said to have originated this idea, and Mulla Sadra to have endorsed it. *Trans.*
7. *Kitab-i Milal va Nihal*, vol. 2.
8. Henry Corbin believes that this word was used for the first time in the Islamic world near the turn of the third-fourth centuries by Ibn Wahshiya. See Seyyed Hossein Nasr, *Three Muslim Sages* (Cambridge, Mass., 1964), pp. 63 and 151, n. 22. [Nasr cites for his source H. Corbin, *Les Motifs Zoroastriens dans la philosophie de Suhrawardi* (Tehran, 1946), p. 18. See also Henri (*sic*) Corbin, *Histoire de la philosophie Islamique* (Paris, 1964), p. 285. *Trans.*]

   Sayyid Hasan Taqizada, in his "Yad Dashtha-yi Tarikh-i 'Ulum dar Islam" ("Notes on the History of the Sciences in Islam"), in *Majalla-yi Maqalat va Barrasiha* ("Monographs and Researches Bulletin"), 3 and 4, Tehran, Publications Group of the College of Theology and Islamic Sciences, p. 213, after mentioning an unknown book attributed to this Ibn Wahshiya, says:

   > Another book by Ibn Wahshiya the Nabataean has occasioned much discussion, titled *Al-Falahat an-Nabatiya* ("Nabataean Agriculture"), which has also been attributed to a sage of Babul named Quthami and which quotes older books from Babul, such as the writings of Zagrith and Yanbu

Shad. Even Ibn Khaldun, with his flair for research, attributed this book to the Nabataean scholars and saw it as an Arabic translation from the Greek. But finally, through the researches of the German scholars Gutschmid and Nöldeke and especially of the Italian Nallino it grew clear that this book is a fabrication and full of balderdash; Nallino goes so far as to hold that no Ibn Wahshiya ever existed and that Abu Talib Zayyat compiled all these fantasies and attributed them to an imaginary person. Researchers believe that such books are works of the Shu'ubiya, who sought to prove that the sciences belonged to non-Arab peoples and that the Arabs had no part in them.

It is not unlikely that the source of Suhravardi's error was *Al-Falahat an-Nabatiya* or some similar work of the Shu'ubiya. This book is not available to us at present, so we cannot compare its contents with what Suhravardi has said on the subject.

9. Muhammad 'Ali Furughi, *Sayr-i Hikmat dar Urupa,* 3 vols. in 1 (n.p., n.d.), vol. 1, p. 20.

10. Bertrand Russell, *A History of Western Philosophy* (New York, 1945). See especially pp. 119–143.

11. For further study of Pythagoras, see ibid., pp. 105, 120, 126, and Shahristani, *Kitab-i Milal va Nihal,* vol. 2.

12. *Tafsir al-Mizan* (Arabic text), vol. 7, under the *sura* An'am, verse 59.

13. For a detailed study of Mulla Sadra's thought, see Fazlur Rahman, *The Philosophy of Mulla Sadra* (Albany, N.Y., 1975). *Trans.*

14. There is no question here of a systematic distinction between being and existence. I merely have used the two English words to correspond to the two contexts in which being is discussed here. *Mahiya* has appeared throughout this work as identity, but here only essence serves the context. *Trans.*

15. *Mahiya* is an Arabic word, a contraction of *ma huwiya.* The phrase *ma huwa* means "What is it?" With the final letters *ya'* and *ta' marbuta,* it becomes the verbal noun *mahuwiya,* which is contracted to *mahiya.* Thus, *mahiya* means "what is it-ness," or "whatness."

16. See Rahman, *The Philosophy of Mulla Sadra,* pp. 27-34. *Trans.*

17. Here is how the *hukama'* have expressed this point: A thing's need of cause hinges on possibility, not on createdness in time." For detailed dicussion of this point, see my *'Ilal-i Girayish bi Maddigari* ("Causes of the Turn to Materialism"). Mashhad, 1350 Sh./1971 [also many subsequent editions. *Trans.*]

18. Unknown. *Trans.*

19. See "Asl-i Tazadd dar Falsafa-yi Islami" ("The Principle of Contradiction in Islamic Philosophy") in my *Maqalati-Falsafi* ("Philosophic Essays").

20. This determinism is not opposed to free will in the case of man, and should not be confused with the form of determinism that is. The necessity of the system of the universe is not inimical to man's free will.

Spirit, Matter, and Life

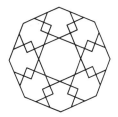

Spiritualism (The Substantive Reality of the Spirit)

Many scholarly questions have had the good fortune not to be discussed outside scholarly circles. Others have been dragged into every assembly and forum and handled by every group, thus giving them an altered aspect, making the work of students and researchers difficult or even tending to throw them off the track from the first. The questions of spirit and body and God and the world belong to the latter group. Perhaps no one has not raised these questions for himself and somehow resolved them for himself. The first questions man, with his inquiring nature, asks himself are What am I? and What is this world I am in? Man must satisfy himself somehow vis-à-vis these questions. Accordingly, everyone forms a kind of egology and world-view.

Because the question of spirit and body is one of these shopworn questions, one which everyone has heard about from birth, first from nurse, mother, and grandmother, and later from preachers, poets, and public speakers, everyone has accumulated impressions and associations concerning the subject, along with a special way of thinking about it. Therefore, many may be prepared to read that the spirit is a mysterious, invisible being that, "providentially" hidden behind the veil of the body, masking itself in it, and carrying out interventions more mysterious and irregular than those ascribed to jinn and ghouls from behind its palpable mass, accomplishes everything from behind this outward, artificial, and borrowed curtain that is the body. Much of our poetry immediately brings this picture to mind: The spirit is a celestial bird, and the body is only an ephemeral cage built for it through special causes. The spirit is a falcon dwelling in a lote-tree that unexpectedly has come to lodge in the torturous alcove of the body. It is a king who has chosen the hovel of the body for his castle and may grant more importance to this hovel than to himself and who may cover its exterior with brocades and himself sit naked and unadorned.

I do not mean to criticize the language of poetry, which is what it is and could not be anything else. The language of poetry, like that of sermon and pulpit, is different from the language of science and philosophy because its object is different. The language of any discipline is a key made for that discipline. A key is useful only in that lock for which it was designed.

Persons who have a compound personality speak in more than one language. One who is both poet and philosopher speaks in the languages of poetry and philosophy, which remain separate. For example, compare how and in what language Avicenna discussed spirit, body, and the relation between them in his books of philosophy (such as the *Shifa'* and the *Isharat*) on the one hand and in his famous " 'Ayniyya" *qasida* on the other, whose opening line is "It descended to you from the highest locus,/ [And grew] filled with pride and refusal." We must distinguish the languages of science and philosophy from the languages of poetry and the pulpit so that we do not, like so many atheists and materialists, become faced with grave and unpardonable errors.

In fact, philosophers have theories that correspond with what appears in the language of poetry. For instance, Plato holds that the spirit is an eternal substance preexistent to the body. When the body is ready, the spirit "descends" from its level and is "attached" to the body. This theory is totally dualistic in that it regards spirit and body as two separate and disjoined substances and sees their relation as something accidental and nominal, like the relation of bird and nest or of rider and mount. It recognizes no substantial and natural connection representing a kind of unity and essential connection between them.

But before long, Plato's student, Aristotle, demolished this theory. Aristotle noted that Plato and his predecessors had focused on the aspect of duality and contrast between spiritual phenomena and physical phenomena but ignored their unity and interdependence. Aristotle noted that one cannot regard the interrelation and interdependence of spirit and body as superficial, like that of bird and nest or that of rider and mount, but that the relation of spirit and body is certainly more profound and natural. Aristotle regarded the relation of spirit and body as belonging to the species of relation of the form to the matter in which it originates, with the difference that, because the rational faculty is abstract, it is a form with matter, not a form in matter. The idea that the spirit is an eternal substance *in actu* does not persist into Aristotle's philosophy. The spirit is not eternal; it is created in time. At first it is purely potential. It acquires no sort of prior knowledge; it actualizes all its knowledge in this world. The same idea in a slightly different form is reflected in Avicenna. The duality, separation, and alienness in Plato's philosophy has been largely obviated in the philosophies of Aristotle and Avicenna, in which this matter has been based on the well-known Aristotelian theories of hylomorphism and of generation and corruption.

Although Aristotle's theory is most noteworthy for its advantages over its predecessor, especially for its rejection of the spirit-body duality and its advocacy of a kind of real and substantial unity and interrelation of spirit and body, it nonetheless is not devoid of major ambiguities and difficulties. These difficulties pertain to the question of how the natural relation of matter and form is to be depicted and to the question of generation and corruption. Further steps in the worlds of science and philosophy were necessary if the curtain were to be lifted from over this mystery or if the topic were even to be addressed in a rational and satisfactory way.

The precursors to this intellectual and scientific transformation appeared in Europe and created a revolution in the fullest sense of the word. Revolution threw out the good with the bad. All past foundations and structures were cast down at one stroke. The revolutionaries designed a new scheme for everything. The famous French philosopher, Descartes, articulated a new scheme of spirit-body dualism that in time became the one scheme to accept, reject, or revise.

Descartes admitted three realities: God, the soul, and the body. In conceiving that the soul has thought and intelligence but not dimension and the body has dimension but not thought and intelligence, he came to believe that soul and body are separate things. The objection raised, first by other Europeans, against Descartes's theory is that he had considered only the aspects of duality, difference, and contrast obtaining between spirit and body, but offered no explanation of how spirit and body, which he says represent extremes of disparity and contrast, came to be conjoined. It is important to consider how they connect and are united, what sort of relation obtains between them.

Descartes's theory is in this respect a kind of regression, a reversion to Plato's theory. We seem to be back to the story of the bird and the nest. Because Descartes entertains conceptions of innate qualities and essences and so regards the soul as a phenomenon *in actu,* his theory resembles Plato's.[1] His theory falls as far short as Plato's of explaining the relation between spirit and body.

This regression or reversion turned out to be very costly. The essential and natural relation of body on the one hand and spirit or spiritual qualities on the other is not something one can ignore; one cannot content oneself with noting their discrepant and contrastive aspects. Intelligent people after Descartes sought to discover the relation of these two entities. Modern philosophers labored to discover what sort of relation physical phenomena have with spiritual, and in the course of their labors highly divergent schools and theories arose, marked by all kinds of excess. Some have even denied all duality of spirit and body in regarding all psychical phenomena as normal and natural properties of material compounds, and others have denied all such duality in regarding body and matter as unreal, as a mere phantasmagoria displaying itself to the spirit. Still others have wearied of the search and declared the subject beyond man's power to explore.

Although modern scholars and philosophers have gotten nowhere in studying the identity of spiritual phenomena and the nature of the relation of spirit and body, researchers in all fields, especially biology, physiology, and psychology, have had tremendous and amazing results. They at times may not have noted the implications of their findings for spiritual questions or for questions of the nature of the relation between spirit and body, but their work has opened the way for study of these questions.

Among post-Avicennan Islamic philosophers, no original research into this question was done directly, but enormous transformations and advances occurred in the most general and basic questions of first philosophy, that is, the questions surrounding being.[2] These advances had an indirect but tremendously important effect on most other philosophical questions, among them questions of motion and of the unity versus the duality of spirit and body.

Mulla Sadra, who spearheaded this transformation in the approach to questions of being, concluded from the new, excellent, and powerful principles he had forged that, in addition to the overt, accidental, and sensible motions governing the superficial phenomena of the world, there is a deep, substantial motion inaccessible to the senses that is the principle of these overt and sensible motions. If one is to postulate hylomorphism, one must postulate it only on the basis of this motion. The appearance and formation of physical species are based on the law of motion, not on that of generation and corruption. The soul and the spirit arise in accordance with this law of motion. The soul is formed within the matrix of physical matter. Matter has the capacity to nurture an entity in its lap that is on the plane of the supernatural. No wall or membrane exists between the natural and the supernatural, and there is nothing to prevent a material being from transforming into an extramaterial being through a gradual evolution.

Neither Plato's nor Aristotle's conceptions of the source for the formation of the soul and the nature of its relation to the body is correct. The nature of the relation between life and matter, or between spirit and body, is more natural and more substantial than they supposed. It is like the kind of relation between a stronger and better developed stage of a thing to a weaker and less well developed stage of it. Or to put it perhaps more aptly, it is like the relation of one dimension to the other dimensions. That is, matter in its transformation and evolution expands in a new direction additional to the three physical or spatial dimensions and to the temporal dimension by which essential and substantial motion is quantified. This new direction is independent of the other four, the spatiotemporal directions.

In calling this direction a dimension, I do not mean it is a kind of extension or that it is susceptible to mental analysis, like other quantifiables. Rather, I mean only that matter finds a new direction to expand into, one in which it wholly sheds the quality of materiality.

We are now in a position to address this question: Are spiritual properties the product of an admixture or a synthesis of material elements, like the other properties that matter exhibits in isolation or in compound entities? Or does physical matter, insofar as it is physical and material, lacks such properties and effects, such that they appear only as matter evolves in its essence and substance, coming to have in its essence a degree of being according to which it is extramaterial and extraphysical? Spiritual properties would relate to that degree of being and reality. I now have no need to confine our discussion to the human spirit and the psychical phenomena of man, as is conventional. I can start lower and extend this discussion to vital phenomena and effects as such.

The difference that can be allowed between mental effects and other vital effects, that the one is abstract and the others not, is not at issue here. What concerns us is the idea that the spirit is not a property or effect of matter, but a substantial entelechy that appears for matter and is in turn the source for effects more numerous and various than those of matter.[3] This is true of all life. Whatever the reality of life, whether or not it is possible for us to perceive the inner reality and core of life, those beings we call living or animate, the plants and animals, have activities and effects not witnessed in other, dead or inanimate, beings.

Beings of this class have the property of self-preservation and place themselves at a remove from the effects of environmental factors. They use a wholly internal power to equip themselves for life in a particular environment and so array their internal defenses as to be able to combat factors in that environment or to use them to further their survival in it.

A living being has the property of adaptation to the environment, which arises from its internal processes. An inanimate being, however, has no such property, and if it is placed in an environment containing factors destructive to it, it can exhibit no activity oriented to its survival and in fact cannot combat environmental factors. For example, a living being has the property of acclimation. If it encounters a stressful external factor, at first it is heavily affected and distressed, and its equilibrium is lost; but it gradually acclimates and acquires a sort of immunity to the external factor. This immunity is an effect of internal functions and of the property of adaptation to the environment, which it acquires to the extent of its capacity. If a plant, an animal, or even a member of an animal's body is placed in an environment wherein it contacts something injurious, something that poses a threat to its equilibrium and survival, it gradually arms itself to resist that factor in that environment. When a human hand that is soft and fine is first faced with carrying a hard and rough material such as brick, it is unable to stand up, but gradually that hand acclimates; that is, an internal power in its tissues brings about changes that enable it to resist the new factor.

A living being has the power of assimilation. Under the influence of an internal factor, it automatically draws external materials to itself and, through special processes of decomposition and resynthesis, uses them for its own survival. However, this property does not exist in inanimate beings.

Wherever living beings and organic factors appear, they gradually grow, renew themselves, and evolve. They augment their power until they are ready to reproduce; thereafter they wane and disappear, having given perpetuity to their existence in their progeny.

Whenever life appears, it predominates over environmental conditions and triumphs over the lifeless elements of nature. It alters nature's compounds and makes of them a new synthesis. Life is designer, modeler, engineer, and artist, and it evolves in these very capacities. Life has goals and makes choices. It knows its way and its object. It slowly follows the road it adopted millions of years ago, toward a definite object and destination that will be unattainable save at the utmost degree of perfection.

All these properties exist in living beings and not in inanimate beings. In the words of A. Cressy Morrison, "Matter has no initiative, but life brings into being marvelous new designs and structures."[4] Here we perceive fully how life itself is a special force, a separate entelechy, and an added process that appears in matter and that exhibits various further processes and effects.

Invaluable research has been carried out in the area of life and the properties of living beings, research that makes quite plain the substantive reality of the vital force. Many researchers have perceived this truth and referred to this substantive reality of the vital force in their work.[5] They have noted that this vital force is an extramaterial force in nature and that biotic phenomena are the effect of this force and not simply of the synthesis, the addition, subtraction, and combination, of material constituents. These latter processes are a necessary but not sufficient condition for the emergence of life. Then there were those like the famous biologist, Lamarck, who denied the substantive reality of the vital force and formally declared that living nature must be studied from the standpoint of mechanics. What impelled them to deny the substantive reality of the vital force was their equation of such a reality with a duality, an existence for the vital force separate from matter and its effects. They supposed that if the vital force had a substantive reality, this fact would entail its being independent of the environment and environmental factors, its being the same in all environments, its unsusceptibility to influence by environmental factors, and its independence of the physicochemical processes of the body. Scientific observations have demonstrated the contrary in each instance. Lamarck said life is nothing but a physical quality. All the qualities of life depend on physical or chemical causes and originate in the organism's structure. Lamarck evidently supposed that if the vital force had substantive reality, this fact would necessitate its being independent of physicochemical causes and its not having its origin in the organism's material structure.

Descartes's dualistic theory, his regression or reversion to Plato's theory, wound up being very costly because it obliged scientists to conclude that whenever they contemplated a substantive reality for the vital force, they were denying the substantial and essential connection of life and body and were thinking of them as two opposing poles. Descartes himself, in arriving at this dualism of body characterized by dimension and soul characterized by thought and intelligence and in positing a deep gulf between the two, was compelled to deny life as a substantive force in other-than-human beings. Incredibly, he regarded the structure of all animals—except man—as purely mechanical and denied all perception and feeling in animals. He claimed animals have no perception, no feeling, no pleasure, no pain. When they move or call out, this behavior does not arise from feeling or will. These machines have been so constructed as to display these effects at these times, whereas we imagine that they result from feeling or will![6]

Modern scientific research supports the theory of the substantive reality of the vital force. The theory of evolution of species further supports the concept of the vital force and its governance of and predominance over matter and the inanimate forces of matter. Darwin, the original champion of this theory, did not seek to demonstrate the substantive reality of the vital force but rather at first based his work on natural selection, which he saw as the result of random, undirected changes in nature. But as he inquired closely into the secret of evolutionary advance and the ordered evolution of species, he was obliged, as he says, "to admit a character for living nature." He spontaneously arrived at this conclusion, to such a degree that some of his contemporaries said to him, "You speak of natural selection as if it were an active force or a supernatural power."[7]

Those who study the psychical aspects of man, without intending to show the substantive reality of human life or to derive a philosophical conclusion from their researches, have arrived at such a conclusion. Freud, the psychologist and founder of psychoanalysis, set off a revolution in psychology. He concluded from his studies and clinical work that the researches of the physiologists and the anatomical studies of the brain with its convolutions constituted an inadequate approach to mental illness. He discerned a hidden system of intelligence relative to which man's overt and everyday intelligence and self-awareness are superficial. He noted that the diseases of the spirit that arise from complexes themselves have a substantive reality and give rise to organic illnesses. One must approach the treatment of these illnesses spiritually and resolve these complexes, and thus even their physical symptoms will often be alleviated.

The treatment of physical illnesses by spiritual means and even the treatment of some organic diseases by spiritual means represent no new discovery—such physicians as Muhammad ibn Zakariya Razi and Avicenna used it—but today this technique has found extraordinary breadth of application.[8] It wholly affirms the substantive reality of life and especially of the spirit. But what is noteworthy in Freudianism is the discovery of the hidden mind and also of a range of complexes. Formerly, moral and physical afflictions were explained simply as a range of engrams ('adat). An engram is a state resulting from the repetition of an act and is said to be a quasimaterial process. When we first bend a straight stick, it returns, but not quite fully. After we repeat this process many times, the stick remains bent. An engram was said to be something similar, something like the folding of a sheet of paper. Through repetition of an act, permanent effects, called moral virtues or sins, would be left on the furrows of the brain. But the theories of a hidden mind and of complexes demonstrated that the dynamics of morality involve quite different processes.

Freud did not seek by his theory to demonstrate the substantive reality of the vital force or life's governance of matter. Rather, where he moves from the area of scientific researches in which he shows such mastery, to the area of philosophical inference, in which he shows no such competence, he arrives at certain objectionable theories unworthy of his stature. This does not detract from the value of his scientific researches.

Some of Freud's students, such as Jung, wholly disagreed with their master over the method of deriving philosophical conclusions from psychological theories. They did much to throw light on the substantive reality of the vital force in their theories; they imparted a "supernatural" dimension to Freud's theory.

What is most difficult here is not to see the difference between body and psyche or between matter and life. Even before the European researchers provided such clear evidence for the substantive reality of the vital force, superficial observation revealed these differences plainly enough. What is more difficult is to arrive at a sound conception of the relation of body and psyche. This difficulty has led many scholars to withhold belief from the substantive reality of the vital force. This difficulty has been resolved in the finest way in the philosophy of Mulla Sadra.

The question of the substantive reality of the vital force has a supernatural aspect. If life were an effect and property of matter, it would have no such aspect, in that it would exist as a latent effect of matter in the elemental state or in compounds. When a living organism appears, nothing would actually be created; no entelechy would be created in matter. But according to the theory of the substantive reality of the vital force, matter in its essence lacks life; life is created and added when a capacity appears in matter. In other words, matter becomes alive in the course of its movement toward perfection; it gains an entelechy that it had lacked. In consequence, it gains effects and modes of activity that it had lacked. Therefore, the being that comes alive actually has been created.

Although inanimate matter in the elemental state does not have the property of life, what is there to prevent this property from emerging in consequence of the interaction of these material constituents? When several material or extramaterial constituents are compounded and interact, each yields some of its effects to the others and receives some of the others' effects. An intermediate temper results. It is absurd that through the synthesis of several constituents an effect should appear other than the combined effects of the constituents or a quality intermediate to their effects, unless the synthesis of these constituents makes it possible for a faculty or a force higher than those of any of these constituents to come into being as a substantial entelechy and to impart a real unity to these constituents. Therefore, if it is asked what there is to prevent the property of life from appearing in consequence of the synthesis and interaction of material constituents, this question calls for further clarification. If it is meant that, in consequence of the interaction of material constituents, the capacity appears for a substantive force, the vital force, and so this force does come into being, and with it the properties of life, this is correct. But if it is meant that, in the absence of a vital force, properties of life appear inconsistent with the properties of any of life's constituents, this is absurd and impossible.

Another hypothesis might be proposed. Although matter lacks life in its essence and life is a force superior to material and inanimate forces—just as, according to scientific research, there is in the physical universe a certain fixed quantity of energy and the formation and disappearance of inanimate entities does not constitute creation but rather consists of a set of coalescences and dispersals of material constituents and transfers of energy—so we may posit a special mode of energy for life, such that, like other forces, vital forces would not be created. Rather, through these coalescences and dispersals and transfers of energy, they would be concentrated in certain instances. Thus, animation would not involve creation.

The concept of vital energy must be clarified. Is this energy inanimate or animate in its essence? If it is animate, does an entity *have* life? Is life a thing apart from the entity, which has been compounded or conjoined with it? Or is this entity life itself? If the energy is animate or inanimate, there is no difference between vital energy and other energies in respect to this question (of how animacy is to be explained and how this energy produces life), in that either this energy is not alive at all (the first hypothesis) or the agent of life is a thing external and added to the entity's essence. If this entity is life itself, an abstract being (life, or the vital force) has descended a level and, preserving its effects, has become matter, which is absurd. What the philosophers call "descent" when they say that nature and matter have descended from the supernatural is not this transfer and transduction of energies.

If we deny that there is creation in inanimate matter but hold that the appearance of these entities is nothing more than the coalescence and dispersal of material constituents and the transfer of energies, we are saying something scientists agree is incorrect in reference to animate beings. The character of life is such that one cannot hypothesize that there is some certain fixed quantity of it; one cannot regard the appearance of animate beings as a transfer of life from one locus to another, as, in truth, a kind of transmigration. The phenomenon of life cannot be assigned a certain fixed quantity; it has been on the increase since the day it appeared on earth. If at times much life has perished in a mass extinction, this power did not concentrate elsewhere. Life and death are a kind of expansion and contraction, but an expansion and contraction arising from above the plane of natural being. They constitute an emanation coming from the unseen and returning to the unseen. As Oswald Külpe says in criticism of materialism:

> Materialism stands in contradiction to a fundamental law of modern natural science, the law of the conservation of energy; according to which the sum of energy in the universe always remains constant, and the changes that take place all about us are simply changes in the distribution of energy, and involve an absolutely uniform transformation or exchange. The law evidently implies that the series of "physical" processes is a closed chain, in which there is no place for a new kind of phenomenon: the "psychical" or "mental." Brain processes, e.g., despite their extreme complexity, must be included in the circle of causes and effects, and all the changes produced in the brain substance by outside stimulus conceived of as propagated and diffused in a purely chemical or physical way. A theory of this universal validity leaves the mental side of things "all in the air"; for how the secondary effect of mentality can be produced without any the least loss of energy upon the physical side, is difficult to say. The only logical thing to do is to coordinate mental processes, as representing a special form of energy, with the ordinary chemical, electrical, thermal and mechanical energy, and to assume that the same uniform relation of transformation and exchange obtains between them as between the various "physical" energies. But apart from the fact that this view is nowhere mentioned, still less worked out in any detail, in materialistic literature, there are several objections to it upon general grounds, all leading to the same conclusion, that the idea of energy as defined by natural science is inapplicable to mental processes.[9]

A. Cressy Morrison says:

> The rise of man the animal to a self-conscious reasoning being is

too great a step to be taken by the process of material evolution or without creative purpose.

If the reality of purpose is accepted, man as such may be a mechanism. But what operates this mechanism? For without operation it is useless. Science does not account for the operator, nor does Science say that it is material.

Matter has never done more than its laws decree. The atoms and molecules obey the dictates of chemical affinity, the force of gravity, the influences of temperature and electric impulses. Matter has no initiative, but life brings into being marvelous new designs and structures.[10]

The *hukama'*, in discussing cause and effect or the odder phenomena of nature (as Avicenna does in the tenth section of the *Isharat*), speak of spiritual influences and forces. Mulla Sadra composed a chapter of the *Asfar* on the subject of cause and effect titled "On the Fact that Thought and Imagination are Sometimes the Origin for the Creation of Phenomena." In this chapter, he seeks to demonstrate the governance, predominance, and effect of thought and imagination, which are phases of life, upon matter. He introduces various subjects in this chapter, among them that of the effect of the suggestion and imagination of health or of illness in actually producing either condition.[11]

Today no place remains for the ancient Democritean idea that the universe is a purely mechanical one and that creation consists solely in the coalescence and dispersal, or the combination and synthesis, of particles.

Scientific research has thoroughly deflated the materialists' hubris. No longer may someone say, as did Descartes and others, give me matter and motion, and I will construct a universe. The warp and woof of the universe have too many threads for being to be confined to matter and the sensible and accidental motion of matter.

The Qur'an and Life (The Qur'an and a Question Regarding Life)

Repeated mention is made of life in the Noble Qur'an. The following are mentioned in its verses repeatedly as signs *(ayat)* of divine wisdom and providence: the animation of beings, the successive appearance of living things, the evolution of life, the system of creation of living organisms, and the properties of life—comprehension, intelligence, perception, hearing, sight, guidance, inspiration, and instinct. Each is a very interesting subject in itself.

One of the points the Qur'an makes about life is that life is in God's hands; it is God Who gives life and takes life. The Noble Qur'an, with its special logic, is saying that life is not at the disposal of any other than God; no one else can give or take life.

In the *sura* Baqara, Abraham is related to have said to a contemporary tyrant, "It is my Lord Who gives life and death" (2:260). The *sura* Mulk describes God as "He Who created death and life" (67:2). There are many verses in the Qur'an that speak of God simply as the Giver of Life and the Giver of Death and that predicate these functions directly to Him. That is, they exclude agents other than God from them. Likewise, the verses that attribute acts of reanimation of the dead to certain prophets stipulate that these acts occur "by God's permission." An example is Al 'Imran: "And [appoint him] a messenger to the Israelites [with the message], 'I have come to you with a sign from your Lord: I create for you out of clay the figure of a bird. I breathe into it, and it is a bird, by God's permission. And I heal the born blind and the lepers, and I raise the dead, by God's permission' "(3:49).

Overall, this is one of the points of difference between theists and materialists, the theists regarding the origin and creator of life as something external to nature and the materialists regarding matter itself as creative of life.

There is a subtle yet vast difference between the logic of the Qur'an as to God's being the Creator of Life and the standard logic of theists in this matter. It exemplifies the miraculous quality of this Noble Book. If theistic scholars were to familiarize themselves with this logic, not only could they extricate themselves from the materialists for good, but they could free those unfortunates from the clutches of supposition and error as well.

Usually, when scholars seek to relate life to *tauhid* and God's will, they bring up the issue of life's appearance on earth and raise the question of how it first appeared. Clear scientific evidence shows that life has a beginning on earth, that is, that no species of living organism, plant or animal, has existed into the indefinite past, in that the earth itself has a finite and ascertainable age and has not been capable of sustaining life over the whole of its many millions of of years of existence. By what means did these organisms first appear? Our immediate experience is that an individual is always born of another individual of its own species. Wheat springs from wheat, barley from barley, horse from horse, camel from camel, human being from human being. Nature forbids the spontaneous generation of, say, an animal or a tree from a mass of pure earth. Living organisms always have their origins in other living organisms; for instance, they are released as germ cells or seeds to grow in a suitable environment. How did this process begin? Does each of these species have its origin in a single individual? If so, how did this individual appear? Nature forbids that an organism should be unpreceded by an egg and a sperm or by some material released by a prior organism. One would therefore be forced to say an exception, a "miracle," had occurred, that the hand of divine power had emerged from its sleeve to create that individual.

Or do all these species have a common origin? Do they all relate as a family? Assuming all these various organisms trace through one or more lines to a single unicellular organism, how did this organism appear? Has not science demonstrated that no organism appears except through other organisms? So has an exception, a miracle, occurred? Has the divine will intervened such that a suddenly a single cell has appeared?[12] Here the partisans of the materialistic theory see themselves compelled to advance a hypothesis that not even they can accept. The theists take this point as proving the existence of a creator, saying that certainly a supernatural power has intervened to cause the appearance of this first life; certainly, God's will has manifested itself to bring it into being. Likewise Darwin, personally a theist, having resolved the question of speciation to his own satisfaction and considering the one or more organisms that first appeared on earth, without deriving from other lifeforms, said that these have found life through the divine breath.[13]

A. Cressy Morrison says on this same subject:

> It has been suggested by some that life arrived from some planet as a germ which escaped unharmed and after an eternity in space settled upon the earth. Such a germ could hardly survive the absolute zero temperature of space, and if it did, the intense short-wave radiation

would kill it. Here, if it survived, it must have found the right place, the ocean probably, where an amazing combination of circumstances brought about its rebirth and the beginning of life here. Besides, this puts the question back one step, for we can ask how did life originate on any planet. It has been generally held that neither mere environment, no matter how favorable to life, nor any combination of chemical and physical conditions which could be brought about by chance, can bring life into existence. Disregarding this question of the origin of life, which is, of course, a scientific mystery, it has been suggested that a little speck of matter, a giant molecule, but still so small that no regular microscope could even glimpse it, added atoms, upset its cohesive balance, divided, and the separate parts repeated the cycle, and thus took on the aspects of life; but no one yet claims it took on life itself.[14]

Here Cressy Morrison seeks to demonstrate that, because life cannot be explained through material and natural causes, it must have appeared through the intervention of a creator. He considers the first appearance of man, the great transformation that led to the appearance of a rational and thinking being, a being with an extraordinary capacity for thought, the power to produce sciences: "The rise of man the animal to a self-conscious reasoning being is too great a step to be taken by the process of material evolution or without creative purpose."[15] What Morrison says exemplifies the manner of thinking and deductive reasoning that has been applied to the question of the relation of life to God's will.

For all man has tried, he has been unable to form the constituents of a living organism by scientific means. He has not, for instance, succeeded in producing a synthetic grain that would have the property of life, that would grow and seed if planted, from chemicals. He has been unable to produce an animal or human germ cell that could become an animal or a human being. Scientists, however, have spared no effort in this attempt, and it is yet not fully clear to them whether they will succeed one day or this feat is wholly beyond the power of human science and industry.

This question of the future, like the question of the beginning of life has created a stir in the world. Those theists who say God is the author of life and who address the relation of life and God's will in the manner exemplified by Morrison's work have held that human effort along these lines is futile because life is not by the hand of man but depends on God's will: Man cannot of his own volition, by the means of science and industry, create life whenever he pleases. The prophets, in animating dead matter, did so through God's permission. It is impossible and absurd for someone to do such a thing without God's permission. If he wishes to do so with God's permission, he must join the ranks of God's prophets and perform miracles, for God does not enact miracles except through the instrumentality of His prophets and saints.

These theists have taken this present incapacity of man as proof for their position: See what would happen if man should form a grain of wheat that did not differ from natural wheat in its chemistry, that would be identical with it, but that lacked life. This would be the case because life depends on God's will and must appear by God's permission, which He has not given to any other than His prophets.

The Noble Qur'an, too, says explicitly that God is the Author of life and denies that any other can intervene to create life. But nowhere do we find the Qur'an invoking the beginning of the life of man or of other animate beings to demonstrate this point. On the contrary, it calls this existing and observable system to witness and regards this very system in process of life as the system of creation and perfection. The Qur'an says that God is the Author and Creator of life, but in ascribing life to God's creatorship, it does not refer to the first day and contrast it to later days. It says that these very systematic transformations of life constitute the creation. For instance, it says in the blessed *sura* Mu'minin: "Truly We created man from an extract of clay, then We made the droplet into a clot, and then We made the clot into a little lump, and then We made the little lump bones and clothed the bones with flesh, and then We produced it as another creation. So blessed be God, the best of creators!" (23: 12-14). This noble verse refers to the transformation and evolution of the embryo according to a determinate system and says that ongoing acts of creation follow this same evolutionary pattern. It is said in the *sura* Nuh: "What is the matter with you, that you do not look to God for dignity, while He has created you by stages?" (71: 13-14).

It is said in the *sura* Zumar: "He creates you in the wombs of your mothers, creation after creation, in a threefold darkness" (39:6).

It is said in the *sura* Baqara: "How is it you disbelieve in God when you were dead and He gave you life! Then He will give you death, then life again, and then you will return to Him" (2:28).

It is said in the *sura* Hajj: "It is He Who gave you life, will give you death, then will give you life again" (22:66).

There are many other verses to this effect, in all of which this same system we witness in process is called the system of creation. The opening of a seed under the earth, the growth of herbs and the foliation of trees in the spring are all spoken of as the new creation, the ongoing acts of creation of God. Nowhere do we see the Qur'an holding that creation and God's will to produce life are confined to a single first human being or first animal that appeared on the earth as the sole creature of God or product of God's will.

Mention is made in the Noble Qur'an of the creation of a first human being, but not in demonstration of *tauhid* or to argue that the existence of a first human being shows that the hand of divine power emerged from the sleeve to manifest God's will in the act of creation. The hand was never in the sleeve and never will be.

In telling the story of Adam, the Qur'an alludes to many moral and edifying teachings, such as: man's worth to reach the station of divine creativity, man's abundant capacity for knowledge, the angels' humility before knowledge, man's capacity to outstrip the angels, the detrimental effects of avidity and arrogance, how sin causes man to fall from the highest planes of being, how repentance saves man and returns him to the station of nearness to the Truth, and admonition to man not to be led astray by Satanic temptations. But the special and exceptional circumstance of Adam's creation is in no way related to the subject of *tauhid* and recognition of the Creator. Because the object in telling the story of Adam consists in a series of moral and edifying teachings, not in a calling to witness the beginning of life in testimony to *tauhid,* mention of the first human being is felt to suffice, and no mention is made of how the other species of animals found life on earth.

When theists consider the first living being and find no way to account for its life, they say, "It came into existence through the divine breath." But just as the Noble Qur'an regards this divine breath as the life of the first human being, it regards it as the life of all other human beings, which take shape through the system in process.

At one point, God says to the angels regarding the first human being, "When I have set him in balance and have breathed into him of My spirit, do fall down in prostration to him" (15:29, 38:72). Elsewhere He says, "And We created you, then shaped you, then told the angels, 'Prostrate to Adam'" (7:11). Plainly, in this verse, the creation, the inbreathing of the spirit, and the humbling of the angels have been generalized to all human beings.[16] It is said in the *sura* Sajda: "He Who has made everything He has created good— He began the creation of man with clay, then He made His progeny from an extract of despised fluid, then He fashioned it and breathed into it of His own spirit. And He gave you hearing, and sight, and hearts. Small thanks you give!" (32:7-9). As exegetes have said, and as the context indicates, the pronoun *hu* (it) in *sawahu* (He fashioned it) refers to *nasl* (progeny), not to *al-insan* (man).

Theists turn to the first appearance of life when they seek to attribute life to God's will. The Noble Qur'an never takes this turn in its method of *tauhid*, but treats life with its evolution as such as the direct product of God's will, without distinguishing between the beginning of life and its continuation. This difference between the Qur'an's logic and others' logics springs from a more fundamental difference. These theists seek to know God through the negative aspect of their knowledge, not through its positive aspect. That is, when they are confronted with an unknown, they drag God into it. They always seek for God amid what they do not know. That is, they always look to those things for which they know no natural cause, and when they come up with some striking instance of such a thing, they at once exclaim, "*This*, certainly, has come into being through God's will!"[17] It follows that the more unknowns they rack up vis-à-vis the natural causes of things, the more evidence they see for their conception of *tauhid*, and the more they learn of these causes, the more their faith diminishes. For some theologians and adherents to the school of *tauhid*, the supernatural is like a storehouse for their ignorance: Whatever they do not know, do not understand, or have not found a natural cause for, they at once ascribe to the supernatural.[18] They see the traces of the supernatural in instances where, as they believe, something out of the ordinary has occurred and the natural order has been disrupted and has broken down. Because they have not found the natural cause for an event, they substitute a supernatural cause for it, failing to note, first, that the supernatural also has a logic and law and, second, that if a cause should supplant a material and natural cause, it too must be material and natural, on a level with matter and nature, not supernatural. Nature and the supernatural are aligned longitudinally, not latitudinally. A natural cause cannot supplant a supernatural cause, and a supernatural cause cannot occur on the plane of a natural cause.

The Qur'an never cites cases in which it would appear the natural order has been disrupted and has broken down in demonstration of *tauhid*. It cites cases having natural elements and causes familiar to people; it calls the system itself to witness.

In the special case of life, the logic of the Qur'an is premised on life's being wholly a sublime emanation from a plane above that of sensible bodies, by means of whatever law and reckoning the emanation takes place. Therefore, the evolution of life is creative and perfective. According to this logic, it makes no difference whether life appeared on earth in an instantaneous creation or gradually, in successive creations. This logic is premised on the assumption that sensible matter is essentially lacking in life and that life is an emanation, a light, that it must be emanated from a higher source. Thus, the laws of life in any form represent this law of creation.

The difference in plane of being between matter and life is a demonstrable scientific fact. If we seek to discover a supernatural basis for life by reference to this difference in plane of being, we shall have proceeded from the positive aspect of our knowledge, not from its negative aspect. We shall no longer need to draw down the supernatural from its own level to supplant the natural whenever we are at a loss for the natural cause of something. Rather, we shall have to surmise that a natural cause, which our knowledge has yet to encompass, is at work.

In the "Safar-i Nafs" section of the *Asfar*, Mulla Sadra takes Fakhr-i Razi to task on this point, saying, "I am amazed at how whenever this man and those like him seek to demonstrate the principle of *tauhid* or some other principle of religion, they go looking for some situation where the natural cause is unknown, where as they suppose the order of the universe has broken down and calculations collapsed."[19]

According to the Noble Qur'an, creation is not an instantaneous phenomenon. An animal or a human being continuously undergoes creation in traversing the stages of evolution. The whole universe is continuously undergoing creation. The contrary idea is that creation is confined to a moment. In considering the creation of the universe, one has reference to that first moment in which the universe was created and emerged from nonexistence. It is as if the universe cannot be viewed as created except on such an assumption. Similarly, in considering the createdness of life, one is supposed to have reference to that first moment in which life began. This is a Jewish way of thinking. "The Jews say, 'God's hand is shackled.' May *their* hands be shackled and may they be accursed for what they have said" (5:67). This conception of the relation of life to God's will, that inevitably seeks to relate it to God's will by reference to its beginning, is a product of Jewish thought. This Jewish conception gradually has spread everywhere, and, unfortunately, the *mutakallimin* of Islam have come under its influence. This "moment" has no place in Qur'anic teachings.

I noted earlier that some have asked if man is capable of making a living being. Will he be able, for instance, to fabricate a human zygote that, after implantation in a womb or other suitable environment, will develop into a complete human being? Some theists, who see the relation between life and God's will as restricted to the first appearance of life and other exceptional instances, vehemently deny this possibility. But, in Qur'anic teachings, there is nothing to prevent it.

The immense structural complexity of living organisms must be considered. Will man one day be capable of discerning all the mysteries of the material organization of a living cell and of discovering the natural law whereby such a cell is produced? I can express no opinion on such a question; it is outside my competence. Scientists say that higher and more profound than the creation of earth, planets, solar systems, and all else is that of the substance called protoplasm.

If one day man discovers the law of the creation of living things —just as he has discovered the laws of many other entities—if he achieves all the conditions and assembles all the material constituents for synthesis of a living organism, will that synthetic being be alive? It will definitely be alive. It is absurd that the conditions for the existence of an emanation should be fully met and that emanation not be realized. Is not the Essence of Unity eternally self-sufficient, absolutely perfect, and absolutely effulgent? Is not the Necessary Being in Essence necessary from all standpoints and in all respects?

Where does the idea that God is the sole Author of life, that beings other than God are excluded from the acts of giving or taking life, fit in? The Noble Qur'an itself makes this point. If one day man is graced with success in this area, what in the final analysis he will have accomplished is to bring about the conditions for life, not to create life. Man will not be giving life; he will be perfecting the capacity of matter to receive the emanation of life. He will be the agent of motion, not the source of being.

If one day man is graced with such a success, this will be a major work of scientific discovery, but it will be no more an intervention in the creation of life than that of the father and mother in creating the life of the child through copulation or that of the farmer in creating the life of the grain through planting. In none of these instances is man the creator of life; he is the one who brings about the conditions for some material substance to receive life. The Noble Qur'an expresses this point in the best possible way in the blessed *sura* Waqi'a: "Have you seen that which you emit? Do you create it or are We the Creators?" (56:58–59).

The miracles of the prophets represent acts of which man is incapable through his normal knowledge and power. The prophets did not arrive at this knowledge and power by normal means; they bore an extraordinary degree of knowledge and power that carried them above the plane of nature, enabling them to be sources for such magnificent acts. If people should one day succeed in [producing life], they will not be accomplishing what the prophets accomplished through God's permission. If ordinary people should one day gain the ability to bring about the conditions for life, it will be similar to the way people today can destroy the conditions but cannot cause life to withdraw. The emanation of life is in God's hands. One might say that man could bring about or remove the capacity of matter to receive life by discovering the laws of the emanation and withdrawal of life.

I have said that life is not the act of man, that it is beyond the realm of human action, since to give or to take life is in the hands of God. And I have said that man may be able to bring about the conditions for life.

I am not, however, suggesting a division of labor, some works belonging to man and not to God and others belonging to God and not to man. Rather, I have delimited and qualified human action, not delimited and qualified God's action. God's action is absolute and unlimited; what is qualified and limited is the action of the creature. This point has far-reaching implications. For further discussion, I refer you to *Usul-i Falsafa va Ravish-i Ri'alism,* volume 5.

Tauhid and Evolution

In order fully to understand this section, the reader must bear in mind the contents of the two preceding sections. In "Spiritualism," I made the point that life is a reality accompanying matter under certain special conditions. A duality does not govern the relation of matter and life, and they are not two conjoined realities, but matter and life are two levels of one being, each level having special properties. At certain stages of its evolution and under special conditions, matter transforms into life. As everything transforms from a less perfect to a more perfect form, the less perfect being of inanimate matter transforms into the more perfect form of the living organism. Life is not the creation or effect of inanimate matter but an entelechy or activity that is added to it. Matter in its essence does not possess life, such that it could express or manifest it. Matter has a receptivity vis-à-vis life that becomes apparent under certain conditions, not the property of creating or giving life.

In other words, matter cannot create or give life. This system of living organisms we see before us is a system of receptivity from the standpoint that it is associated with matter and a system of creativity from the standpoint that it is associated with a higher plane.

Life transforms, intervenes in, governs, and makes matter behave as a function of its own determinations. If life were the creation, effect, or product of matter, it would not be able to so influence its own cause and origin or to have determinations superior to the determinations of inanimate matter able to govern them. Biologists and psychologists, without seeking to arrive at a conception of the substantive reality of life, have arrived at results that demonstrate such a reality. Even the theory of natural selection, seen by most authorities as having a materialistic character, when gone into more deeply, demonstrates the governance and substantive reality of life.

In "The Qur'an and Life," I considered the mode of relation between life and the supernatural, or God's will, and I explored the marvelous logic that is one of the features of the Noble Qur'an. I dwelt on two points in particular. First, that an erroneous idea of Jewish origin as to the meaning of the creation has appeared in the world. It inevitably attaches the creation to a moment. That is, whenever one attempts to visualize the creation of the universe or of life, one begins by asking, "At what moment did it emerge from nothingness; when did it begin?" The question of this moment never arises in the logic the Noble Qur'an first propounded.

The second point is that innumerable persons approach the question of *tauhid* and theology by attempting to know God by negative means. They seek for God amid their ignorance, not amid their knowledge. Whenever they are at a loss to explain the cause of an event, they drag God into it. Thus, in dealing with the question of the createdness of life or that of the createdness of the universe, they dwell on the moment of its first appearance because in their view nothing is less known than how life or the universe appeared. This idea of negative theology amounts to the basis for the idea that creation is confined to a moment.

This Jewish idea on the one hand and this negative idea on the other have resulted in a tendency to predicate the question of *tauhid* on the matter of the moment on the one hand and on the unknown causes of events on the other. If the matter of the moment of the creation of life or of the universe is placed in doubt or if the unknown causes of events come in time to be known, then the ideas of *tauhid* and theology in time come into doubt and discredit.

An example of the miraculous nature of the Noble Qur'an consists in the fact that no trace of this Jewish idea or of this negative idea is to be found in it, notwithstanding the fact that these two paralyzing ailments are so pandemic in human intellectual history that none but the few who have drunk deeply from the Qur'an have escaped them.

This fact is confirmed by a close examination of the intellectual history of pre-Islamic philosophers as well as that of the *mutakallimin* of Islam and that of the European philosophers of the modern period as a body. The Qur'an is the sole teacher of *tauhid* that introduces

God to man within the extant and observable system, within the process of operative causes, effects, and norms of the creation, not by reference to its beginning, and through the clear and demonstrable, not by the negative means of resort to unknown causes.

I shall not go into the subject of *tauhid* per se, rehearse the proofs for *tauhid* that have appeared in books of *kalam* or of philosophy, or go over all that has been said or might be said on the subject. Nor shall I discuss the evolution of living beings, committing the same error others have committed in seeking to defend the bounds of *tauhid* by denying and attempting to falsify the principles and laws of evolution, thus inciting those who take a materialistic approach to philosophical problems to leap into the fray and obliging them to treat even the more questionable aspects of evolutionary theory as definitive in order to attack the theory of the existence of the Creator. This wrangling is pointless for two reasons. First, the principles of *tauhid* and the principles of evolution in nature in all its forms, including the transpecific evolution of living organisms, do not negate and oppose but affirm and complement each other. The supposition that these two principles contradict each other is born of ignorance. Second, it is not for just anyone to hold forth on this subject. Only those scientists who have devoted their lives to research on this question and have approached it by the correct scientific method can more or less reasonably discuss what the flickering flame of science is able to reveal.

Transpecific evolution is a recognized scientific fact. The gradualistic model of evolution, which the ancient Greek philosophers advanced, which Lamarck and Darwin sought to demonstrate scientifically, and which prompted their fanatical followers earnestly to search for the ancestors of horses and human beings and their assumption that man is descended from the apes, has been displaced by the punctuational model of evolution.[20]

But consideration of this question is the task of biologists. Theists and materialists alike must await the results of scientific research to see whether it accords with their principles.

Accordingly, I shall treat directly neither *tauhid* nor evolution, but the complement to these topics, the relation of *tauhid* and evolution. I seek to see whether these two ideas are mutually exclusive or mutually supportive. For instance, if someone should be convinced of the principle of *tauhid* through rational proofs, does this entail his rejecting the principle of the evolution and speciation of living beings? If he comes to believe in speciation, does this impair his belief in *tauhid*? And likewise, if someone has accepted the principle of transpecific evolution, if he is convinced that species of living beings derive from others in some manner, does this entail his casting aside the key principle of *tauhid* and turning into a materialist? My citations of the proofs of *tauhid* or of the principles of evolution in this section are directed toward answering this question.

The idea of the contradiction between *tauhid* and evolution, like the idea of the creation's being tied to a moment or that of negative theology by resort to the unknown has spread across the globe. Bizarre, even unbelievable, specimens of such thinking that can only sadden a Muslim thinker have appeared in the histories of European science and philosophy. Study of the modern history of biology and the sciences in general shows that this contradiction exists in the thought of almost all European scientists. Thus, an ambiguity or distortion, which materialists have had no small part in creating, has come about.

We are obliged to study this intellectual current to see why, as modern thought has developed, a materialistic and antitheistic aspect has been imparted to the theory of evolution. Why have both parties to the conflict taken this aspect of the theory for granted? Why have *tauhid*, theism, and acceptance of the principle of creation been thought synonymous with the theory of constancy of species? Is there really a logical contradiction between the idea of *tauhid* and that of evolution, or has one or more particular causes led to the supposition that there is?

In studying the works of scientists in this field, I have always striven to discern the roots of their thinking from the tenor and phraseology of their writing and to apprehend just what has prompted them to approach a problem involving philosophical inference in a particular way. What assumptions have they taken for granted and based their subsequent views upon? The main reason for divergencies in philosophical views is that each thinker tacitly begins from a set of assumptions. Each supposes that these assumptions are beyond question and to be taken for granted, not only in his own mind, but in others' minds. In fact, the assumptions are nothing but idiosyncrasy and fallacy.

What has led to this conception of a contradiction between the idea of *tauhid* and that of evolution is the Jewish idea of creation and the negative theology at its root. If we study the history of science or biology or refer to the books of philosophy written, on the one hand, to defend the bounds of *tauhid* and refute the theory of evolution or, on the other, to defend the school of materialism, we see the specter of that Jewish idea everywhere. The idea of negative theology appears to be the source of the idea of the momentary character of creation. The idea of the momentary character of creation is the source of the idea of the contradiction between *tauhid* and evolution.

From ancient times until comparatively recently, scholars have debated this point: Does the organism with all its members and organs exist in miniature yet fully formed from the beginning in the female ovum or the male spermatozoon, these organs thereafter to grow in proportion? Or is the matter that is the source of the members of the organism at first simple and uniform, only later to be differentiated into various organs and members? In modern times, not in the middle ages, for about two hundred years, most scientists held to the former belief.

This is more or less the same split in opinion that once existed between Aristotle and Hippocrates, with their respective followers, concerning the germ. Hippocrates held that sperm collected from all the body, and so each portion of it gave rise to a member. Aristotle believed that germ is uniform.[21] It is not clear from what Hippocrates has written whether he held that there was an actual homunculus in the germ. (His opponents said that such an unsound inference follows from his assertion.) Beginning in the seventeenth century, however, scientists formally held to preformation and preexistence.

One of the wonders of the creation is this appearance of the most diverse beings with all their various members from a simple, uniform substance that is the same in appearance for all of them. One of the best testaments to the existence of a dominical guidance and a divine sovereignty is this very diversity and this structure within which beings progress from uniformity to diversity and from simplicity to complexity. It is said in the Noble Qur'an, "It is He who forms you in the womb as He pleases" (3.6). As Sa'di says: "He gives the germ a Peri's form/Who's painted images on the water?"[22]

Many seventeenth-century scientists contributed to this theory of preformation without having any scientific proof or analytical evidence. They claimed that, from the first creation of the human species, all individuals have been created with all their organs and members whole and entire, if minute. They were present in the seed of the first human being and have been transmitted from generation to generation, growing into visible form with each generation. Pierre Rousseau says:

> William Harvey affirmed in 1651 that every creature arose from an egg, and, dissecting the does of Windsor Park at regular intervals, he discovered the embryonic calves at the various stages of their development. Some years later, in 1672, the Dutchman Régnier de Graaf (1641-1673), sacrificing in the same way a series of rabbits, believed he had laid his hands on the secret of the eggs of mammals. And in 1689, Malpighi, studying eggs not yet sat on by hens, declared he had seen the forms of chicks there. This was the point of departure for the extraordinary theory of *preformation.*
>
> Seeing that the as yet unfertilized egg contains a complete being all ready to develop, that being, that embryo, must itself contain eggs that in their turn contain each a complete being, and these too must contain other eggs containing other complete beings, and so on.
>
> "Consequently," added Swammerdam, "the body of Eve contained, nested one within another, all the eggs and all the germs of future humanity."
>
> But a voice was raised in contradiction—that of Leeuwenhoek, who, in 1679, had just discovered *spermatozoids*: "This is all wrong," he wrote. "It is not the egg that contains the preformed being, but the spermatozoid."
>
> "The proof," exulted Fr. de Plantades, secretary of the Academy of Sciences of Montpellier, "Is that I have seen, under the microscope, a spermatozoid open, and a tiny but fully formed man emerge from it!"
>
> Was this believed? The biologists *(sic)* placed their faith in this audacious tall tale and went on gravely discussing whether the germs of humanity had been lodged in the ovaries of Eve or the spermatozoids of Adam.[23]

Rousseau recounts the opposition of a couple of scientists to the theory of preformation and continues: "Yet, the theory of preformation, commended by such grand savants as Haller and Charles

Bonnet, continued to rally the near-unanimous support of men of science. Even Cuvier [the great biologist of the second half of the eighteenth and first half of the nineteenth centuries] was a johnny-come-lately partisan!"[24]

Pierre Rousseau offers no explanation as to why so many scientists held to this senseless theory. I believe that this hypothesis was intended to account for the fact of the creation; these scientists sought by this means to demonstrate that every living being is the creature of God. That they hypothesized that every human being and even animal came into existence completely formed, if minute, on the first day its most remote ancestors came into being shows the influence of the Jewish idea.

How vast is the difference between this way of thinking and that way which, when it seeks to express God's creatorship, says it is God who gradually formed and shaped a shapeless, characterless, simple, and uniform substance in the womb. "It is He Who forms you in the wombs as He pleases" (3:6).

Usually, when the subject of the origin of life, the nature and character of its appearance on earth, is approached by works of biology, works of so-called philosophy, or even textbooks, various hypotheses are offered, none of which has any scientific corroboration. One of these is called the creation hypothesis. It holds that all species of beings were created whole and entire, with no antecedents. This interpretation therefore implies that, if any of the other hypotheses are valid, there is no creation. What has led to this position, which holds that, if the appearance of living things was instantaneous and without antecedents, then creation is demonstrated, but if this was not the case, creation if refuted?

A chapter of *Farziyaha-yi Takamul* ("Hypotheses of Evolution"), beginning on page 9, is devoted to the subject of the origin of life. After an introduction, the author says, "We shall now note the hypotheses that are worthy of mention and that have had widespread acceptance for some time."[25] He then notes several hypotheses, such as that the first living organism came to earth by chance from another planet, spontaneous generation, and that of entities arising through volcanism or lightning. The first hypothesis he names he calls the creation hypothesis. He suggests implicitly that, if living organisms were spontaneously generated from inanimate matter, then no creation is involved. If the ultimate origin of living organisms is some other planet, then the living beings found on earth have not been created. One can only say that the living beings on earth are God's creatures if none of the previously-mentioned conditions hold, if living beings first appeared out of stillness and with no antecedents. In the small mind of the author of this book, creation can have no other meaning than this.

As the history of biology shows, Cuvier, who had a tremendous influence on his contemporaries' scientific thought, rejected gradual transformation of living beings. Seeing that the fossil record shows that animals had not maintained the same structure through various periods, Cuvier proposed and defended the hypothesis of a series of geological revolutions and catastrophes. He proposed that, in consequence of these catastrophes, the species living in one geological era had become extinct, and God had created newer (and, of course, more perfect) species to replace them on the earth.[26]

There is an article in the Azar 1338 [November 1959] issue of *Sukhan* that consists of the recorded remarks of Mahmud Bihzad, a scholar from Tehran, at a meeting commemorating the centenary of the publication of *On the Origin of Species*. He says:

> Cuvier in comparing fossils of extinct faunas noted their gradual development with the passage of geological eras. He also perceived that the animals of any given era are comparable to those of previous eras in their structural organization, but since he believed in the constancy of species and their periodic mass extinction, he sought to explain his observations through the hypothesis of "the plan of creation." Cuvier maintained in this hypothesis that a general plan exists for the creation of living beings, and that this plan is consulted on the occasion of each renewed creation: the reason for the basic resemblance among the faunas of different eras is the existence of such a plan.[27]

Elsewhere, too, whenever reference is made to Cuvier's theory on the partitioning of the organisms of one era from those of another, it is called the theory of successive creations. One would have to ask Cuvier himself, or at least his followers, what led him to suppose that we can speak of creation only in the event of the absence of genetic relation among organisms. Why should creation otherwise be meaningless?

Pierre Rousseau writes:

> When the Darwinists had resolved—they thought!—the prob-
> lem of the origin of man and animals, they no longer sensed any
> limit to the all-power of their science, so they merrily attacked
> another question, one which the German naturalist Emile du Bois-
> Reymond (1818–1896), successor to Jean Muller, had classed, in a
> famous discourse given in 1880 at the Academy of Sciences of
> Berlin, among the seven enigmas of the universe: the question of
> the origin of life. There was a very perplexing point here, for if one
> were to reject the creationism of the Bible and of Cuvier, if one were
> to deny that only divine intervention could make living matter
> appear from nothing, one was as good as admitting that living
> matter had been created all by itself. In other words, one was as
> good as shaking hands with spontaneous generation, which Pasteur
> had condemned justly in the name of experimental science.
>
> We must confess that, since that epoch [the time of the material-
> ists' hypothesis on the origins of life, which was discredited by
> Rousseau's time], not much progress has been made on the prob-
> lem. It always consists in finding by what means many hundreds or
> many thousands of atoms of carbon, hydrogen, nitrogen, and oxy-
> gen were able to agglutinate to form a molecule of living matter. . . .
> The probability of the appearance of a single cell rests on a phenom-
> enon of pure chance, a chance so prodigious that it approaches a
> miracle.
>
> Is one thus obliged to have recourse to divine creation? "No,"
> responded the French de Monlivault in 1821, and "No," responded
> the German Richter in 1865, followed by Lord Kelvin and Helm-
> holtz. Since positive science admits neither creation nor generation,
> it remains for us to suppose that the earth has been inoculated like a
> petri dish. "Good God, inoculated by what germs?" "Well, by
> bacteria come from other worlds and sailing across interstellar
> space."[28]

Rousseau, who claims conversance with all the world's scientific
knowledge from ancient times to the present age, believes that
positive science accepts neither creation nor spontaneous generation. He is right to believe this because his conception of the meaning
of the creation is unsupported by science. His conception, and that
of all scientists who think along the same lines, is, according to firm
and indubitable philosophical demonstrations, impossible and

absurd; such a thing never has occurred and never can occur. That conception of the creation rests on wild, haphazard surmise. God's creation does not take place except through specific and definite norms, whether or not they are known to us.

You may suppose that Pierre Rousseau and others speak for science, propounding and explaining what science has shown them, and that my objections amount to objections to the progress of science. What I have sought to show in these examples is that the hypotheses so expressed do not rest on concrete observations and objective experiments. The trend of scientific experiment can be otherwise explained and interpreted, but the particular conception scientists have of the creation and the particular sort of philosophy that holds sway over their minds have resulted in the above-named questions being addressed as they have throughout the history of science. Despite what the title of his book suggests, what Rousseau addresses is not just the history of science and of empirical observation, but a hybrid history of science and European philosophy. The most tragicomic aspects of this situation pertain not to the history of the modern sciences, but to that of philosophical thought in Europe. European scientists conceive of the creation in terms of a form of the Jewish conception and of God in terms of the negative theology I have discussed in "The Qur'an and Life." That is, they seek for God amid their ignorance.

By now you should able to guess why the materialist school so flourished in Europe. The faulty logic on questions of divinity that has held sway over scientists at large was doomed and bound to fail and disappear from the very beginning. As I study the history of science in recent centuries and note the peculiar coloration given pure science simply by scientists' special turn of philosophical thought, I grow saddened and discouraged. I wish scientists could become acquainted with the fine caliber of philosophical thought that has evolved in the lap of the Noble Qur'an over the last fourteen centuries and the limpid water of science would not remain polluted by that Jewish way of thinking. I am especially saddened to see those youths newly introduced to science and lacking the power of analysis who, reading works of modern philosophy, works on the history of science, or even textbooks, assimilate a conception of scientific progress adulterated by that way of thinking. They are persuaded that scientific observation discredited the hypothesis of the creation and of the existence of God years ago. They think that the hypothesis of a creation and a Creator lives on only in the darkness of inherited beliefs and that not a trace of it remains to be seen in the clear light of science.

Perhaps what has led scientists to adopt this mode of thought is not what I have termed the Jewish way of thinking, but reverence for the contents of the Book of Genesis. Doubtless, its contents have had a profound effect, but at the most, the Book of Genesis has propounded the character of the creation in a special manner. It has not suggested that, if organisms have come into being in any other way, creation has no meaning. Basically, the Book of Genesis cannot impart a particular conception of or way of thinking about the meaning of the creation. The history of scientific thought on this question indicates that scientists, theists and materialists alike, have been unable to consider the creation from any other standpoint than the one I have described.

Even after rejecting the conception of the creation given in the Book of Genesis, scientists continued to regard the meaning of the creation as before. Therefore, some other cause is at work. I believe that cause is a pandemic way of thinking characteristic of the Jews and stemming from Jewish scholastic theology, not from the Book of Genesis. They lack the correct, clear, and logical way of thinking characteristic of those raised with study of the Noble Qur'an.

After noting Cuvier's theory of catastrophism, Bihzad says:

> It is not unamusing to note that Louis Agassiz (another student of Cuvier and opponent of evolution), in order to accommodate the evolution of faunas observed in the fossil record to the theory of the constancy of species, arrived at a bizarre theory that is in a class of its own and, if closely examined, sheer unbelief. Agassiz proposed that the cause for the development of faunas from era to era, or otherwise their gradual evolution, resulted from the evolution that has taken place in the thought of the Creator Most High from the first era of time to the present.[29]

This quotation shows how deeply rooted this Jewish idea has become, not as a principle of religious observance, but as a philosophical assumption, so deeply that it is easier and more acceptable for one scientist to conceive of evolution occurring in the mind of

God than, gradually, in the creation. Is the theory of catastrophism also found in the Book of Genesis? Does the Book of Genesis say that God's knowledge gradually has evolved?

Notes to "Spirit, Matter and Life"

1. For an explanation of this point, see *Usul-i Falsafa*, vol. 2.
2. For a more extensive treatment of this topic and of the historical development of questions of being, see *Usul-i Falsafa*, vol. 3.
3. Concerning the history of the entelechy concept in biology, from Aristotle to Hans Driesch, see Arthur Koestler, *Janus* (New York, 1979), pp. 222-226. *Trans.*
4. A. Cressy Morrison, *Man Does Not Stand Alone* (New York, 1944), p. 35.
5. For discussion of vitalist currents in modern biology and for further references, see Koestler, *Janus*, p. 224-226; Arthur Koestler, *The Ghost in the Machine* (New York, 1976), pp. 196-221; Karl R. Popper and John C. Eccles, *The Self and Its Brain* (Berlin, 1981), pp. 28-29, 68; C.H. Waddington, *The Nature of Life* (London, 1963), pp. 115-122; Richard Grossinger, *Planet Medicine: From Stone Age Shamanism to Post-Industrial Healing* (New York, 1980), pp. 116-123; and Rupert Sheldrake, *A New Science of Life: The Hypothesis of Formative Causation* (Los Angeles, 1981), pp. 43-52. Ludwig von Bertalanffy perceptively analyzes and criticizes vitalistic theories in his *Problems of Life* (New York, 1960). Most present-day biologists, although they may not advocate a substantive reality of the vital force, hold that biological phenomena cannot be fully analyzed in physicochemical terms. This rejection of explanatory reductionism is embodied in the ideas of holism and organicism and reflected in systems theory. Especially interesting work along these lines is reflected in Erich Jantsch, *The Evolutionary Vision: Towards a Unifying Paradigm of Physical, Biological, and Socio-cultural Evolution* (Boulder, Colo., 1981). See also the various writings of Gregory Bateson. In *The Growth of Biological Thought* (Cambridge, Mass., 1982), p. 52, the eminent biologist Ernst Mayr suggests that vitalism per se is a dead issue among biologists but notes that it has many defenders among physicists and philosophers.

   Some modern physicists who appear to advance vitalistic ideas are Werner Heisenberg (see his *Physics and Philosophy: The Revolution in Modern Science* [New York, 1962], pp. 102-106), David Bohm, (*Wholeness and the Implicate Order* [London, 1981], pp. 193-196), and J.A. Wheeler (with C.M. Patton, "Is Physics Legislated by Cosmogony?" in Ronald Duncan and Miranda Weston-Smith, *The Encyclopaedia of Ignorance* [Oxford, 1977], pp. 19-35). *Trans.*

6. This belief is preserved to this day among the behaviorists. For an extensive refutation, see Donald B. Griffin, *The Question of Animal Awareness: Evolutionary Continuity of Mental Experience* (New York: 1981).

   The Qur'an ascribes rational being to animals in 24:45–46, verses whose significance Mahmud Taleghani discusses in *Society and Economics in Islam* (Berkeley, 1982), pp. 166–167. *Trans.*

7. Mahmud Bihzad, *Darvinism*, 5th ed., p. 99.

8. See Kazimzada Iranshahr, *Tadavi-yi Ruhi* ("spiritual healing").

9. Oswald Külpe, *Introduction to Philosophy: A Handbook for Students of Psychology, Logic, Ethics, Aesthetics, and General Philosophy* (London, 1901), p. 122. [Gregory Bateson has stressed how inapplicable such physical concepts as energy and force are to mental phenomena. See especially his *Steps to an Ecology of Mind* (New York, 1972, paperback edition), pp. 448–465, 478–487, and *Mind and Nature: A Necessary Unity* (New York, 1979), pp. 217–223. *Trans.*]

10. Morrison, *Man Does Not Stand Alone*, pp. 34–35.

11. Readers can refer to the various works that have been written on suggestion and its effects, among which I recommend especially Iranshahr, *Tadavi-yi Ruhi*. [A balanced and comprehensive treatment of these areas in English is Grossinger, *Planet Medicine. Trans.*]

12. See Pierre Rousseau, *Histoire de la science* (Paris, 1945), pp. 687–681.

13. This is surely a paraphrase of part of the concluding passage to Charles Darwin, *On the Origin of Species*, 1st ed. (London, 1859), p. 490: "There is a grandeur in this view of life, with its several powers, having been originally breathed into a few forms or into one." *Trans.*

14. Morrison, *Man Does Not Stand Alone*, pp. 39–40.

15. *Ibid.*, p. 96.

16. The second-person objects here are all plural. Also, the context is of an address to peoples and communities. *Trans.*

17. Note Chuang Tzu's dictum: "In the world everyone knows enough to pursue what he does not know, but no one knows enough to pursue what he already knows." (*The Complete Works of Chuang Tzu* [New York, 1968], p. 113.) *Trans.*

18. The context suggests that the author means to include monotheists at large here and in similar references in these articles. *Trans.*

19. See *Usul-i Falsafa*, vol. 3, p. 220.

20. The punctuational model was first clearly formulated by Ernst Mayr in 1954 and has been given its best theoretical elaboration to date in Steven M. Stanley, *Macroevolution: Pattern and Process* (San Francisco, 1979). It does not radically alter the scientific picture of human origins. It proposes that major evolutionary change occurs relatively rapidly, in small, isolated populations.

It is also possible that the author's term *takamul-i daf'i* translates the theory of saltationism, advocated by Richard Goldschmidt in *The Material Basis of Evolution* (New Haven, 1940). It held that a new species could arise in a single generation, as a bird from a dinosaur's egg. *Trans.*

21. See Mulla Sadra, *Asfar*, vol. 4, and Avicenna, the *Tabi'iyat* of *ash-Shifa'*.

22. Exact place of occurrence not found. *Trans.*

23. Rousseau, *Histoire de la science*, pp. 371-372.

24. *Ibid.*

25. Unknown. *Trans.*

26. For a view that Cuvier's thinking was chiefly influenced by the Platonic doctrine of essentialism, see Ernst Mayr, *The Growth of Biological Thought* (Cambridge, Mass., 1982), especially pp. 363-371. *Trans.*

27. Mahmud Bihzad, "Darvin va Nazariya-yi Takamul" ("Darwin and the Theory of Evolution"), *Sukhan*, vol. 10 number 9 (Azar, 1338), p. 947. *Trans.*

28. Rousseau, *Histoire de la science*, pp. 678-679.

29. Bihzad, "Darvin va Nazariya-yi Takamul," p. 947. *Trans.*

Index

A

'Abd al-Jabbar, Qazi, 153
Abi'l-Khayr, Abu Sa'id-i, 152
Abraham
  on God, 196
  on worship, 88-89
Absolute, God as, 75, 83
Abu 'Ubayda, 153
Actions. *See* Acts
Active worship, 82
Acts
  of devotion, anxieties obviated by, 46
  as signs, 82-83
  tauhid in, 86-88
Adam, object of story of, 200-201
'Adl-i Ilahi (Divine Justice), 17, 116, 121, 125
Agassiz, Louis, 215
Agency, *shirk* as regards, 109-10
Akhundism, 114
'Alam al-Huda, Sayyid Murtaza, 154
'Alavi, Hakim Nasir-i Khusraw, 41
Alexander of Aphrodisias, 150
Alexandrian school, 150
'Ali
  on attributes of God, 86
  dual goals of, 94
  on enslavement by Pharaohs, 105
  God seen in everything by, 113
  on hereafter, 119
Al 'Imran, on creation, 196
Al-Jam' Bayn Ra'yay al-Hakimayn (Farabi), 147
Al-Kindi, 151
'Allaf, Abu'l Hudhayl, 153
Al-Milal wa'n-Nihal (Shahristani), 148
Al-Munjid, on dual role of Islam, 93-94
Ammonius Saccas, 150
Angel of Death, 109

Animals
  awareness and desire in, 25-26
  Descartes' view of, 190
  humanity vs. animality, 28-31
  man vs. 25-31, 67-68, 91-92, 110
  as pleasure-oriented, 48
  vital force in, 188, 190-91
Anjuman-i Mahana-yi Dini, 14-15
Anjumanha (Islamic associations), 14
Ansari, Khwaja 'Abdullah, 152
'Aql-i Surkh (Suhravardi), 152
'Arabi, Muhyi'd-Din Ibn, 152
Arani, Taqi, 12
Archetypes, ideas and, 146
Aristotle
  on body and spirit, 150, 184-85, 187
  on causation, 173
  on change and constancy, 167-68
  Hippocrates vs., on germ, 209
  metaphysics studied by, 141
  peripatetics as followers of, 146
  Plato's ideas opposed by, 146-47, 148
  rebelled against Sophists, 163
'Arshiya (Mulla Sadra), 155
Art, need for, 38
Asceticism, as path to wisdom, 146
Asfar-i Arba'a (Mulla Sadra), 154-55, 156
  on cause and effect, 195
  Imam Khomeini lectures on, 11
  motion discussed in, 170
  on natural cause, 202
Ash'ari, Shaykh Abu'l-Hasan, 153
Ash'arite beliefs, 103, 107, 108, 109, 153,154
Ashna'i ba 'Ulum-i Islami (An Introduction to the Islamic Sciences), 17
Ash-Shavahid ar-Rububiya (Mulla Sadra), 155

221